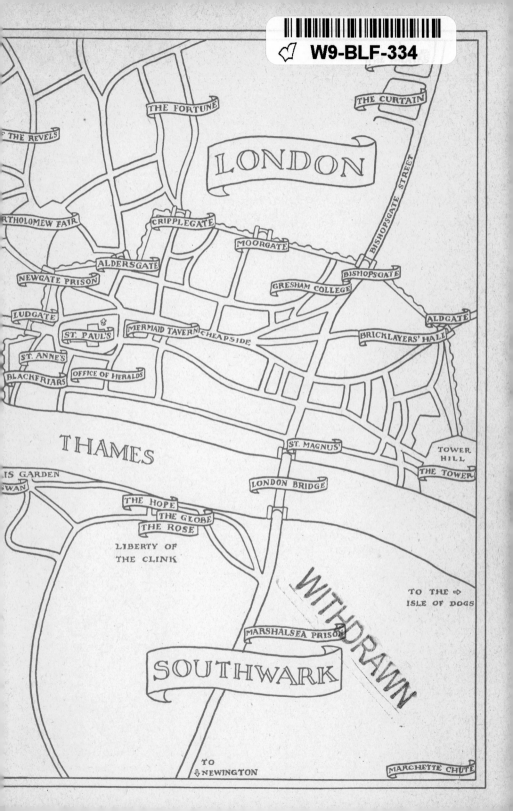

# Ben Jonson *of Westminster*

## By *MARCHETTE CHUTE*

THE SEARCH FOR GOD

GEOFFREY CHAUCER OF ENGLAND

SHAKESPEARE OF LONDON

BEN JONSON OF WESTMINSTER

E·P·DUTTON & CO. INC

1852  1953

CREATIVE · 101 YEARS · PUBLISHING

DEEST QUOD DUCERET ORBEM

# BEN JONSON

## OF

# 𝔚estminster

## MARCHETTE CHUTE

*New York*
E. P. Dutton & Co., Inc.    Publishers
1953

To The New York Public Library,
*with affection and respect*

*Give me a spirit that on this life's rough sea*
*Loves t' have his sails filled with a lusty wind*
*Even till his sail-yards tremble, his masts crack,*
*And his rapt ship runs on her side so low*
*That she drinks water and her keel plows air.*

—George Chapman

# Ben Jonson *of Westminster*

# Chapter 1

IN THE DAYS OF QUEEN ELIZABETH THE FIRST, the little village of Charing stood halfway between two cities. If anyone climbed the steps of Charing Cross and looked eastward he would see the walled city of London, and if he looked towards the south he would see the ancient and royal city of Westminster.

The city of Westminster had already begun to spread northward and was engulfing the village of Charing, and there was a time coming when London would engulf Westminster. But in the late sixteenth century they were two separate cities and possessed very different temperaments.

London was the city of the middle class. Packed inside the walls and already spilling out into the suburbs were nearly a quarter of a million ordinary citizens. It was a city of haberdashers and bankers and jewelers and booksellers and actors and housewives, with comparatively few lords in it and comparatively few beggars. It was a city of buying and selling, manufacturing and finance, and although most of the wealth of England was concentrated there it was shared by many people and constantly changing hands.

The city of Westminster was much smaller than the expanding giant to the east of it, and in comparison with the sprawling vigor of London it was both medieval and motionless. Westminster was dominated by the two institutions that had made it a city—the Court and the Church—and it had developed a rather hothouse, specialized atmosphere that was unlike anything else in England.

London had its cathedral church of St. Paul's, but no one could say that St. Paul's dominated the city. The Londoners treated it as a kind of comfortable, overgrown parish church and they even found it a convenient place to conduct their business affairs. Unlike St. Paul's, the church of Westminster was given over to affairs of state and to tourists rather than to ordinary people; and no one would have dared put up an advertisement or meet a client among the ancient painted tombs of what was officially known as the Collegiate Church of St. Peter but usually called Westminster Abbey.

Westminster Abbey dominated the life of the city, for the Dean of Westminster was the head of the city government. Assisting him was the High Steward of Westminster, a post that always went to a member of the nobility. With the Church and Court securely established in the top positions, the rest of the government machinery was handled by twenty-four burgesses, selected by the Dean from among the local tradesmen.

There were not many tradesmen to choose from in that aristocratic and churchly city, for Westminster did not possess many members of the middle class. The city was inhabited by two extremes, the very rich and the very poor, with the latter naturally in the majority. One melancholy report of the period said that most of the people of Westminster were "of no trade . . . and become poor, and many of them wholly given to vice and idleness, living in contempt of all manner of officers." This rabble of the poor lived in a network of choked alleys off the beautiful main street of the city, and their activities made the seat of the English government a very difficult place to control. On the other hand, this mushroom growth of cheap tenements was partly the Dean of Westminster's own fault. The city was built on drained land from what had once been an island, and Westminster Abbey, as the owner of the land, had been unwilling either to sell it or to rent it out on long leases. As a result, no one felt any incentive to invest in adequate housing, and Westminster remained a city of a few beautiful buildings and a great many slums.

Ordinary citizens came to Westminster in crowds four times a year from all over England, during the four terms when the law courts were in session; and another and smaller group of Englishmen made it their headquarters when Parliament was in session. This floating population of the middle class competed for the limited number of hired lodgings, but they made no permanent impression on Westminster except to foster an unusually large number of taverns around Westminster Hall. In general, Westminster was a city without ordinary citizens.

There was one institution, however, in which the Church and Court united to bridge the great gulf between the Westminster rich and the Westminster poor. It was an institution which reflected great credit on everyone concerned—a public grammar school for the small boys of Westminster, with forty free scholarships for the most deserving. Its official name was the College of St. Peter's, but everyone called it Westminster School.

As far back as anyone could remember there had always been a free school in connection with Westminster Abbey. But Queen Elizabeth, as one of the first acts of her reign, set it up in revised and permanent form, complete with charter, seals and a long list of statutes. She set aside the revenue from several large estates to maintain it and hoped that it would ultimately rival Eton.

The Dean was the official head of Westminster School, and he governed it with the assistance of a board of twelve prebendaries, "all professors of theology." But its unofficial head was Lord Burghley, the Queen's great secretary of state, who kept a careful eye on everything connected with the Crown and who had suggested the school foundation to Elizabeth in the first place. Burghley loved learning, and when he was a student at Cambridge he had hired a bell ringer to wake him at four o'clock every morning. There was no longer any room in his crowded life for studying Greek and Latin but he still kept his profound respect for scholars and for scholarship. Moreover, he loved children, and it was charmingly said of him that whenever he was surrounded by children "he was then in his kingdom."

Since Westminster School was so closely allied to the Court, its "forty poor scholars" had a closer view of royalty than usually comes to grammar school boys. Elizabeth visited the school from time to time to see how the boys' studies were progressing, and when the Queen's Scholars presented the annual Christmas play that was required by the statutes, they borrowed whatever silks and velvets they needed from the royal Office of the Revels. If the boy actors needed a rapier onstage it could be borrowed from an earl; their backdrop was designed by a professional, and their audience might include not only the Queen and her high government officials but even a visiting princess from Sweden.

Not every boy that went to Westminster School became a Queen's Scholar, to be fed and housed and supplied with clothes and books at royal expense. There were a hundred and twenty boys in the school, from among whom the forty Queen's Scholars were chosen, and the remaining eighty were divided with pedagogical neatness into three categories. There were the Pensioners, mostly sons of good families who were put in charge of members of the governing board or of the schoolmaster. There were the Peregrines, sons of less important families who stayed with friends or relatives while they went to school. And there were the Oppidans, whose families lived in Westminster already and who did not need to be boarded.

Among the small Oppidans was a boy named Benjamin Johnson, who walked to Westminster School each morning from his home in an alley near Charing Cross. When he died he was buried next door in Westminster Abbey, as one of England's greatest poets and dramatists and the dean of English letters, but he could never have forced his life into this pattern of triumph if he had not, as a small boy, gone to Westminster School.

# Chapter 2

U NLIKE WILLIAM SHAKESPEARE, Ben Jonson is a hard man
to trace back to his beginnings. The date of his birth
is unknown, except that it was late in 1572 or sometime during the first six months of 1573. And the place of his
birth is unknown, except that it was not in Westminster. Westminster had only two parishes in those days, and neither one
has any record of his baptism.

Nor is there any record of his ancestry, except what comes
from Jonson himself. He believed that his family came originally from Annandale and he took pride in his Scottish ancestry.
He must have enjoyed encountering the definitive history of
the British Isles and reading there of the glory of the Annandale
family: "In this territory the Johnstons are men of greatest
name, a kindred ever bred to war." Jonson assumed the coat
of arms of the Annandale branch, and there is no doubt that he
carried on its warlike spirit. No man in the history of English
letters ever started more fights or continued them with more
wholehearted enthusiasm, and his warlike ancestors from the
vale of the river Annan should have been proud of him.

According to Jonson his grandfather came from Carlisle,
south of the Border, and it was his impression that his grandfather
was a member of the gentry and had served under Henry the
Eighth. It may have been true. It may equally have been true,
as members of the Shakespeare family contended, that one of
their ancestors was a member of the gentry who had served
under Henry the Seventh. It was a period in which the matter

of birth was taken seriously, and everyone naturally wanted to have as distinguished an ancestor as possible. Lord Burghley, whose achievements were magnificent but whose antecedents were not, saw to it that the Office of Heralds evolved a set of ancestors for him that were suited to his position in life; and if it pleased Jonson to feel that his family belonged to the gentry there is no reason why a biographer should try to take the distinction away from him, as long as there is no proof to the contrary.

Jonson also believed that his father had once possessed a considerable "estate," which he lost when he was imprisoned in the days of Queen Mary. He had probably been imprisoned for religious reasons, for Jonson's father was a minister. His son never knew him, since he died a month before Benjamin was born.

It would be interesting to know who decided on the child's name, which was an unusual one in the sixteenth century. Perhaps the minister wanted his son to have a Hebrew name. Moreover, if he was no longer a young man when the child was conceived the name would have been an especially suitable one. As a writer of the following century remarked, many clergymen were older men when they married. "Their children then are all Benjamins, I mean the children of their old age."

Or it may be that the minister chose a distinctive name like "Benjamin" to counteract the commonness of the "Johnson." England was full of Johnsons, and one reason why it is so difficult to trace the poet's family is the fact that the parish records are full of other people of the same name. Benjamin himself, when he grew up, found a way of separating himself from his hosts of fellow Johnsons by dropping one letter out of his name. Almost from the beginning of his career his name appears as "Jonson" whenever he had any control over the activities of the printer, and this is done so consistently that it appears to have become a settled policy with him.*

* It was a policy to which his contemporaries paid no attention. His friends and his enemies went on spelling his name with an *h,* and even the printers

Not long after the minister's death, his widow and his little son came to Westminster and established themselves in the village of Charing. Jonson's first biographer, Thomas Fuller, reported that when Jonson was "a little child he lived in Hartshorn Lane near Charing Cross, where his mother married a bricklayer for her second husband." Hartshorn Lane was an alley east of Charing Cross leading down to the Thames, one of the clutter of small back roads that connected the main thoroughfare with the river.

To be the wife of a minister was one thing, and to be the wife of a bricklayer was quite another. It is true that bricklaying was an ancient craft, with its own guild, and that the bricklayers of Hull had opened their book of ordinances with a magnificence to match any minister's: "All men are by nature equal, made all by one Workman of like mire; and howsoever we deceive ourselves, as dear unto God is the poorest beggar as the most pompous prince." In practice, however, the bricklayers belonged to one of the lowliest of the guilds, and when the Elizabethan courts released them from the provisions of the labor statute it was on the rather insulting grounds that their trade required no intelligence to speak of and "rather ability of body than of skill."

A bricklayer could not be expected to concern himself with the education of a small stepson who, in the nature of things, could have no loftier future than to become a bricklayer in his turn. Nevertheless Benjamin succeeded in learning his letters, crossing each morning the heavily traveled main road that was called the Strand to go a few paces down St. Martin's Lane. The parish church of St. Martin's maintained a small schoolhouse, big enough to have at least one window, and there Ben

---

stopped co-operating as soon as Jonson was no longer there to watch them. Later critics like Dryden and Pope went on with the spelling he had tried so hard to abandon, and he would probably have it still if another distinguished man of letters had not appeared with the same last name. Ben Jonson and Samuel Johnson could be kept apart much more easily if their names were not spelled alike, and by 1840 Jonson had won his final victory. From that time forward his name has been spelled without the *h*.

Jonson took the first step into his kingdom. It was probably his mother who helped him get as far as this on his long, difficult road into the world of letters, for she had been the wife of a minister and she would have valued education.

The next step in Benjamin's education was Westminster School, and this was much more difficult to achieve. He would not be eligible for a scholarship until he had been there a year, and in the meantime there was the expense of schoolbooks, paper, ink, tallow candles and other educational equipment, to say nothing of the fact that the average Westminster schoolboy managed to wear out a pair of shoes each month. In addition, the teachers at Westminster School were not especially well paid. The headmaster received only twenty pounds a year, which is no more than he would have been given in a little town like Stratford, and the undermaster less than eight. Both men supplemented their incomes with the gifts their students gave them at Christmastime, and although in theory these were free-will offerings, in practice they were compulsory. It is unlikely that the bricklayer in Hartshorn Lane would be able to afford all this, even if he had been willing to let his stepson have so expensive a luxury as a grammar-school education.

If Ben Jonson had lived in Stratford, he could have had a grammar-school education for the asking. The Stratford school was supported out of town funds, and the same education was available to every small boy in town. A Stratford boy like William Shakespeare, who was ready to leave school at about the same time Ben Jonson was entering, got his education almost automatically, but a boy from the city slums could go to grammar school only if someone helped him.

Fortunately, while Westminster might be a city of slums it was also a city of contacts; anything could be achieved if one knew the right people. Westminster School was a church school, and perhaps Jonson's mother had some useful ecclesiastical connections through her late husband. Or perhaps someone noticed the small boy learning his letters in the little parish schoolhouse and became interested in Benjamin himself. At any rate, Jonson was able to take the next upward step in his education. He was "put to school by a friend" and enrolled at Westminster.

When young William Shakespeare walked to school each morning he passed a few shops and the houses of some of his friends, with nothing more impressive along the route than the Market Cross and the Stratford town hall. But when Ben Jonson went to school each morning he walked through the grounds of the royal palace of Whitehall.

There was only one real road in Westminster, a continuation of the Strand that curved from Charing Cross down to Westminster Abbey and was known as King's Street, and on its way it passed through the cluster of buildings that made up Queen Elizabeth's palace. In the old days the kings of England had lived in Westminster Hall, next door to the Abbey, but as the years went by the premises became increasingly crowded with government offices. The situation was further complicated by a bad fire and Elizabeth's father finally took over the town residence of the Archbishops of York and made it his own. Wolsey had spent a great deal of money on the place, and Henry the Eighth made himself extremely comfortable in it.

Later on, Ben Jonson was as familiar with the royal residence at Whitehall as he was with the contents of his own desk, for it grew to be a normal part of his working hours. Yet even as a schoolboy he knew it well. On his left was the glassed Banqueting Hall where his own masques were later to be presented, and as he entered under the great gate that Hans Holbein had designed he passed on one side of the street the tilt yard and the tennis courts where the young men played at games and on the other the Queen's garden with its orchards and its fountain. South of Whitehall, at the foot of King's Street, stood the ancient bulk of Westminster Abbey, and next to the Abbey was Jonson's school.

The hundred and twenty boys who made up Westminster School were packed into a small building that was already "too low and too little to contain the number of scholars." There were plenty of other rooms available in the monks' old quarters but they needed repairs, and it was not until the end of the century that the Dean and Chapter managed to raise enough money to give the school larger accommodations.

In the wintertime little Benjamin had to make his way through Whitehall when it was still dark, for school never began later than seven in the morning. In spring the hour was put back to six, although one kindhearted schoolmaster admitted that it was "hard for little children to rise so early." The small scholars were allowed an hour for breakfast at eight, and if they were overcome with sleepiness in the middle of the afternoon they could get formal permission to drop their heads on their desks. Since the school day lasted until six, there was also a short recess in the middle of the afternoon, but this humane Westminster custom was felt to be a daring innovation. One schoolmaster remarked that if he tried to introduce the same idea in his locality, the parents would accuse him of running a school in which the children did "nothing but play."

It may have been these long hours that led to the widespread custom of flogging. There is a limit to the amount of sitting still that a roomful of vigorous small boys can endure, and the average Elizabethan teacher took the easy way out. He did not try to interest small boys in learning. He beat them into it. As one schoolmaster said feelingly, "The Lord be merciful unto us all who are in this calling, even for this sin; for it is no small matter to moderate our passion, and our correction." It was this same schoolmaster who believed that the classroom should be a place of "play and pleasure . . . not of fear and bondage," but he was a long way ahead of his day. The average schoolmaster of the period laid a heavy hand on his roomful of small boys, and the idea that they might be encouraged to love learning never entered his head. He himself had been beaten into an education and he proceeded to use the same method on his pupils.

The headmaster of Westminster School was thoroughly convinced of the usefulness of flogging. His name was Edward

Grant and in his field he was a very distinguished man, a prominent scholar and a specialist in Greek. The Dean and Chapter
found him wholly satisfactory but one of his pupils left a different report for posterity. Richard Neile said wistfully that
he might have achieved a real mastery of Latin if Edward Grant
had not whipped him so often.

The boys in the lower forms did not see very much of the
headmaster. Their lives centered around his assistant, the undermaster, and it was the greatest piece of single good fortune in
Ben Jonson's life that when he was a small boy he should have
come under the influence of that wise and good man, William
Camden.

Camden was still in his late twenties when Ben Jonson entered Westminster School, and no one knew that he was going
to become one of the greatest of England's antiquarian scholars.
Outwardly he was a gentle young man—"a very good-natured
man, very mild and very charitable"—who needed all his charity
since he bore the chief share of handling a hundred and twenty
boys. He did not escape from his charges even at night, since he
was a kind of house mother for the forty Queen's Scholars, who
slept two in a bed in a dormitory adapted from the old granary
of the monks.

Camden lived almost entirely surrounded by boys and yet
he succeeded in keeping a part of his life wholly to himself.
Up in his tower rooms he labored at the dream of his life and
sometimes it must have seemed to him an impossible one. He
was trying to write a book about Britain of a kind that had
never been written before, giving a complete description,
county by county, of everything that could be found out about
his native land.

In Camden's day the early history of England was still
wrapped in a thick mist of legend and conjecture, and yet in
dozens of English towns, in Roman coins and Saxon stonework,
lay the actual records of the past. A brother of the Dean of
Westminster who knew that Camden was ardently interested
in antiquarian research not only bought him whatever books

were available on the subject but also financed the field trips
in which the young schoolteacher burrowed through ancient
ruins in Norfolk and went digging for coins in Colchester.
Lord Burghley, who had an archaeological collection of his own,
became interested in the project and Camden began to corre-
spond with some of the great scholars on the Continent. He
wrote long letters to Abraham Ortelius, the Antwerp geogra-
pher who had been the first to encourage him with his book,
and confided to him his longing "that some light might arise
over our ancient Britain which is so enveloped in darkness."

Camden admitted that he had embarked on a very difficult
undertaking. "What toil is to be taken, no man thinketh, so no
man believeth, but he that hath made the trial." Even the most
leisured scholar might have been forgiven for shrinking from
so monumental a task, and Camden was a hard-working teacher
who cared for his boys as much as he cared for his book. He
said that he worked on the book only when he had "any spare
time," and that was little enough.

Camden wrote the book in Latin, since it was a learned work
and he was addressing an international circle of scholars. He
dedicated it to Lord Burghley, who shared his love of English
history, and he published it in 1586 while Ben Jonson was
probably still at Westminster.

*Britannia* was an instant success and established its author as
one of the foremost scholars of the age. It went through several
editions on the Continent, and after it was translated it went
through six English editions in Camden's lifetime. When he
died, heavy with age and honors, the monument that was
erected to him in Westminster Abbey showed him with
*Britannia* in his hand.

Camden was not an ambitious man. He had done the work
for the work's sake, and he said truly that he had never "desired to soar higher than others." After the book came out he
went on placidly teaching at Westminster, "contented" to be
there and doing the best he could for the boys. It was the boys
who boasted about him, as one of their number admitted. "I

remember when I was his scholar, we heard news continually that our master had letters from beyond seas, and we his scholars were wont to brag in what esteem he was beyond seas." Camden was held in esteem everywhere, and deservedly, for he was a wise, honorable scholar and a good man.

This was the teacher who received Ben Jonson when he came to grammar school each morning and who opened the world of letters to the small boy from a Westminster alley. The rest of Jonson's life was lived in the blaze of a single, intense and burning ambition, and although the fire was already laid it was Camden who supplied the spark that set it alight.

Ben Jonson did not forget to be grateful. When he himself became a towering figure in the world of letters he wrote a tribute to his old teacher in which he thanked him for everything he himself had attained.

> Camden, most reverend head, to whom I owe
> All that I am in arts, all that I know . . .

# Chapter 3

VERY GRAMMAR SCHOOL IN ENGLAND taught each little Elizabethan schoolboy the same thing. It taught him Latin. Sometimes an exceptional school like Westminster went a step further and taught one other subject, and in that case the subject was Greek. The explanations in the Greek grammar were of course in Latin, for the boys of Westminster School were expected to use nothing but Latin in their school hours. If anyone forgot and spoke in English it counted against him as much as three mistakes in spelling.

It might be said in general of the Tudor school system that its aim was to turn out little Roman-Christian gentlemen who could write exactly like Cicero. To this end the boys struggled through the Stoic precepts of the *Disticha* in the first form, learned elegant Latin colloquialisms from Terence in the second, and emerged on the great plateau of Cicero—"the very foundation of all"—in the third. Throughout, there was a stern emphasis on the two great principles of Tudor education: the gentlemanly Christian virtues on the one hand and a sound Latin style on the other.

The emphasis on character development was not new, and Ben Jonson started school with the same moral maxims that had been inculcated in young Geoffrey Chaucer. The teaching of Latin, however, had changed. Chaucer was taught a Latin over which the dust of centuries had been drifting; no one knew exactly what "correct" Latin was supposed to be and no one cared. But by the time Ben Jonson went to school it had been decided that "correct" Latin meant the Latin that Cicero wrote. The blurred medieval theories on vocabulary and syntax were replaced by a single standard, and the great Roman orator became the emperor of all the English schoolrooms of Queen Elizabeth's day.

The situation would have pleased Cicero, since he had trained himself to write ideal Latin and had coolly and methodically shaped the rather unformed Latin of his own day into a medium for literary art. Cicero had studied the best Greek models and he transmitted to Latin the delicate architectural balance of clause against clause that the Greek orators had used so effectively. He also learned from the Greeks a respect for order and form, and he taught in his own turn the doctrine of artistic self-control that came to be called "classical." It was Cicero who quoted with approval a remark of Roscius that might almost be said to be the guiding principle of classical writing: "A sense of fitness, of what is becoming, is the main thing in art."

Education is a curious thing. All over England the wriggling young Elizabethans sat in their classrooms and studied the classical ideal of gravity and control. They learned elegance and restraint from Horace; they learned a balanced and antithetical prose from Cicero; they learned the tight rules of dramatic construction from Terence. And then they went forth and produced the tangled, loose, barbaric magnificence of the Elizabethan drama.

The average Elizabethan writer agreed in theory that the classics were very valuable and important, but in practice he used his classical education chiefly as a way of showing off. Writers like Thomas Nashe and Robert Greene, who were university graduates, scattered bits of classical lore through their writings like children playing with bits of colored glass. There was hardly a dramatist in London who could resist dragging in references to Hector or Hannibal or Hercules, and poetry was never merely poetry but always that classical lady, "the

Muse." A superficial classicism of this kind was one that any intelligent Londoner could acquire in a week if he settled down with a copy of Aesop's *Fables*, a handbook on mythology and an anthology of classical quotations. No doubt men like Nashe and Greene could have recited whole pages of Cicero and Horace from memory, but neither of them had any idea what those disciplined Romans were talking about.

Part of this was a matter of temperament. The Elizabethans were a volatile, excitable and experimental race and they were not attracted to the idea of sobriety in their writing. They were as unwilling to bow themselves to a set of literary rules as they would have been to wear togas, and they had no real sympathy with the solid and weighty notions of Cicero. No doubt the riotous experimentation of the average Elizabethan style would have benefited by a little Roman dignity, and certainly a proper understanding of classic principles would have put a much-needed stiffening into the loose Elizabethan sentence structure. But the Elizabethans ignored their grammar-school training as soon as they escaped from it, and the average Elizabethan dramatist remained as untouched by the classic ideal as though his long years of wrestling with Latin in the schoolroom had never existed.

Yet it was something more than the Elizabethan temperament that fixed a gulf between Ben Jonson's contemporaries and the theory of classicism. It was, even more, the way in which classicism was taught. The average schoolmaster did not understand the principle upon which a study of Greek and Roman literature was based. He did not realize that it was a liberating force, not a confining one, and he conducted his classroom in the same way that his medieval ancestors had done before him. He made no attempt to awaken the curiosity or interest of his pupils, since he had none of his own, and he walked through the mighty landscapes of Greece and Rome with his eyes closed to everything but grammar and discipline. If his charges did not learn he beat them, and if they still refused to learn he merely beat them harder.

There had been a time, early in the Renaissance, when it looked as though things might be otherwise and that a golden age was dawning for schoolboys everywhere. During the early years of the fifteenth century, when all Europe was excited by the ancient manuscripts that were being unearthed, an Italian archaeologist discovered in a neglected monastic library a complete copy of one of the greatest educational treatises ever written. It was Quintilian's *The Training of an Orator*.

Quintilian was the kind of teacher that most schoolboys encounter only in their dreams. He was so influential that he was made the head of the first public school in Rome, so popular that he had to protest against his students' "excess of enthusiasm," and so good a teacher that he thought always of his pupils and never of himself. Quintilian disliked the Roman custom of flogging because it made the boys lose heart, and he maintained that there could be no successful education "unless teacher and taught are in perfect sympathy." He implored the teachers of his own day to arouse the pupils' understanding and interest, instead of forcing them into mechanical learning as most of the Roman schools were doing; and when Quintilian's book was rediscovered at the end of the Middle Ages it became a kind of spearhead for the group of men who were trying to loosen up medieval education.

Quintilian gave these men a wonderful goal. They could see a time coming when education would not consist of barren memory work and equally barren rules, but when each teacher would open up to his students the great world of Greece and Rome and the whole heritage of the past would be available to modern Europe. Men like Erasmus or like the wise Spanish educationalist, Juan Luis Vives, knew that the New Learning would never thrive if it remained the property of a few trained scholars and was imprisoned in dogma. It should be thrown open to schoolboys as a thing of delight rather than as a penance, and it called for teachers who were not dusty grammarians but men of the broadest culture. Flogging would be unnecesary because the boys would be eager to learn, and Erasmus could see the whole face of Europe becoming transformed by a combination of enlightened Christianity and an intelligent reading of the classics. "The world is coming to its senses as if awakening out of a deep sleep."

In England at the beginning of the sixteenth century the center of this educational enthusiasm was St. Paul's School in London. Its founder, John Colet, knew both Vives and Erasmus and had even hoped that Erasmus might become its first headmaster. "Teach what thou hast learned lovingly" was the keynote of Colet's educational theory. Since no satisfactory Latin grammar was available for his school he worked out one of his own, going on the principle that nothing could be made "too soft or too familiar for little children, especially learning a tongue unto them all strange." Erasmus helped Colet with the grammar and so did the school's headmaster, William Lily, and when it was finished it came to be known as Lily's Latin Grammar.

This grammar of Colet's, worked out by a group of humanists to supply English schoolboys with a key to the great learning of the past, became the chief instrument of bondage in the English school system. As the official Latin grammar it was set before the boys to be learned by rote, with a beating every time they failed, and the only difference which was made by a better set of rules and a wider use of classical authors was that there was more for the children to learn and more possible mistakes to be made.

The ideal remained, but there was no one to bring it to life. It was much easier for the average hard-working schoolmaster to beat a set of rules into a boy than to operate as the guide and friend that Quintilian had advocated, and the great liberating force of classicism closed in to become a prison house again. Vives and Erasmus had succeeded in easing the lot of the little prisoners somewhat, for they had both written charming exercise books for beginners, cast in dialogue form, that were incorporated into the Tudor school system. But as far as the average Elizabethan schoolboy was concerned the great wave of excitement that had spread over Europe with the rediscovery of the ancient manuscripts of Greece and Rome might never have existed. The boys learned classical Latin instead of medieval Latin, but they were still taught by the same methods and beaten for the same faults. Their minds were dulled when they should have been stimulated, and it is not surprising that most of Ben Jonson's contemporaries were not interested in classicism.

Yet for Ben Jonson the miracle happened and those early days of excitement returned. Somehow, in the crowded schoolroom at Westminster, William Camden managed to give his small pupil a vision of the ancient world. It was a vision that leaped over the intervening years and the quarreling grammarians and it brought the bricklayer's stepson into the serene, golden atmosphere of which the earlier humanists had dreamed.

It is hard to say how much of this can be credited to Camden, since he taught hundreds of small boys and only produced one real classicist. Nor was the achievement the result of any special quickness or cleverness on Jonson's part, since England was full of clever little boys who were superficially good classical scholars, able to parrot correct Latin by the hour and turn out yards of hexameters on request. What made Jonson exceptional was the way his mind reached out for the principle behind the rules. He became the one Elizabethan dramatist who was concerned with the spirit of the classics rather than the outward trappings and who was drawn to the world of which Erasmus had once dreamed—a serene, steady, ethical world made luminous by the principles of reason and order.

Apart from opening out the classic world to Jonson, Camden gave him a series of lesser gifts that were useful to him as a writer. He taught him handwriting, and young Jonson labored over ruled paper with a homemade pen until he had perfected his decorative and individual script, which he could turn out with such steady precision that his pages have the neatness of a professional scribe's. Camden also taught Jonson to keep a commonplace book in which he jotted down passages from his reading, a familiar Elizabethan habit which became so ingrained in

Jonson that his notebooks were a storehouse and his own writings an intricate tissue of the great passages he had loved.

Camden taught Jonson to write poetry by the method that was standard during this period. The idea was first written in prose, to make sure that it was clear and complete, and then it was turned into verse. When the average Elizabethan poet stopped writing school exercises in Latin verse and turned instead to his native English, he abandoned this slow and rather prosaic way of working in the same way he jettisoned nearly everything else he had learned in grammar school. But it was characteristic of Jonson that he kept it up throughout the whole of his life. He habitually wrote his poetry "first in prose, for so his master Camden had learned him."

Unlike most schoolmasters, Camden had a profound respect for the art of poetry. The average Elizabethan schoolteacher was only too likely to think of poetry as being "nothing but the turning of words forth out of the grammatical order . . . in some kind of meter." Poetry was designed "rather for ornament than for any necessary use" unless it served a commendable purpose such as describing the funeral of a nobleman. Archbishop Usher admitted that when he was a boy "he was extremely addicted to poetry and was much delighted with it, but afterward, growing to more maturity and consideration, he shook it off as not suitable to the great end of his more resolved, serious and profitable studies." Young Ben Jonson, equally resolved and serious, might have fallen into the same illusion if his schoolmaster had shared the contempt for poetry that marred so many Renaissance scholars. But Camden was a poet himself and he never lost his respect for that most powerful and ancient of the arts. "Poets were the first politicians, the first philosophers . . . They are God's own creatures."

It was probably Camden who gave Jonson his profound sense of the moral dignity and value of poetry. Great writing was not a light amusement but a civilizing force, and the poet was not a pleasant versifier but, as Camden said, a philosopher. This had been the point of view of the ancient world, for although the Greeks disliked preaching they had never attempted to separate ethics from art; and the Romans, who encouraged preaching, were wholly convinced that any skillful user of words was under an obligation to teach morality.

As Horace pointed out, the poet had the advantage of being an irresistible instructor because he gave delight, and Horace's twin doctrine of "delight and teach" became the watchword of literary theory in the Renaissance. A Christian nation like England obviously could not concentrate on pagan authors in the classroom unless some kind of moral purpose was involved, and when the plays of Terence were included in every school curriculum it was not primarily because "his words be chosen so purely, placed so orderly, and all his stuff so neatly packed up." It was chiefly because his comedy was "a mirror of man's life," where evil was not taught but exposed. This may not have been quite what Terence himself had in mind when he wrote his smooth and skillful comedies of manners, and it may not have been the quality that interested the Westminster school-boys when they memorized one of his plays to present it to the Queen. But the classic Latin authors would never have been permitted inside the Tudor schoolrooms unless it was felt that they were not merely good writers but guides, moralists and philosophers.

Somewhere and somehow, the ambition was implanted in Ben Jonson to be just such a writer himself. He would be like one of the great Romans of the Augustan Age, remote, disciplined and calm, and by the force of his example he would rescue the Elizabethan world of letters from its sloppy and emotional ways. He would bring back the ancient days of order and reason and rebuild in England the massive glory that had once been Rome's.

Jonson's humanist vision of the man of reason, the moral being who inhabited a calm, stable and reasonable world, was probably incapable of being realized at any time in the world's history. It could certainly not have been realized in Elizabethan England, whose special literary virtues were its liveliness, its emotionalism and its irrepressible, youthful bounce. But the more hopeless it became, the more fiercely Jonson longed for it. Stubborn, vigorous and strong-willed, he was determined to make Elizabethan England see his vision; and Elizabethan England, with equal stubbornness, refused.

What Jonson saw as enlightened helpfulness on his part, his fellow writers interpreted as unwarranted conceit in a writer no better than themselves. They did not understand that Jonson was not acting in his own person but as a kind of champion for the whole of antiquity, and they considered him an insufferable upstart who had no better purpose in life than to insult his elders. Jonson, for his part, saw himself as a warrior with the mighty spirits of Horace, Cicero and Quintilian ranged behind him, and he could not understand why his fellow Elizabethans seemed so willfully to misinterpret him.

Jonson would have liked to behave with the dignified calm of some ideal Roman gentleman. He pictured himself living far removed from all thoughts of petty strife, inhabiting a philosopher's world of wise words and judicious actions. Perhaps if his colleagues had given Jonson the respectful attention he considered his due, he might have been able to attain this ideal. But instead he found himself surrounded by disrespect, and it drove him to fury.

In an age full of touchy writers, there was not one who managed to get into as many fights as Ben Jonson. He leaped from feud to feud with such intensity that occasionally he was involved in several at once, and he laid about him with a vigor that was as impressive as it was undignified.

It was Jonson's furious devotion to the ideals of classic calm that started most of these wars, for he would never admit that he had given himself an impossible task when he tried to transplant Augustan Rome to the resistant soil of Elizabethan England. He tried to impose the Roman theory of classical restraint both upon his excitable self and upon the equally excitable world of letters that surrounded him, and while he failed in both cases it was at least a magnificent attempt.

# Chapter 4

ONCE EVERY YEAR, seven men of wisdom and rectitude gathered together at Westminster School to single out the little boys who were worthy to receive scholarships. They were all gentlemen of high standing and included the Dean of Westminster and two representatives each from Oxford and Cambridge. Moreover the system of choosing the Queen's Scholars was well handled. The boys were judged on the basis of "their teachableness, the goodness of their disposition, their learning, good behavior and poverty." No influence was to be brought to bear on the judges, an innovation which many parents deplored.

Ben Jonson was exactly the kind of boy who should have received one of the school scholarships, and his hopes must have been high when he entered the competition. Perhaps he tried too hard. Perhaps the "goodness" of his disposition could not be conscientiously recommended. Or, more probably, he lacked the superficial cleverness that does so well in examinations. Roger Ascham, one of the wisest and most experienced of Tudor schoolmasters, said that learning was "both hindered and injured" by school examiners who chose boys like children choose apples and judged them by their pleasant manners and quick wits. "This I know, not only by reading of books in my study, but also by experience of life abroad in the world, that those which be commonly the wisest . . . when they be old were never commonly the quickest of wit when they were young." Ben Jonson

may have been one of these. At any rate, the most ardent
scholar that Westminster School ever produced was not given
a scholarship, and Ben Jonson never became one of the favored
forty whose tuition was paid by the Crown.

The loss of a scholarship was not a complete disaster in the
earlier years of Jonson's education, since a friend was helping
with his tuition and he could eat and sleep at home. But the
problem became really serious as he grew older. Unless he could
find some way of being sent to either Oxford or Cambridge
he would almost certainly, considering his stepfather's profession, end his life as a manual laborer.

All over England, anxious parents were saving and struggling
to send their sons to Oxford or Cambridge. A university education was the one lever that could lift the boys into a higher
sphere of life, the open door to preferment and honors. Sometimes the parents or a friend of the family supplied the money,
but in the case of a clever boy it was usually done through a
scholarship. Christopher Marlowe, for instance, went to Cambridge on a scholarship, and without it he might very well have
spent the rest of his days in Canterbury at his father's trade
of making shoes.

Westminster School gave six scholarships annually, three to
Oxford and three to Cambridge. Unfortunately, only the
Queen's Scholars were eligible to compete for them, and since
Jonson had not succeeded in becoming a Queen's Scholar this
avenue was closed to him.

On the other hand, there were other ways in which a Westminster boy could get a university education. Richard Neile,
for instance, was the son of a tallow chandler who had died
poor, and the best that the Westminster headmaster could suggest to the boy's mother was that she apprentice him to a bookseller. Luckily Lady Burghley became interested in the case.
She was a Greek scholar, a woman "of more learning than is
necessary to that sex," and she shared her husband's warm interest in Westminster School. She sent young Richard Neile to
Cambridge, where he flourished mightily, and in time he him-

self became Dean of Westminster. As Dean he was a member
of the board that assigned the Westminster scholarships, and he
financed several private scholarships of his own since he knew
how easy it was for promising boys to be passed over by the
examiners.

Richard Neile went to Cambridge in 1580, when small Ben
Jonson was just beginning to discover the glories of the printed
word. It would have been natural enough for Camden's new
pupil to start dreaming of the time when he too would go to
Oxford or Cambridge and enter one of the great universities as
a free citizen of the world of learning. He would leave the
alleys of Westminster behind him forever, and there would be
nothing to check him except the limits of his own mind.

The dream vanished. It may have been destroyed by lack of
money, lack of patronage, his stepfather's hostility to education,
or, more probably, by a combination of all three. At any rate
it was destroyed. While Ben Jonson's school friends went on
to Oxford and Cambridge, Jonson himself was apprenticed to a
bricklayer.*

It is possible to feel a certain sympathy for Ben Jonson's new
master, saddled with a hot-tempered, bookish youngster in his
teens who did not wish to learn anything about the art of laying
bricks. Jonson hated coercion, and the whole system of Elizabethan labor laws was founded upon coercion. Even a loyal
Elizabethan like Sir Thomas Smith admitted that an apprentice
was not much better off than a slave. "He must do all servile
offices about the house, and be obedient to all his master's com-
mandments, and shall suffer such correction as his master shall
think meet . . . his master being bound only to . . . teach him his
occupation." This relationship lasted by law for seven years,
and if master and apprentice were not in sympathy it could be

---

* Jonson's first biographer, Thomas Fuller, says that "he was statutably admitted into St. John's College in Cambridge . . . where he continued but few
weeks for want of further maintenance." There is no way to check the accuracy of this statement, since the records of admission to Cambridge for this
period are missing, but in any case a "few weeks" at Cambridge would have
been small comfort.

a remarkably uncomfortable period. Sir Thomas said cheerily that all this control was justifiable, since it was "only by covenant and for a time." But it was a covenant Jonson had not wished to make and it led to a future he did not desire. All he learned during his seven years of bondage was how to lay bricks, and he did not wish to learn any such thing. As he told a friend, many years later, he "could not endure" bricklaying.

If Jonson could have resigned himself to leading the life of a laborer, he might conceivably have enjoyed being a stonemason. His writing shows the solid workmanship, the careful fitting-together of parts, of a man who could have made a good stone wall. But bricklaying was routine work, with no element of choice or sense of achievement, and every aspect of a bricklayer's life was thoroughly regimented. His hours of work and his behavior were covered by law, and even his bricks had to be exactly nine inches long.

The Tudor labor laws had been worked out by the employers and they naturally operated to the employers' benefit. The system not only guaranteed each master bricklayer a supply of free labor but it also prevented younger men from setting themselves up in competition against their elders. Each apprentice had to be twenty-four years old before he could leave his master's service, a provision that was frankly designed to prevent "over-hasty marriages and over-soon setting up of households of and by the young folk." In return for working seven years in another man's household, the apprentice eventually reaped his reward. He became a member of the guild and could take apprentices in his turn, and, in the London area, he became a citizen of London.

A man who lays bricks twelve hours in the summer and from dawn to dusk in the winter does not have much time for reading. But every laborer got an hour off at noon and half an hour at three o'clock, and if a young apprentice wanted to keep a candle burning late at night while he went on with his education there was probably no one to stop him. A legend of the seventeenth century says that Jonson worked on a new building at Lincoln's Inn with a trowel in his hand and a book in his pocket. No buildings were erected at Lincoln's Inn during the period of Jonson's apprenticeship but he may have helped with the brick wall that was erected "at the upper end of the backside toward Holborn." As for the book in his pocket, it is likely enough. Since he could not go to Oxford or Cambridge he had to go on studying by himself, and he ended by becoming the most learned poet in England. He had very little time to himself, but he offset it by his determination and by what must have been a remarkable memory. Even when he grew older and his memory had weakened he was able to say, "I can repeat whole books that I have read."

There was a short period during his late teens or early twenties when Ben Jonson was in the army. This episode in his life is usually pictured as a young man's adventurous fling, a brief and enthusiastic foray into a gallant life of arms. But it is much more likely that Jonson, like most of his fellow Elizabethans, was drafted.

The war that Queen Elizabeth and her subjects were waging with equal reluctance was in the Low Countries. It had started in 1585 when Jonson was a schoolboy and when it became evident that the United Provinces of the Netherlands could never hope to win their heroic revolt against Spain unless some other Protestant power helped them. Elizabeth issued a state paper, published simultaneously in four languages, in which she mentioned the tyranny of Catholic Spain and her responsibilities to God Almighty; and then, with the bitter reluctance of a woman who hated war as much as she disliked unnecessary expenses, she sent English troops abroad under the command of the Earl of Leicester.

England was still near enough to the days of feudalism and the glitter of the chivalric ideal so that the troops were headed by men as excited as boys. All was drums and glory, and the Dutch greeted them with interminable classical pageantry, with triumphal arches and with banquets, to show that they, too, understood the amenities. What Camden called "a tickling desire of command and glory" filled everyone from the commander down, and there was only an occasional voice raised in protest. One of these voices belonged to a European friend of Sir Philip Sidney's, who loved him so much that he tried to persuade him the chivalric ideal was an absurdity. "You and your fellows, I mean men of noble birth, consider that nothing brings you more honor than wholesale slaughter."

But Sidney went with the rest. He set aside his dream of establishing an American colony of free men that would offset the bondage of Spanish rule in the New World and went off instead to fight the Spaniards in the mists before Zutphen, dying of gangrene from a bullet that shattered his thigh. All England mourned him, as well it might, that "lovely joy" of all honorable men who had lived so gallantly and who died in a badly planned, useless skirmish.

Sidney left behind him his uncle, the arrogant and tactless Earl of Leicester, who succeeded in pleasing no one. The allies quarreled more or less continually with each other, as allies are likely to do, and the fine chivalric glow with which the war had begun faded rapidly. By the time Ben Jonson entered the army, no one was enjoying the war except an assortment of clerks, captains and government officials who were quietly making fortunes out of graft.

The root of the difficulty was the fact that England had no experience in military matters. In the old days she had raised her troops by feudal levies, and now that the feudal system had vanished Queen Elizabeth saw no reason to set up a professional army in its place. It cost too much and she was trying to avoid war in any case. The result was that the harassed and confused Privy Council was trying to run a military machine without either money or experience, and it is remarkable that Lord Burghley and his colleagues succeeded as well as they did.

Everything plagued Elizabeth's ministers. They struggled with shipowners who did not want to carry the soldiers abroad and with victualers who supplied bad rations. They wrestled with uniforms that shrank and surgeons who knew nothing

about gunshot wounds, and with an inflation that made everything cost more than it should. They also struggled with the
problem of modernizing an army that had been brought up on
archery, and they must have thought wistfully of those happy
days when an Englishman could be sent forth to battle with a
longbow that cost only a few shillings instead of having to be
supplied with a musket that cost as much as two pounds. Moreover muskets were hard to handle, difficult to use in wet
weather and forever disappearing out of the soldiers' hands—
lost in battle, pawned or otherwise vanished. Meanwhile the
ordnance department, which was composed of a number of
separate officials with no one in complete control, spent its time
squabbling over precedents and had no real interest in the conduct of the war.

The worst problem the Privy Council had to face was the
question of graft. It was everywhere, like rats in grain, and the
well-meaning government never caught up with it. The ordnance department was riddled with corruption, and the war
treasurer was busy making sixteen thousand pounds a year in
addition to his regular salary. This was bad enough, but the
problem became heartbreaking on the lower levels. The money
and supplies that were intended for the men were issued
through the captains, who were paid very little, and the company clerks, who were paid nothing at all. A dead soldier was
obviously more useful than a living one, since his pay could be
pocketed and his uniform pawned, and it was financially profitable for a captain to allow his men to be killed and then fail
to report it. This system of "dead pay" was notorious, but no
one seemed to be able to do anything about it.

Every man in England, from sixteen to sixty, was liable for
military duty and nearly everyone evaded it if he could. Many
of the men who were conscripted escaped the first chance they
got—before the march to the coast, during the long wait for
ships in the port towns, or by bribing the clerk of the company
to take the name off the rolls. The deserters may have been
lacking in patriotism but it is difficult to blame them, since even

if a soldier was fortunate enough to serve under an honest captain it was almost impossible to save anything out of his pay. He was expected to buy his own rations, and as the victim of food profiteers he often paid more than the market price and got bad pork and cheese in exchange. He was supposed to pay for any powder and shot that he might be so incautious as to use up in battle, and only the most respectable of soldiers could escape paying fines. A conscript was fined the enormous sum of five shillings if he was caught swearing, and a day's pay if he failed to go to church.

Winter uniforms were theoretically available by the first of November, but if the captain was dishonest they were never distributed at all. When they were, they were often made of cheap materials by incompetent contractors, and even the warmest of shirts and doublets would not have reconciled the shivering English soldiers to the Dutch weather, with its damp and its cold winds. As Lord Burghley's son Robert wrote to a friend in England, "Your nose would drop off . . . if you were as cold as we have been." Parts of the once-prosperous land had become so devastated by war that the sentries were attacked by wolves, and although there were many men, both English and Dutch, who made money out of the war it did not profit the average soldier.

Yet Ben Jonson remembered his own part in it with some pride. Young, lively and an excellent swordsman, he succeeded in fighting a successful duel with an enemy soldier "in the face of both the camps." Such duels were not unknown but neither were they common, and it is characteristic of Jonson that he managed to inject an irrepressible note of individualism into a war that most conservative Englishmen felt was deplorably unlike those "well-ordered wars betwixt emperors, kings and commonwealths" that took place in the good old days.

Some years later, Jonson wrote a set of verses, "To True Soldiers," in which he made it clear that his frequent satires on military men did not include any of the decent ones.

Strength of my country, when I bring to view
Such as are mis-called captains, and wrong you . . .
I swear by your true friend, my Muse, I love
Your great profession, which I once did prove
And did not shame it . . .

Jonson looked back on his days in the army with quiet pride and even, like many demobilized veterans, with affection. It was easy to forget the boredom and the inefficiency, and to remember instead the comradeship, the occasional excitement, and the half gallon of beer that was issued to each man every day.

The returning soldier was watched by the government with an anxious eye, and elaborate plans were drawn up to dispose of those whose lives, in the tactful government phrase, had not "otherwise been disposed of by the Almighty." When Ben Jonson arrived back in England his name and equipment were listed by the port authorities and he was issued a pass which gave him just enough time to get back to London and no more. If he had stopped off on the way he would have been arrested as a vagrant, for the Elizabethan government was terrified by the prospect of masterless men roving about the countryside. Its ideal was to have everyone tucked into his own proper niche in his own particular town, and the sooner each returned soldier was back at his old job the better the government was pleased. But the employers did not always want the men back and the men were sometimes too restless to return, so that the country was full of old soldiers whose activities must have haunted the dreams of the Privy Council at night. There was a very wide gap between the Elizabethan theory of total conformity and the Elizabethan practice of lively individualism, and the more rigidly the ideal was upheld in theory the less it seemed to work in practice.*

* For instance, in Jonson's home town of Westminster no stranger was permitted to move in unless he brought two certificates of good conduct from his last place of residence, one for himself and one for his wife. If he lacked a certificate, even his landlord could be brought into court and fined. If the burgesses of Westminster had had their way, the place would have had the regimented neatness and propriety of a toy village—a quality which it conspicuously lacked in practice.

When Ben Jonson returned from the wars, the governing powers had his life all mapped out for him. He was to settle down in his little niche as a bricklayer and spend the rest of his life obedient to the machinery of his local guild. But Jonson, who was a true Elizabethan, promptly went in reverse.

In the first place he married. Marriage was of course very right and proper in its place, since it supplied the government with loyal little subjects and a future string of ratepayers, but as an apprentice Jonson was not free to marry until he was twenty-four. By the time he was twenty-four Jonson was not only married but he had a son.

Very little is known about Jonson's family or about his private life. The lives of most Elizabethan writers are shadowy enough, since the age of biography had not yet dawned, but Jonson is especially hard to trace since his name was so common. Still, there was apparently only one "Benjamin Johnson" in London at the time; and a parish record, discovered by Mark Eccles, shows that Benjamin Johnson and one Anne Lewis were married on the 14th of November, 1594, in the parish church of St. Magnus the Martyr near London Bridge. Anne was apparently a Londoner, since an Elizabethan marriage usually took place in the bride's parish. Jonson himself was still living in Westminster, for when the parish church of St. Martin's was collecting money, three years later, to have the pews fixed, Jonson as a parishioner was assessed eighteenpence.

No evidence has survived about Anne Johnson, except for a casual remark made by her husband a quarter of a century later. He said that she "was a shrew, yet honest." When Jonson called his wife honest he was giving her a high compliment, since "of all styles he loved most to be named honest" and treasured more than a hundred letters in which various correspondents had applied the term to him. As for being a shrew, she must have presided over a lively household, for Jonson was very quick-tempered himself. Moreover, she had reason for her shrewishness, for Jonson was not faithful to her. He was, as he cheerfully admitted, "given to venery," and he regarded his exploits in that field with the same happy pride with which he looked back on his successful duels. He was not what would be called a domestic man, and on one occasion he and his wife lived apart for five years.

Several children were born of the marriage, and it would seem that Jonson loved them deeply. There is a beautiful epitaph he wrote for his baby daughter Mary, in which he describes the grief he and his wife felt over the loss of "the daughter of their youth"; and when his seven-year-old son Benjamin died of the plague Jonson wrote one of the saddest and most personal of his poems. Another "Benjamin Johnson, son of Benjamin" was christened five years later, following the Elizabethan custom of giving the same name to a second son if the first one died. This child died also, when he was only three years old. Earlier, there had been a "Joseph, the son of Benjamin Johnson," born at St. Giles, Cripplegate in 1599. No doubt there were others, but it is not possible to trace them with any certainty.

Whatever the number of his children, it is clear that Jonson emerged from his seven years of apprenticeship with a family to support. A cautious wife would have encouraged him to keep to the trade that would guarantee him a living, but Anne Johnson was apparently lively enough to be willing to take a chance and it may even be that she had some connections with the theatre. The parish of St. Magnus was directly across the river from Southwark, and Southwark was the center of the Elizabethan theatre. In fact, the year that Jonson married the foundations were being laid in Southwark for the newest and largest theatre in England, a magnificent building called the Swan.

Three years after his marriage, Ben Jonson was an actor at the Swan. He did not settle down to the life that had been intended for him, as an orderly and obedient cog in the Elizabethan labor machine. Instead he entered the world of the theatre, and even in that tempestuous atmosphere few people managed to stir up as much excitement as Ben Jonson.

# Chapter 5

B Y 1596 THE ELIZABETHAN THEATRE was in a flourishing state. It had triumphed over the enmity of the city fathers, who saw in the actors a threat to all legitimate business. It had triumphed over the plague, which for two years had closed every playhouse in town. It had triumphed over the loss of some of its best playwrights—Marlowe's sudden murder in a tavern and Greene's slower death through disease and drink. It was as lively and vital and tempestuous as the great city of London that gave it birth, and most of the writing talent in England poured into the one profession where there were no rules to speak of and plenty of ready money.

When Ben Jonson entered the theatre, two great acting companies dominated the London horizon. Of these two, the Chamberlain's company had the more intelligent organization and the longer life, for the actors were close personal friends as well as experienced men of the theatre and they operated as a self-contained democratic unit. William Shakespeare belonged to this company and remained with it as long as he stayed in the theatre. Another member was Richard Burbage, who was rapidly becoming the most popular performer in London and who scored a personal triumph in the lead of Shakespeare's *Richard III*.

The other major company in London was the Admiral's, whose special asset was that brilliant actor, Edward Alleyn. Alleyn had been the idol of the theatregoers in the previous

decade, especially for his overwhelming performance in Marlowe's *Tamburlaine*, and he was still young enough and vigorous enough to challenge competition from Richard Burbage.
The Admiral's company had another asset in Alleyn's father-
in-law, Philip Henslowe, the first great businessman of the
theatre. Henslowe built the company's playhouse, financed its
costumes, lent money to the actors, and in general kept the
whole organization tightly locked in his account books. The
Chamberlain's company had no one to fall back on when a new
play failed or the weekly profits dropped to a dangerous level,
but the actors in it had much more professional freedom than
the ones Henslowe financed.

Neither company had been allowed to build a theatre inside
the city walls, where it might divert money from the pockets
of the London shopkeepers. If a playgoer wanted to see the
latest play of the Chamberlain's company, he went north on
the great thoroughfare that ran through east London and followed it out to Shoreditch. In the crowded suburb of Shoreditch stood the oldest theatre in England, built in 1576 through
the faith and fury of James Burbage, father of Richard. It was
named the Theatre and just south of it stood the Curtain,
erected a short time later and operating under the same general
management. If, on the other hand, the playgoer wanted to see
the Admiral's company, he went south on the same thoroughfare and followed it over London Bridge into Southwark. In
Southwark stood the Rose, which dominated the south bank
of the river. Its only rival on that side of the Thames was a
theatre at Newington Butts, which was too far out of town
and too poorly kept up to be of much importance.

A London businessman named Francis Langley eyed the
profits of the Rose and decided to build a theatre of his own
on the south bank of the Thames. He already owned a piece of
land west of the Rose, the old manor of Paris Garden for which
he had paid eight hundred and fifty pounds; and when the
plague subsided and the theatres reopened Langley concluded
that the time had come to put up his new playhouse.

The mayor of London found himself faced with yet another den of iniquity and wrote a letter to Lord Burghley as head of the Privy Council, asking him to put a stop to it. But Langley's brother-in-law, Sir Anthony Ashley, was one of the clerks of the Privy Council, and in any case the government had no real objection to another theatre. Queen Elizabeth was an ardent playgoer and the actors clearly had to try their plays out somewhere if they were to be available for the Christmas season at Court.

Langley called his building the Swan and he made it more splendid than the Theatre, the Curtain or the Rose. A Dutch traveler who was touring England in 1596 was much impressed by all four theatres and said they were all of "notable beauty." But he added that "the largest and most magnificent is the one of which the sign is the swan . . . for it accommodates in its seats three thousand persons." The traveler was especially interested in the wooden columns, which had been painted in "excellent imitation of marble," and he made a little sketch of the interior of so remarkable a building.

It took more than clever paintwork to fill the huge theatre. What the Swan really needed was a permanent organization of actors that could challenge the supremacy of the Chamberlain's company at the Theatre and the Admiral's company at the Rose. No such company existed, but one could be formed. Early in 1597 Langley signed a contract with two of the leading actors at the Rose, Richard Jones and Thomas Downton, who agreed to play at the Swan for a year or forfeit a hundred pounds apiece. Langley made a similar agreement with three other actors, Robert Shaa, Gabriel Spencer and William Birde, and after many "conferences and communications" the new company moved into the Swan. Its patron was the Earl of Pembroke and it was called Pembroke's company.

Apart from these leading actors, who had joint control of scripts, costumes and properties and were known as sharers, there was a larger group of minor actors who were paid a regular salary but had no direct share in the profits. There is no list of these minor actors in the agreement with Langley since they were not important enough to put under bond, but among them was Ben Jonson.

Jonson apparently entered the acting world through a provincial touring company, since a fellow playwright later jeered at him for having been "a poor journeyman player" who ambled beside "a play-wagon, in the highway." There were shoals of these minor acting companies all over England, usually headed by some London actor who could no longer get leading roles and who was reluctant to tour the Continent. A company that was inadequate by metropolitan standards could sometimes do very well on the road, even though it had to compete both with the well-established local companies and with the summer tours of the Londoners. These minor companies used old scripts and piled their costumes and properties into a wagon. Jonson speaks of actors who go about with shoes "full of gravel . . . after a blind jade and a hamper, and stalk upon boards and barrel heads, to an old cracked trumpet," and it is a fair description, if a rather bitter one, of the life of a small touring company.

Jonson had no special training as an actor, but he had a vigorous body and a magnificent memory. His exploit when he was in the army indicates that he was an excellent swordsman, able to take an effective part in the multitude of duels and battle scenes that set the Elizabethan stage awash with mimic deaths. He had even had some training in music, that very important part of an actor's trade, since each student at Westminster School spent two hours a week studying music under the choirmaster. There was nothing else about his training that fitted Jonson for the trade of strolling player but at least it was a more interesting occupation than laying bricks. Moreover, the world of the theatre was a flexible one and it was not impossible for an actor to become a playwright too. Richard Tarleton, the famous comic actor, had written at least one successful play, and the Chamberlain's company owed part of its popularity to the scripts that were supplied by one of its members, William Shakespeare.

The new company at the Swan was especially anxious to get good scripts since it had none of its own. There had been an earlier Pembroke's company but it collapsed during the plague period and was forced to dispose of its stock of costumes and plays, so that the new company had to start over again from the beginning. Francis Langley advanced his actors a large sum of money to invest in new costumes, but that did not solve the problem of laying in a stock of good, playable scripts.

There was one playwright in London who had survived as the last representative of the brilliant young group of university men who had brightened the theatre for a decade. His name was Tom Nashe, a minister's son who had come to London in his twenties and had startled even that tolerant town with his lively disrespect for his betters and his irresistible flow of words. Everyone enjoyed Nashe's impudence, including himself, and he had been one of the most brilliant of the university wits who had dominated the literary scene before the plague. He wrote a tragedy with Marlowe and a comedy with Greene, and he attended the banquet of pickled herring and Rhenish wine that took place a month before Greene died. When Gabriel Harvey was so incautious as to attack the dead dramatist, Nashe leaped to Greene's defense and bestowed a series of insults upon his enemy which were so vigorous and so imaginative that Harvey must have had the greatest difficulty in living them down.

Nashe was thirty years old when the new company at the Swan asked him for a script. All his old comrades were dead and in theory it was time for Nashe to settle down. But he still possessed a strong streak of youthful mischief and it emerged in his new play, which he called *The Isle of Dogs*.

Nashe had a collaborator for his play, the young actor at the Swan whose name was Ben Jonson. Nashe later maintained that he himself had written the first act only and that the other four were done without his knowledge or consent. This may have been a convenient fiction that Nashe used to protect himself as soon as the play got him into trouble or it may have been the truth. A lively, independent young man like Ben Jonson may very well have been the one who carried the play over the narrow borderline that separated impudence from sedition.

Possibly Jonson thought that the world of the theatre was subject to fewer controls than the army or bricklaying. If so, he promptly found out otherwise. The Privy Council heard that *The Isle of Dogs* contained some "very seditious and slanderous matter" and stopped the play, going so far as to trace and suppress even the copies that the actors had lent to their friends. The Council also imprisoned the actors, and the only one who escaped punishment was the wary Nashe. He already knew a good deal about the inside of London prisons and retreated among the herring at Yarmouth, leaving the Privy Council to search among the papers in his lodging for possible criminal intent.

The government sent Ben Jonson to Marshalsea prison, as being "not only an actor but a maker of part of the said play." With him went two of the leading players in the company, Robert Shaa and Gabriel Spencer. Not content with this, the government sent a board of expert inquisitors, headed by the notorious and vicious Richard Topcliffe, to persuade the three actors to give evidence that would involve "the rest of their fellows." There was also an attempt to plant informers in the prison when direct questioning had no effect, and Jonson still remembered with bitterness, years later, the "two damned villains" who tried to trap him into some kind of admission of guilt.

Although the script of *The Isle of Dogs* has not survived, it would probably seem harmless enough to a modern reader. It did not seem harmless to the Privy Council, since England was operating under a one-party system and any criticism of the government was automatically looked upon as seditious. Moreover the government happened to be in an extremely touchy frame of mind in July of 1597 when *The Isle of Dogs* was produced. The end of the decade was darkened by a depression which was already making itself felt in food shortages and high prices, and the Privy Council was on the alert for any signs of popular discontent. Only the year before the mayor of London had forestalled a minor case of sedition, as he proudly reported to the head of the Council. He had sent a publisher to jail for issuing a ballad on the scarcity of grain, since he feared that "thereby the poor may aggravate their grief and take occasion of some discontentment." Apparently the ruling classes felt that the shortage of food would not be really serious as long as no one was allowed to talk about it.

The Privy Council must have been deeply disturbed over *The Isle of Dogs* since in the first heat of the moment it decreed that every theatre in town was to be destroyed. Orders were sent to the justices of the peace in Surrey and Middlesex to superintend the wrecking of the stages and the seating arrangements, with instructions that the buildings were to be defaced so thoroughly that they could never be used again.

Fortunately this drastic order came to nothing. The Lord Admiral and the Lord Chamberlain, the patrons of the two major companies, were members of the Privy Council, and the Queen herself was a confirmed playgoer. The theatres were closed briefly but they were not demolished, and after a decent interval the Theatre, the Curtain and the Rose were all able to reopen.

The Swan, however, did not reopen. Francis Langley found himself unable to get a license. It may be unjust to feel that Philip Henslowe, owner of the Rose, had a hand in this, but Langley had lured away two of his best actors and Henslowe had moved with remarkable speed to retrieve them. The Privy Council had not yet had time to alert Richard Topcliffe and the other inquisitors before Henslowe had Richard Jones back in the fold again, bound by a three-year agreement to prevent any further straying. Jones' fellow actor, Robert Shaa, who had also left the Rose to work at the Swan, was not able to sign a similar agreement with Henslowe because he was in Marshalsea prison and so Jones signed it for him. Henslowe also suc-

ceeded in getting the other three main actors from the Swan—
Spencer, Downton and Birde—and although Langley brought
suit for breach of contract he was never able to get any of them
back again.

Ben Jonson also entered Henslowe's employ and it was in this
same month of July that his name makes its first appearance
in Henslowe's account book: "Lent unto Benjamin Johnson,
player, the 28 of July, 1597, in ready money the sum of four
pounds."

Perhaps Jonson needed the money for his family, since an
actor cannot earn a living while he is in the Marshalsea. Or
perhaps he needed it for himself, since an Elizabethan prison
was a kind of evil boardinghouse in which the prisoner was
obliged to pay for everything he got. He paid for his food and
his bed and even for the irons with which he was manacled,
and the wardenship of Fleet prison was such a profitable position that it was possible to raise a mortgage on it. When a
formal complaint was made against the Fleet in the House of
Commons, the prisoners did not object to the fact that they
were charged over two shillings a week for their lodgings.
What they were objecting to was the fact that they were
packed in ten to a room and had no "room to spit but on each
other's beds."

Ben Jonson was released from prison in October by order of
the Privy Council, having spent more than two months in the
Marshalsea. Robert Shaa and Gabriel Spencer were released
with him and took their places as members of the Admiral's
company at the Rose. If Jonson himself did any more acting
there is no record of it.

It was as a playwright that Jonson went to work for Henslowe at the Rose, and two months later Henslowe advanced
him twenty shillings for a new script. Jonson had worked out
the plot of a play, the company had approved it, and he had
promised to have the finished manuscript in the actors' hands
before Christmas.

Unlike James Burbage, that other builder of playhouses,

Jonson's new employer could not be called a man of the theatre in the dedicated and professional sense of the word. Instead he was a man of business, who respected money and knew exactly where to find it.

Philip Henslowe had originally come up to London to be apprenticed to a dyer. He served his full seven years, so that he became "citizen and dyer of London," and then he took a familiar Elizabethan short cut to business advancement by marrying his late master's widow. The money that he acquired was invested in a variety of ways. He ran a pawnbroking venture in which part of the work was done by his disorderly nephew, he manufactured starch and he made a great deal of money out of bear-baiting. As far as Henslowe was concerned, the building and management of theatres was just one more way of making a living.

Henslowe built the Rose in 1587, in what had once been a rose garden near his home in the Liberty of the Clink. He shared expenses with a London grocer, and they agreed to divide the profits and allow "their friends to go in for nothing." Henslowe did not lavish on the Rose the valuable timber and the expensive plastering that James Burbage had insisted on for his beloved Theatre, and as a result he faced some extensive repairs five years later. He had to spend more than a hundred pounds on workmen's wages and bought a vast number of hinges and nails from the ironmonger at the Sign of the Frying-pan. But the Rose repaid him by making a great deal of money, and it became the permanent home of the Admiral's company under the brilliant leadership of Edward Alleyn.

The most attractive aspect of Henslowe's life in the theatre is his close relationship to Alleyn. The same year he remodeled the Rose he acquired the great actor as his son-in-law, for in 1592 Alleyn married Joan Woodward, who was the daughter of Henslowe's wife by her first marriage. Alleyn left London almost immediately to go on tour and Henslowe sent him a series of affectionate letters on the small doings of the household he had left behind. The two men remained close and loyal friends all of Henslowe's life, and he spoke no less than the truth when he said that they were "not as two friends but as two joined in one."

Part of Henslowe's success in the theatre came from his partnership with Alleyn and part of it came from his careful, businesslike respect for money. He kept an account book, thriftily using the blank sheets of one already started by his brother in Sussex, and towards the beginning he allowed a certain amount of irrelevant material to creep in. He noted down that a man might cure hydrophobia by writing a magic formula on a crust of cheese and he trustingly recorded a recipe for curing deafness that involved the juice of ants' eggs. Then he settled down, more realistically, to business, and most of the book is a record of loans made for costumes and scripts to the men of the Admiral's company. The only touch of eccentricity lies in the extraordinary spelling, which makes Henslowe notable even in an age of highly imaginative spellers.

Since Jonson's fellow actors at the Swan were now at the Rose, their names appear and reappear in Henslowe's pages. Robert Shaa borrowed ten shillings to get a friend out of jail. Richard Jones borrowed forty to buy a bass viol and some other musical instruments for the company, and Thomas Downton got another thirty shillings for the same purpose. Downton required forty shillings for the costume his boy apprentice wore in *Cupid and Psyche,* and Gabriel Spencer sent his servant to pick up ten shillings so he could buy a plume. Stage costumes were expensive and accounted for a large part of the company's expenses. The taffeta for a single gown cost as much as the salary of a hired actor for fifteen weeks, and even a robe "for to go invisible" represented a considerable investment.

Another heavy expense was the scripts, for the company never paid less than six pounds for a script and ordered a great many. The Rose was a large theatre, and a different play had to be supplied every afternoon. If the play was successful it would be repeated later on in the week, but a run of twenty-two performances for even the most successful play was uncommon. In general there was a steady stream of new scripts, and Henslowe counted on novelty and a rapid turnover to keep his theatre filled with paying customers.

This meant that the playwrights had to be kept working at high speed, turning out scripts with the same efficiency that Henslowe's other workmen turned out starch. The usual system was for one writer to supply the plot and a group of others to write it, apparently taking an act apiece. The payment was not necessarily divided equally among the collaborators (when *Fair Constance of Rome* was finished one of the five playwrights got only eleven shillings) but the money was paid promptly and Henslowe's men learned to write quickly. Thomas Dekker, for instance, worked four years for Henslowe at the rate of nearly a script a month, and Michael Drayton, that gentle and distinguished poet, produced seventeen scripts for Henslowe in a single year.

Henslowe was generous enough according to his lights. He was ready with a cash advance as soon as the plot had been approved, and fat Henry Chettle was always borrowing small sums from him for work not yet completed. The four playwrights who worked on *Sir John Oldcastle* were not only well paid for the script but also given an extra bonus of ten shillings after the successful opening. Moreover, the writers could always count on a few drinks to bind the bargain, and when Henslowe advanced four pounds to Drayton, Dekker, Chettle and another successful writer named Wilson for their latest script he spent five shillings "at the tavern in Fish Street for good cheer."

Henslowe kept in general to the same group of playwrights. He worked them hard but he paid them fairly, and the same names occur over and over again in his accounts. Ben Jonson joined a group of experienced, overworked men whom Henslowe sometimes called "poets" and sometimes "gentlemen" but who actually operated as literary hacks.

Some of Henslowe's employees were probably contented enough. Men like Dekker and Chettle had had enough experi-

ence in literary London to know how precarious it was to try
to make a living with a pen, and they could appreciate the value
of Henslowe's prompt payments. Minor writers like Porter and
Day and Hathway had no special literary gifts, and a man like
Anthony Munday would do anything for money. Munday happened to excel in thinking up plots, and one of his frequent collaborators was Michael Drayton. Drayton was a very fine poet
who was already well known in London for the "purity and
preciousness of his style." But the praise of his contemporaries
and inclusion in the poetry anthologies could not earn Drayton
a living and it was better to work for Henslowe than to starve.

Until Ben Jonson went to work for the Admiral's company,
the oddest fish that Henslowe had caught in his net was George
Chapman. This vigorous, opinionated and brilliant writer had
come up from Oxford and made his reputation in London with
"The Shadow of Night," a subtle, intellectual poem that was
so obscure that many people could not understand it at all.
Chapman started writing for Henslowe and unexpectedly
showed a gift for turning out enormously popular plays. His
*Humorous Day's Mirth* was one of the hits of the season and
*The Blind Beggar of Alexandria* had an enormous run.

*The Blind Beggar* was published in 1598, the same year in
which Chapman brought out his translation of the first seven
books of *The Iliad*. It was the dream of Chapman's life to produce a complete translation of Homer, and not even the drain
of his hack work for Henslowe could keep him from working
on the project with furious intensity. But Chapman knew that
if he could find a rich patron he would be released to devote
all his time to Homer, and he spent his life in a bitter and un-
availing search after patronage.

The problem of finding a patron was a melancholy one in
Elizabethan times. The old concept of the gracious and wealthy
nobleman who was willing to support a retinue of poets had
not been able to survive the change from a feudal to a mercantile
civilization, and the matter had become further complicated
by the host of new authors that had sprung up since the inven-

tion of printing. As one author frankly put it, "The multitude of writers in our age hath begotten a scarcity of patrons." Whenever any promising young aristocrat made his debut at Court there was a rush of poets dedicating books to him, and a stupid youngster like the Earl of Southampton could hardly come of age before there was a cluster of anxious writers hoping to be admitted to the magic circle of his purse strings. The case of William Shakespeare, who succeeded in getting this particular earl for his patron and then abandoned the relationship, is so exceptional as to stand alone in the history of Elizabethan letters.

The poets did not especially enjoy abasing themselves before these silken young gentlemen. There is a savage scene in a university play of the period in which the needy hero does everything he can think of to ingratiate himself with a patron. "I . . . cast myself down at your worship's toes." He then indignantly reports to his sympathetic friends that it had not been worth it. "When I had pronounced my little speech, with a hundred damnable lies . . . he . . . gave me fiddler's wages and dismissed me."

The young Elizabethan noblemen were not altogether to blame, since they had more alluring ways of spending their money. When they came up to London they found the city spread before them like a vast and glittering show window, and few of them could resist the game of outspending each other. They lavished their money on jewelers and goldsmiths and haberdashers; they paid the enormous rentals that were inevitable in a city as overcrowded as London; they gambled, and they maintained expensive retinues. A young man who owned fifty-eight manors had no difficulty in living beyond his income, and under the circumstances a gift to every needy poet was clearly impractical.

Moreover, the young men of the Court were themselves on the lookout for patrons. They hoped to get government posts or to become the managing directors of various monopolies, and this meant the same sort of abasement and the same pulling

of strings that the poets practiced. It was an age in which everything depended on knowing the right people, and when the
great Lord Burghley wrote out ten rules of conduct for his
son he acknowledged the situation with perfect frankness. "Be
sure to keep some great man thy friend . . . Compliment him
often. Present him with many, yet small gifts . . . If thou have
cause to bestow some great gratuity, let it be some such thing
as may be daily in his sight. Otherwise, in this ambitious age,
thou shalt . . . live in obscurity." There was no bitterness in
these suggestions of Burghley's. He was merely giving ordinary,
practical advice.

There was one Elizabethan who never learned to accommodate himself to this system of shuffling and groveling, and that
was Sir Philip Sidney. He did not like being fawned on and he
respected anyone who could write good poetry, and the combination made him the ideal patron. No one mourned his tragic
early death more than the poets. As Nashe said, "Thou art dead
in thy grave and hast left too few . . . to cherish the sons of
the Muses." But Sidney struck a final blow for the sons of the
Muses even after his death, for he left behind him a manuscript
that called on the young men of his own class to honor poetry
and support the men who wrote it.

For a time the manuscript was circulated among Sidney's
friends and then it passed into the great democracy of the bookstalls. It was published in 1595 as *An Apology for Poetry* and
within the next three years Ben Jonson had read it. His spirit
leaped to meet Sidney's like a man who has found a brother,
and the little book aroused in him the memory of everything
he had dreamed of in Westminster School. Sidney had helped
Camden when they were young men together at Oxford and
now, years later, he helped Camden's pupil. ·

*An Apology for Poetry* reminded Jonson of what he already
knew, that the poet had once been a priest and a philosopher
rather than a mere versifier, and that all antiquity gave him the
honor that was currently being withheld from him. Sidney's
graceful little essay went on to describe, in almost comic de-

spair, the low state of the drama in the early 80's, and Jonson, looking about him, could see that things had been getting steadily worse ever since. His fellow dramatists at the Rose were turning out scripts which not only shattered the classic principles that Sidney advocated but which went out of their way to stamp on the ruins. A successful theatre script was free to leap over the habitable globe and to span whole generations with a flip of the pen, and no one seemed to care that Horace and Cicero and Terence had once laid down the proper rules for a well-made play.

To Jonson, in his young ardor, it seemed clear that the whole confused, vigorous growth of the Elizabethan drama should be hacked away so that only a few pure and classical shoots would remain. The state of the current theatre was rather like the state of Philip Henslowe's property room—a confused jumble of lion skins, crowns, dragons, rainbows, coffins, tombs, swords, steeples, snakes, arms and legs, and bedsteads—and Jonson saw himself replacing this clutter with the classic simplicity that Sidney had advocated.

It seemed possible to Jonson that he could bring back, single-handed, the original function of the poet and dramatist as Sidney had described it and that he could transform the contemporary theatre by raising it to the level of Greece and Rome. His sole experience in the theatre had been as a hired actor and as a hack writer for Henslowe, and seven years of his formal education had been spent learning to lay bricks. Any reasonable person might say that Jonson had given himself an impossible assignment, but Jonson refused to believe that it was impossible. He sat down to write a classic comedy and took up the sword that he did not let drop until he died.

# Chapter 6

WHEN BEN JONSON set himself to write a classic comedy, there was no collection of Greek and Roman comedies that he could study. The only comedies that were available during the Renaissance were those of Plautus and Terence, and both of them had been imitators of the same thing—a late Greek comedy of manners to which they had gracefully and successfully given a Roman background.

Yet if there was a shortage of classic plays, there was no shortage of rules about classic playwriting. For over a century the scholarly theorists of Europe, mostly Italians, had been weaving a tight web of dogma about the whole subject of what was "correct" in drama. They had announced that the unities of time, place and action must be observed, that comedy and tragedy could never be mixed, that tight and decorous limits must be set on characterization, and so on, and they had succeeded in erecting a series of little fences that imprisoned every really conscientious dramatist in Europe. The same rigidity had crept over the subject that had crept over the teaching of grammar, and a classicist in the sixteenth century was not a man who had entered the large freedom of the ancient Greeks but one whose hands were bound by the small rules of the late Italians.

It was generally believed that these rules came direct from Aristotle and Horace, an assumption that would have startled the two men themselves. Neither the Greek teacher nor the Roman poet had set himself up as a supernatural lawgiver from the slopes of Parnassus, since they were both reasonable men who believed in the freedom of the imagination. But their statements had been brooded over and annotated and codified until the spirit of their advice was lost in a rapt contemplation of the letter.

In the case of Aristotle, the Renaissance theorists were obliged to use a difficult and obscure book, the *Poetics*. This seems to have been a collection of lecture notes intended for Aristotle's advanced students at the Lyceum, written for men who had been educated in the same general background and were capable of following the packed, elliptical statements. Moreover, the *Poetics* was written in a complex Greek that proved to be too much for the men who translated it into Latin, so that an obscure text was still more obscure by the time the men of the Renaissance tried to erect a code of rules from its pages.

Aristotle's fellow lawgiver was Horace, who was even more unsuited to the role that had been thrust upon him. Horace's *Art of Poetry* was a very informal piece of work—a letter in verse to two young friends of his who were evidently thinking of taking up writing—and it was written with Horace's usual courtesy and grace. It was not easy to turn so civilized a writer into a literary dictator, but the Renaissance theorists managed to do it. His doctrine of good taste in writing could be dovetailed with Aristotle's more fundamental discussion of first principles, and from them both was ultimately reared the intricate critical theory that had all learned Europe in chains.

The most influential of Renaissance literary theorists was a redoubtable old scholar named Julius Caesar Scaliger. His own *Poetics,* published posthumously eleven years before Jonson was born, was a massive and dogmatic attempt to give the whole subject its final standardization; and Scaliger's remarks were backed by such an array of learning and such a complete absence of doubt on the part of its author that all Europe was awed into accepting the *Poetics* as a basic handbook on the art of writing plays. Scaliger was convinced that "the poetical art is a science," and it was so exact a science that the Greeks themselves frequently failed to measure up to Scaliger's rigid requirements. Homer lacked neatness, Euripides showed grave defects in his choice of plots, and Aeschylus did not understand the principles that guided the correct way to title plays.

Scaliger's heavy shadow lay over Renaissance critical theory from that time forward, and a well-read young man like Sir Philip Sidney knew him well. A mind as graceful and relaxed as Sidney's could accept Scaliger's theories without taking on Scaliger's tone, but Ben Jonson in his twenties was neither relaxed nor graceful. If Jonson's vigorous, dogmatic mind had surrendered itself unconditionally to the teaching of a man like Scaliger and had focused on the exact letter of classicism rather than on its spirit, he would have been unbearable. Moreover, he would have been unreadable, for Scaliger's slide-rule approach to poetry had nothing to do with poetry itself.

What saved Jonson from going to extremes was his dislike of arbitrary rules. His lively, stubborn, independent mind revolted from the whole principle of dictatorship, and he discovered early and by instinct the principle which he later expressed openly and by conviction: "Nothing is more ridiculous than to make an author a dictator, as the schools have done to Aristotle. The damage is infinite." Jonson as a humanist belonged to the liberal tradition of men like Vives and Erasmus, and he did not believe that the great writers of Greece and Rome should be turned into jailers.

Jonson read Scaliger and admired him. But he was armored against the extremes of Scaliger's dogmatism both by his own independent temperament and by the fact that he had found a better teacher in Quintilian. Jonson apparently started reading Quintilian early, possibly as soon as he was parted from Camden and had to continue his education by himself, and the Roman teacher became one of his most treasured mental possessions.

Quintilian was a classicist in an unclassical period, trying to revive in a late, decadent Rome the firmness, dignity and order of the Augustan Age, but since he was a man of sound good

sense he did not try to do it through a set of arbitrary rules. He
said that "rules are helpful . . . so long as they indicate the direct road and do not restrict us absolutely to the ruts made by
others." Jonson was faced by a great many ruts, and Quintilian's serene, steady advice must have been a great help to him.

Unfortunately, Quintilian had no interest whatever in writing plays. His business as a teacher was to train orators, and
while his intelligent suggestions on rewriting and techniques
can be used by any kind of writer, he could offer no special
assistance to a young man of 1598 who wanted to write a classic
comedy. All Quintilian could do was to give Jonson a sense of
the breadth of his goal and reinforce his unwillingness to narrow his work into the rigid groove that went in England by
the name of classicism.

There were plenty of classic plays beng written in England
that Jonson could have chosen for models if he wanted to write
nothing more than a kind of pallid, correct closet drama. Many
learned gentlemen at Oxford and Cambridge were writing plays,
usually in Latin, which even Scaliger would have greeted with
majestic approval, and Sidney's sister, the Countess of Pembroke, had recently organized a group of poets to make translations from a severely classical French dramatist as a gesture
towards elevating the English drama and making it obedient to
the rules of the Italians. Jonson could not have entered this
rarefied atmosphere even if he had wished to. He was a practicing playwright, working for the commercial public stage,
and he did not intend his comedy for a few educated readers
but for the ordinary London public.

One of the most striking things about Jonson, even as a
young man, was his intelligence. Unaided and almost unedu-
cated, he was able to reach back into the past selectively, taking
from it only what he needed and could use; and he was willing
to accept Renaissance critical theory only when it agreed with
what he himself believed to be true.

The basic principle which Jonson accepted from the ancients
and which was reinforced by his reading of Sidney was the

fact that comedy should be what Scaliger called "patterned after real life." Unlike a tragedy, which dealt with far-off, stately and portentous matters, a comedy ought to deal with the familiar and ordinary surroundings that a theatregoer could see about him. Cicero had described comedy, in a famous definition that became increasingly important to Jonson, as "a copy of life, a mirror of custom, a representation of truth." Although both Terence and Plautus used Greek plots they transplanted them to the familiar background of Roman streets and households; and Sidney was echoing the ancient conviction that comedy should mirror daily living when he said that the chief pleasure it provided was to see familiar types "walk in stage names."

The writers of Elizabethan comedy had blithely ignored this classic precept, since they did not wish to be realistic but only to be entertaining; and on this point in particular Jonson was determined to reform the drama. Singlehanded, if necessary, he would bring comedy back to its one true realm and make it what it ought to be, a comedy of manners.

Out of the classical theory about subject matter sprang a somewhat similar theory about characterization. In the comedies of Plautus and Terence the young men were always headstrong, the old men domineering and the slaves wily, so that the audience knew exactly what to expect from them. The interest lay in the unexpectedness of the plot rather than in the unexpectedness of the people, and the characters were supposed to be true to type rather than true to life. Any introduction of the inconsistencies of real people would have blurred the neatness of the classic pattern of comedy and brought an intrusion of real life into the realm of art. A schoolmaster who was not a fussy pedant or a soldier who was not a braggart would have lacked "decorum"—that is to say, he would not have fitted the special pigeonhole in which tradition had placed him. In classic comedy, as it was understood by the Renaissance, each character stood for a single well-defined quality and was not supposed to have its edges blurred by the inconsistencies which make real life so much less tidy than art.

This theory of decorum happened to make a special appeal to a man of Jonson's temperament. Since he was a realist he was quick to accept the theory that a comedy should be a "copy of life" and not concern itself with clowns or fairies. But in spite of his interest in the contemporary scene and his quick, accurate eye, Jonson had a tendency to see his fellow man in sharp, flat, vigorous outline and to overlook the subtleties of shading. If he had been a draftsman he would have belonged to Hogarth's way of thinking rather than Rembrandt's, and his tendency towards caricature found its justification in the classical doctrine of decorum.

A third rule about writing comedy was that it should have a moral purpose, and on this point the whole Renaissance was overwhelmingly in agreement. As Scaliger said, "Those comedies should be prized which make us condemn the vices which they bring to our ears," and Sidney put it much more beautifully in his famous passage of which the end is so seldom quoted. "Our poet . . . cometh to you with words set in delightful proportion . . . With a tale, forsooth, he cometh unto you, with a tale which holdeth children from play and old men from the chimney-corner, and, pretending no more, doth intend the winning of the mind from wickedness to virtue."

This fundamental purpose, the winning of the mind from wickedness to virtue, was the final justification of all art in the eyes of the Renaissance. It was not, however, a point that held any interest for the average Elizabethan showman. It made very little difference to Henslowe whether or not the audience left the Rose in an elevated state of mind, anxious to flee vice and embrace virtue. All Henslowe wanted was a full house, and this seemed to Jonson a barbaric perversion of the real reason for writing comedy.

Jonson also shared with Sidney a distaste for what Sidney called "loud laughter." Sidney even went so far as to suggest that a comedy should not rouse laughter at all, since this was no more than a kind of "scornful tickling" and only distantly related to true delight. Later on in his life, Jonson echoed a current mistranslation of Aristotle and stated firmly that, "as Aristotle says rightly, the moving of laughter is a fault in comedy, a kind of turpitude." Jonson had succeeded in convincing himself that theatregoing was an intellectual exercise in which the rougher and more basic emotions should have no place, and he hoped to find a cultivated audience which would indicate its appreciation with a quiet, inward smile.

Armed with so many theories, and all of them running directly counter to Elizabethan theatre practice, Jonson might very well have failed to attract an audience for his first venture in classic comedy. But he was powerfully assisted by the fact that satire happened to be very popular in London in 1598. Satire has a moral purpose, and its effectiveness comes from the fact that it concentrates on types and mirrors contemporary life. A young dramatist like Jonson, if he took satire out of the bookstalls and transferred it to the stage, had the advantage of capitalizing on a current literary fashion while at the same time being able to obey the chief tenets of classical comedy.

There was a popular catchword that was used to describe the exaggerated types of London citizens with which the satirists were amusing themselves. By 1598 it was no longer fashionable to say that so-and-so was a pedant; instead, he had a "humour" for pedantry. The word was used so loosely that a man who tied his garters in a special way was said to "affect a humour"— a careless use of the word that annoyed Jonson—but in general it was a useful term to describe a man who did not have a balanced temperament.

The word "humours" had originally been a medical one, used to describe the four fluids that were supposed to be kept in balance in a healthy man. It was an excess of one of the humours, such as phlegm or choler, that made a man sick in the eyes of medieval doctors, and it was easy enough to transfer the phrase from the body to the temperament. Even now we speak of a "phlegmatic" or a "choleric" man. By 1598, the man with the "humour" was the man who had permitted his temperament to become unbalanced, so that he permitted "some one peculiar quality" to control his actions. This corresponded very closely to the classical theory of decorum in characterization and satisfied Jonson's own personal bent towards caricature, and he gave his comedy a very fitting title when he called it *Every Man in his Humour*.

Jonson handled his characters well, for he was an observant and experienced young man, with a skillful pen and a quick eye for oddities. The rather shopworn Elizabethan type known as the "gull" becomes in Jonson's play that ridiculous but rather pathetic social climber, Stephano, with his anxious determination to be taken for a gentleman. The even more ancient stereotype of the braggart soldier becomes Bobadilla, a characterization so vigorous and lively that Charles Dickens as an amateur actor cherished it as his favorite part. The plot that Jonson worked out for his comedy is not unlike some of the Roman ones, with the conservative father, the rebel son and the wily servant; but an intricate pattern of subplots was skillfully wound into it to bring a whole series of humours into lively action on the stage.

*Every Man in his Humour* reads like a rather cool play, intelligently constructed but lacking in emotion. It is, on the contrary, a fiercely dedicated play, the first step in Jonson's long and violent crusade to bring the classic spirit into English drama. The effect of coolness is the result of tension; for Jonson was trying to introduce into the theatre the decorous balance and the order that Horace had advocated, and for a man of his temperament it was not easily achieved.

Only once does Jonson's fierceness break through. This is towards the end of the play, when the prose suddenly changes to verse and the hero launches into a long speech on the subject of poetry. Poetry is a holy thing, fit to be seen only by "grave and consecrated eyes," and yet it was currently being travestied and misused in the theatre. The men who wrote the plays were

the ones Sidney had called "poet-apes" and it seemed a shocking thing to Jonson

> That such lean, ignorant and blasted wits,
> Such brainless gulls, should utter their stolen wares
> With such applauses in our vulgar ears,
> Or that their slubbered lines have current pass
> From the fat judgments of the multitude.

It was clear to Ben Jonson that he lived in a "barren and infected age" which was incapable of detecting the profound
difference between "these empty spirits and a true poet." The
indignant dramatist does not say so, but his subsequent career
makes it evident that when he speaks of the "true poet" he is
thinking of himself. Jonson may have learned many of the
Christian virtues at Westminster School, but humility was not
among them.

The sudden violence of this speech is obviously out of place
in a light comedy like *Every Man in his Humour*, and when
Jonson revised the play he omitted the whole passage. But he
was trying to do a difficult thing in his efforts to transplant the
classic tradition to the rambunctious Elizabethan stage, and his
fellow playwrights made no effort to help him. Jonson found
it was impossible to maintain an attitude of classic poise in the
midst of so unpoised and unclassical an atmosphere, and if he
raised his voice to a shout it was because he was determined to
be heard.

All this is very unlike the tone of Sidney's *Apology for
Poetry*, with its well-bred grace and its gentle teasing. Jonson
did not have Sidney's temperament or the advantage of Sidney's
sheltered position. Nevertheless, when Jonson published a revised version of his play eighteen years later he introduced it
with a prologue that is a kind of résumé of Sidney's statements
on the drama, done with a little of Sidney's own lighthearted
grace. It is a thrust at the extravagances and improbabilities of
the contemporary stage and a justification of Jonson's use of
naturalism in his effort to make comedy "an image of the times."

*Every Man in his Humour* heads the list in Jonson's collected works as his first play. It was not, of course, the first play he had written, for he had been turning out scripts consistently for Henslowe and had done enough by 1598 to warrant his appearance on a list of writers who were "best for tragedy." But these were not classic tragedies and Jonson did not wish to have them remembered. *Every Man in his Humour* was his first attempt to write in the classic tradition, and therefore in Jonson's eyes the first that was worth saving.

Jonson dedicated the play to his old teacher, William Camden. It was Camden who had first opened up to him the world of Greece and Rome, and Jonson never ceased to be grateful. "I am none of those that can suffer the benefits conferred upon my youth to perish with my age." Jonson was an honored man, the poet laureate of England, when he published *Every Man in his Humour* in his collected works as the first play he was willing to have preserved. And it was entirely fitting that it should be dedicated, with "thankfulness" to "my honored friend, Mr. Camden."

# Chapter 7

B EN JONSON'S NEW COMEDY was not produced by Philip Henslowe's actors at the Rose. Perhaps he did not offer it to them, or, more probably, they did not want it. It is clear that Jonson had not waited for their approval, sitting down in a tavern to discuss the plot with them before he started on his first act. Nor would Henslowe have sympathized with the ambition of one of his hack writers to reform the English stage.

Whatever the reasons, *Every Man in his Humour* was produced in the autumn of 1598 by the rivals of the Admiral's company, the Chamberlain's men.

The account books of the Chamberlain's company are missing, and very little is known of the method the actors used in buying scripts and commissioning playwrights. It is of course conceivable that they operated on the same principle as the men at the Rose, farming out plots and doling out advances. On the other hand, among the few scripts that have survived out of the many they produced is a complete set written by one of their own number, William Shakespeare. Although there has been much speculation on the subject, there is no direct evidence to show that Shakespeare ever worked with a collaborator or that the company ever put pressure on him to write the kind of plays that would guarantee an audience. Shakespeare had full freedom to experiment or to change his methods, and he seldom followed a successful play with another of the same type. No playwright in English history ever had more liberty than Shakespeare, and it is reasonable to see in his career a reflection of the policy of his company. Moreover, while Jonson wrote plays for most of the London companies, his best ones were produced by the same organization that produced Shakespeare's; and it would seem that the Chamberlain's men followed a policy unlike the Admiral's. When they found a good writer, they trusted him and left him alone.

Jonson was convinced that posterity would take a warm interest in his work, and he formed a habit for which every student of the period is profoundly grateful. He kept a list of the chief actors in each of his plays, and the folio edition of *Every Man in his Humour* ends with a careful notation:

> This comedy was first acted in the year 1598 . . .
> The principal comedians were

| | |
|---|---|
| Will. Shakespeare | Ric. Burbage |
| Aug. Phillips | Joh. Heminges |
| Hen. Condell | Tho. Pope |
| Will. Sly | Chr. Beeston |
| Will. Kempe | Joh. Duke |

Shakespeare heads this distinguished list of players not because he was a great playwright but because he was one of the most experienced actors in the Chamberlain's company. Six years earlier Henry Chettle had noted in print that Shakespeare was an "excellent" actor, and his excellence could hardly have grown less with experience. He had been an actor before he became a playwright and he was evidently happy in the work. He remained an actor as long as he worked in the London theatre, and ten years after his appearance in Jonson's comedy he was still listed as one of the leading "men players" in the company.

Shakespeare was thirty-four years old when he appeared in *Every Man in his Humour*. By then the company possessed more than a dozen of his scripts, including *A Midsummer*

*Night's Dream, The Merchant of Venice, Richard II, Henry IV* and *Romeo and Juliet,* and it might seem to a modern reader that the creator of Falstaff, Shylock, Puck and Mercutio should have been freed from the obligation of portraying other men's characters upon the stage. Such a notion apparently never occurred to Shakespeare and his fellow actors. The stage was not a bondage to them. It was a persistent and stimulating challenge, and each new play was undertaken by the same group of close personal friends and experienced, intelligent craftsmen.

Next in the cast of Jonson's play was Richard Burbage, who was on his way to becoming the best-loved actor in England. He had already created several of Shakespeare's most famous characters on the stage, and he was later to win even greater applause for his performances as Hamlet, Othello and King Lear.

The company's special expert in comedy was Will Kempe, England's most famous comedian since Tarleton's death. Phillips and Pope were also experts in that field, with Pope excelling in low comedy parts. There is an excellent part for Pope in Jonson's play, that of Cob the water carrier, but there is no special reason to believe that he took it. The actors in the company were all versatile men and they did not have to worry about type-casting.

The names of John Heminges and Henry Condell appear in every cast which Jonson recorded for the plays produced by their company. They both had a long and distinguished career in the theatre and towards the end of it the love they bore their "friend and fellow," Shakespeare, impelled them to publish his collected plays in the volume now known as the First Folio. Jonson helped them with the project and brought to a fitting climax the relationship that had started a quarter of a century earlier when Heminges and Condell both acted in *Every Man in his Humour.*

When the Chamberlain's men rehearsed Jonson's script they gave the same careful attention to casting, costuming and so on that they gave to their other productions. But in this case they had a highly opinionated author and a very original script on their hands, and the emotional climate backstage may have been a little more unstable than usual. Nevertheless, when the actors hauled up the playing flag over their Shoreditch theatre, they knew they had done their best and that the rest was up to the audience.

Jonson's play was a success. It might have been a failure in the earlier years of the decade, but the mood of London had been slowly changing. The grandiloquence and youthful excitement that had glittered and surged through plays like Marlowe's had given way in the new crop of young writers to a kind of weary cynicism. This *fin-de-siècle* air of disillusionment was partly the result of the depression, which combined with high taxes and an apparently unending war with Spain to bring about a general feeling of discouragement, and partly the result of a natural swing of the literary pendulum. Young men do not like to imitate their elders, and where the older poets had written love sonnets the younger ones now wrote satires.

These satires seemed to have the dual purpose of showing the depravity of the world and the brilliance of the author, and clever youngsters like Hall and Marston and Guilpin threw themselves into the new fashion under the apparent impression they had just discovered sin. They found an immediate audience for their work, and the bookstalls were so crowded with satires that the following year the Archbishop of Canterbury ordered the whole collection burned.

The Londoners who read books of this kind were a ready-made audience for *Every Man in his Humour*. The play had the further advantage of a lively, well-handled plot, and Jonson was not so devoted to his theories that he had failed to make his "humours" into recognizable people. He had a bright sense of comedy and a quick ear for the turns of ordinary speech, and the average London theatregoer welcomed anything new as long as it was entertaining. *Every Man in his Humour* triumphantly entered the repertoire of the Chamberlain's company and Jonson had the satisfaction of knowing that his first excursion into classical comedy was a complete success.

One play, however, was not enough to earn him a living. Jonson was not in the position of the witty young gentlemen of the Inns of Court, who wrote satires against the comfortable background of a private income. He had a wife and children to support, and the surest way to make a steady living in the theatre was to go on working for Philip Henslowe.

In August, only a short time before the successful opening of his new comedy, Jonson had collaborated with Henry Chettle and Henry Porter on a play for the Admiral's company called *Hot Anger Soon Cold*. He was also selling plots to the Admiral's company, since George Chapman was working on a "tragedy of Benjamin's plot" that October. If these two entries in Henslowe's account book had been invented by an imaginative playwright they could not have been more ironically suitable; for, in the month of September, just between the two entries, a tragedy of Jonson's devising had come into existence in real life and its mainspring was "hot anger."

The central figure in the tragedy was Gabriel Spencer. Spencer was one of the most important actors in the Admiral's company, a young man of great promise whose performances were still remembered years later. But he apparently possessed a vicious and ungovernable temper and less than two years before he had quarreled violently with a goldsmith's son in Shoreditch. The young man picked up a copper candlestick and threatened to throw it, and Spencer lunged at him with his sword, which he had not even drawn from the scabbard. The blow caught his opponent over the right eye with such force that the scabbard went in "six inches deep" and the boy died three days later.

Jonson and Spencer had seen a great deal of each other during the past year. Spencer was one of the actors who had signed up for Langley's new venture at the Swan; he had played in *The Isle of Dogs* and he and Jonson went to prison together. He had become one of the leading actors in Henslowe's company at the same time that Jonson was taken on as one of its writers, and in the small confines of a theatre company there was plenty of opportunity for quarrels.

On the twenty-second of September, at about the same time that *Every Man in his Humour* was being successfully presented at the Curtain theatre in Shoreditch, Jonson and Spencer fought a duel in the fields near the theatre. The reason for the quarrel is unknown, since the report on the coroner's inquest is missing, but it is clear that the two men were not evenly matched. Spencer was several years younger than Jonson and his rapier was ten inches longer. He was a man of great strength, to judge from the candlestick episode, and he succeeded in wounding Jonson in the arm. But in spite of his injury Jonson managed to run in under the actor's guard. He drove his rapier into his adversary's side, and Spencer died instantly.

Duels of this kind were not uncommon in London but from the official point of view Jonson had committed murder. He was taken before the nearest justice of the peace, and since this was an offense for which bail could not be accepted he was imprisoned in Newgate to await trial.

Newgate, unlike the Marshalsea, was a curiously ornamental prison. It was one of the western gates of the city, decorated with towers and statues, with a wide central arch for vehicles and a smaller entrance for foot passengers. The felons of Newgate were packed into the dungeons below and the garrets above, and the limitations of space made it one of the worst prisons in London. Luckily, Jonson spent a shorter time there than he had at the Marshalsea, since the next gaol delivery came on October the sixth.

All the prisoners were tried simultaneously during the Sessions of Gaol Delivery, and the local sheriff had been busy for the past month collecting jurors. In the old days the cases had been tried in the prison itself, but the judges ran so much risk of what was called gaol fever that a special courthouse had been provided in a street called Old Bailey that ran by the prison. The courthouse was surrounded by a pleasant garden, and since it was in use only part of the year the city thriftily rented it out the rest of the time.

The jurors who gathered to consider Jonson's case decided that "the aforesaid Benjamin Johnson feloniously and willfully slew and killed the aforesaid Gabriel Spencer at Shoreditch aforesaid." That is to say, Jonson's crime was murder, and for this the usual punishment was death at Tyburn. But the English law regarding capital punishment was so vicious that it was self-defeating. A man could be hanged for stealing any article worth more than sevenpence, and fortunately, in the case of first offenders, a loophole was provided. A man whose life was in danger could plead "benefit of clergy" and take advantage of a medieval law that had been designed to protect men in holy orders. In the early Middle Ages only churchmen could read, and any first offender who could read was permitted to plead benefit of clergy and have his case placed within the bishop's jurisdiction. This kindly gesture was not extended to women, since they had never been eligible for holy orders, and it made no difference whether they could read or not. The women of London went on being hanged for first offenses, or, in the case of anyone who had killed her husband, burned.

Jonson promptly pleaded benefit of clergy as soon as the verdict of guilty had been handed down, and the bishop's representative at court gave him a psalter. Jonson was allowed to choose his own passage for what was called the "neck verse," and the judge, following the ancient formula, inquired if he had read it like a clerk. *"Legit ut clericus?"* The answer came back from the bishop's representative, *"Legit,"* and the shadow of Tyburn was lifted.

No one could plead benefit of clergy twice, and if the prisoner committed a second capital offense he was hanged. To make certain that he could be identified the second time, the felon was immediately branded with a letter T stamped with a hot iron on the base of the left thumb. It has been hopefully suggested that in the case of a great poet like Ben Jonson the branding must have been done with a cold iron. But Jonson was not a great man in 1598 and the branding was a vital part of the judicial procedure. Eight years later a hangman "was well whipped at Bridewell, for burning a fellow in the hand with a cold iron."

Jonson left prison as soon as he was able to pay the jailer's fees, a branded felon. And he had further managed to complicate his already complicated life by becoming a Roman Catholic.

All Roman Catholics, in the eyes of the English government, were potential or actual enemies of the state, and the London prisons were full of priests and equally full of the people who had tried to shelter them. It was through "a priest who visited him in prison" that Jonson became a Catholic and this probably meant, not that the priest came into Newgate on some kindly errand from the outside but that he was in prison himself and facing death.

These mission priests, as they were called, were young Englishmen who had been trained on the Continent for the single task of saving the souls of their fellow countrymen. Throughout the whole period of their strict seminary training they were never allowed to forget their probable fate, and fresco paintings of the torture room and the scaffold decorated the walls of their college. They came back to England, three or four hundred of them; and since it was high treason to be a priest in England nearly half died as martyrs.

The problem of English Roman Catholics was an extremely difficult one for the English government to solve. A papal bull had announced that no Catholic should give his allegiance to Queen Elizabeth, since she was a heretic, and a cardinal speaking for the Pope went so far as to announce that anyone who assassinated her "not only does not sin but gains merit." Under the circumstances, all Catholics in England had to be looked upon as potential traitors, and failure to conform in religious matters became the same thing as failure to conform in political ones. It was a period in which nonconformity was still considered monstrous, and the idea of more than one religion was as shocking as the idea there might be more than one political party. In England there was one church because there was one state. As Lord Burghley put it, "that state could never be in safety, where there was toleration of two religions."

Burghley had a gentle spirit and hated bloodshed, especially when it was the blood of Englishmen. Moreover he knew that killing Catholics was not the way to get rid of them, "especially in England, where . . . the greatness of heart is such that they will . . . go bravely to death." Burghley and his fellow members on the Privy Council were not crusaders; they were merely trying to hold England together in the only way they knew. Unfortunately the matter did not rest solely in the hands of these moderate and intelligent statesmen. It was handled very largely at the local level, and at the local level there was a fear of Catholicism that amounted almost to hysteria.

In London, for instance, it was nearly impossible for a Roman Catholic to get a fair trial. The jurors remembered the murder of three hundred English Protestants during the reign of Elizabeth's sister Mary. They remembered the Spanish Armada and the confident way the Spaniards had expected the English Catholics to rise to their aid. They remembered the papal bull against their Queen which called her "that guilty woman of England." And in the case of that extreme Anglican sect, the Puritans, they needed to remember nothing. The Puritans hated the Catholics almost by instinct, and Puritanism was increasing steadily in London.

No charge of conspiracy was ever proven against a mission priest, such as the one who visited Ben Jonson in prison, but mission priests were hanged for conspiracy nevertheless. As one of them explained from the foot of the gallows, he could hardly have been conspiring abroad during the time specified since he had spent it in Marshalsea prison. It was other priests who conspired, and it was the heroic mission priests who paid the penalty.

The truth was that the government had put itself in the unhappy position of prosecuting for opinions rather than for actions. And, since thought control is a difficult thing to enforce,

Burghley was obliged to descend to the use of very evil instruments.

The chief instrument against Catholicism in London was Richard Topcliffe, who had been licensed by the Privy Council to torture priests in his own house in order to get confessions from them. Topcliffe possessed that frightening kind of cruelty which is fortified by a full sense of its own righteousness and he apparently got a certain sense of gratification out of torturing the men he called "lewd Popish beasts."

The agents who worked for Topcliffe were not much better, since it was not the kind of work that brings out the best qualities in a man. One of Topcliffe's paid spies for many years was Anthony Munday, who showed the same aptitude for this kind of work that he did for supplying plots to Henslowe's dramatists. Munday was evidently not a very ethical man, since a fellow agent accused him of stealing forty pounds from a widow while he was searching her house for Catholic relics.

The periods of violent anti-Catholic action came in waves, depending on how dangerous Spain looked to England at any given moment. The year that Ben Jonson met his priest happened to be an especially bad one for Catholics, since the King of France signed a peace treaty with Spain in 1598 and England was left facing Spain without the help of her old ally. The number of Catholic executions in England rose promptly, and the priest that Jonson met in Newgate was probably facing the gallows.

The mission priests had trained themselves to become accustomed to the idea of death, and they faced it not only with courage but with grace. The cheerful good humor of John Ingram was characteristic. He wrote an ode on the various prisons he had encountered and spoke with special affection of a small guest of his, a mouse. It was this same Ingram whom Topcliffe called a "monster" because he could not be forced to speak under torture.

This combination of gaiety and courage would have made a strong appeal to a man like Ben Jonson, and a priest who could talk to him about religion would have had an extra attraction if he were a poet and could talk equally well about Horace. Moreover Jonson knew something about Topcliffe, who had been one of the inquisitors sent to examine him when he was imprisoned a year earlier in the *Isle of Dogs* affair. Jonson had no special reason to love the authorities, and since he was never a coward the risks he ran by becoming a Catholic would have made no difference to him. It is reasonable to suppose that he was not moved by an overwhelming spiritual conviction, since he turned Protestant again twelve years later. But he loved brave and good men and something within him rose up to meet the spiritual gallantry he encountered in Newgate.

When Jonson left prison, branded on the thumb, he had theoretically made himself an enemy of the state by becoming a Roman Catholic. But as long as he remained reasonably inconspicuous and did not earn enough money to be worth harassing with fines, it was not likely that anything very serious would happen to him.

A more pressing problem, at the moment, was the perennial one of earning a living. His former employer, Philip Henslowe, could not be expected to be in a very affectionate frame of mind, since Gabriel Spencer had been one of the most valuable members of the Admiral's company. Four days after the duel Henslowe sent a letter to Alleyn, who was staying in Sussex. "Since you were with me I have lost one of my company which hurteth me greatly, that is, Gabriel, for he is slain in Hog's End Fields by the hands of Benjamin Johnson, bricklayer, therefore I would fain have a little of your counsel if I could."

It has sometimes been suggested that Henslowe called Jonson a bricklayer as a gibe, but in fact he was speaking the literal truth. A document of a few months later, discovered by Leslie Hotson, describes him as "Benjamin Johnson, citizen and bricklayer of London." This means that Jonson had completed his seven years of apprenticeship and that he had gone through the subsequent formalities that made him a member of his guild. He had presented himself before the bricklayers' Court of Assistants, accompanied by his former master who was supposed to pay his entrance fee. Then he had gone to the Guildhall and taken up his municipal freedom, which involved the payment of still another fee but which made him a citizen of London.

The normal time for Jonson to have gone through this procedure was as soon as his apprenticeship had been completed, but there is evidence that he did not become a freeman in the company until after his release from Newgate. He would have been eligible a year or two earlier, when he became twenty-four, and why he waited so long is not known. Perhaps he had hoped to avoid becoming a bricklayer and then had been obliged to enter the company and obtain his certificate because of the fear that Henslowe would no longer be willing to employ him.

There is no doubt that Jonson was short of money. He had borrowed ten pounds from an actor the previous April, and when he was released from Newgate he was still unable to pay back what he owed. As a result he was arrested for debt in January of 1599, put on trial and committed to the Marshalsea prison in Southwark.

It may conceivably have been Philip Henslowe who came to the rescue and loaned Jonson the money that released him from this second imprisonment. Henslowe was a good friend to imprisoned playwrights. In March of that year he advanced ten shillings to William Haughton to get him out of the Clink prison, which was also in Southwark; and he had gone bail for Thomas Lodge when a seven-pound debt to a tailor had put that free-spending playwright into the Clink on an earlier occasion.

In any case, it is clear that Henslowe had forgiven Jonson. On the tenth of August, 1599, he advanced forty shillings to Jonson and Dekker for a play they were writing called *Page of Plymouth*. Less than a month later Henslowe paid another forty shillings to a whole covey of writers, including Jonson, Dekker, Chettle "and other gentlemen," for a tragedy on the life of Robert the Second of Scotland. Towards the end of September Jonson collected twenty shillings as a further advance on the same play, so it is evident that he was safely back in Henslowe's employ.

Since the financial pressure on Jonson was so heavy, it would have been reasonable enough if he had given up his dream of reforming the English stage. But anyone who thought he could be beaten so easily would have underestimated Ben Jonson.

# Chapter 8

NEITHER IMPRISONMENT NOR the necessity of working for Henslowe could turn Ben Jonson from his chosen course, and a year after the production of his first classical comedy he was ready with a second. Since he called it *Every Man out of his Humour*, the London theatregoers probably went to it expecting a sequel. But if they thought so, they were mistaken.

Jonson was in the grip of a theory and consequently inclined to overdo things. Every critic had agreed, from Horace to Sidney, that the function of a true poet was to delight and teach, but Jonson in his enthusiasm was prepared to abandon the first of these two aims and concentrate on the second. He was going to teach virtue by making his new play a "comical satire" that would expose the follies of London, and he was going to teach the true art of writing by making the play a showpiece for his theories about the drama.

In pursuit of his first objective, Jonson searched through a newly-published Italian dictionary for a series of names to give his "humours." He called one character Fungoso because the word was defined as "spongy, airy, light, as a mushroom," and he called another Sordido because he was a miser, "a penny-father, a covetous wretch." Most of the characters might as well have remained as definitions in Florio's dictionary for all the reality they achieved in the play, but Jonson was not looking for reality. He was looking for a series of types through which he could expose what he called the "deformity" of his age, and each example of a humour was set up, shown briefly in action and then knocked down again. There is not even a plot in the usual meaning of the word, and what saves the play—insofar as it can be saved—is Jonson's realism. He may have given his characters Italian names but the background is nevertheless London, and since Jonson had an accurate eye for the oddities of his contemporaries he was able to give the London playgoers the pleasure of recognition.

Jonson's second objective, that of lecturing the audience on the principles of classic comedy, was more difficult to achieve. What he would have liked to do was to stand at one corner of the stage and explain each scene as it came along, but neither Aristotle nor Scaliger had ever suggested that the author was free to appear onstage.

Jonson did the next best thing. He put his play within a framework and two spectators appear onstage to comment on the action. One of these is "the author's friend," and he is free to make all the instructive remarks that the author cannot make himself. The author has not followed the unities but his "friend" is able to prove that this is not necessary, introducing the names of obscure Greek dramatists like Susario and Phormus with such aplomb that even the most skeptical spectator should be convinced. It is he who justifies an attempted hanging, which at first glance might seem somewhat out of place in a comedy, by recalling a similar situation in Plautus, and he not only quotes Cicero's definition of comedy in its original Latin but is able to prove that the author has obeyed it. This invaluable man not only justifies the play on learned grounds but also points out any especially good bits of writing that the audience may have missed. At the end of a tavern scene, for instance, he inquires admiringly, "Ha' you heard a better drunken dialogue?"

So many bouquets are tossed to the author, in fact, that it would hardly have been seemly to admit that his name was Ben Jonson. So the author is identified as an individual named Asper, and Asper also makes his appearance onstage. There he makes a speech on those twin subjects so dear to Jonson's heart: the duty of a true poet to scourge vice and the iniquity of those false poets that Sidney called "poet-apes."

Asper is described as a "free spirit," unaffected either by "servile hope of gain or frosty apprehension of danger," and this would be a fair enough description of the real author of the play. But Asper had one advantage that was denied Ben Jonson. He was able to expound his theories to people who listened to him reverently, and he moved in an atmosphere of quiet dignity because no one answered him back. Jonson, on the other hand, had apparently been arguing his theories all over London and been received with steadily mounting exasperation. When Asper announced loftily, "Art hath an enemy called Ignorance," he was agreed with respectfully; but in real life it was hard for Jonson to find anyone who was willing to listen to him as Asper's friends listened to Asper.

As Jonson struggled with his unsympathetic contemporaries in his effort to reform the London stage, he began more and more to see himself as a kind of reincarnation of his beloved Horace. Horace also had been a satirist in his youth, and he had tried to bring his fellow writers back to the high doctrines of Greek classic art. Horace had preached the doctrine of the poet as a dedicated man and he had scorned the easy applause of crowds. Like Jonson he was short of stature and low-born, and like Jonson he was by instinct a critic and a teacher.

Jonson's behavior was very unlike that of the urbane and civilized Horace, but it is only fair to remember that Elizabethan London was very unlike Augustan Rome. If Jonson had been able to shelter himself in the cradling hand of a generous and considerate patron like Maecenas, with little to do except polish his verses, he too might have achieved a reputation for courteous and disciplined calm. But Jonson was being knocked about in a violently competitive climate, trying to earn a living in the rough literary seas of London. He could not live the life of a leisured gentleman, and yet with a touching valor he was trying to write like one. He polished and repolished his lines in the way that Horace advocated and struggled to maintain the high principles of classic art in the cold winds of the market place.

At least Jonson's new script found a good home. It was produced by the Chamberlain's company, a year after the same group of actors had done his first humour comedy, and since they kept it in their repertoire for several years it was evidently not a failure.

*Every Man out of his Humour* was one of the first plays the Chamberlain's men put on in their new theatre, the Globe. The building had been erected by a syndicate made up of the leading members of the company, such as Burbage, Shakespeare and Heminges, and was the first playhouse in London to be owned by the actors themselves. It had been built early in 1599 on the south side of the Thames, not far from Henslowe's theatre, the Rose, and since its owners all had years of experience in the theatre it undoubtedly incorporated all the latest improvements in stage machinery and equipment.

Jonson had no interest in the various stage levels of the Globe, the balconies, the trap doors and the overhead machinery that Shakespeare used with such freedom and brilliance. He could use only a fraction of the resources of the great outdoor amphitheatre, since his firm classical principles kept him confined to the streets and households of old Roman comedy. Jonson believed that the stage should be a "mirror" of ordinary life, and he was convinced that the more educated members of his audience—"the happier spirits in this fair-filled Globe"—would appreciate what he was trying to do.

Since Jonson was so determined a reformer, he could not resist an attack in his own play on a rival kind of comedy that was being currently shown at the Globe. It was inevitable that Jonson should disapprove of romantic comedies, which inhabited a kind of never-never land of their own and were not "familiarly allied to the time." Jonson wanted to see satirical realism firmly established on the stage of the Globe, and instead

he saw the kind of plays which he described as "a duke to be
in love with a countess, and that countess to be in love with
the duke's son, and the son to love the lady's waiting maid;
some such cross wooing, with a clown to their servingman."

This kind of "cross wooing," complicated by disguises and
complete with clowns, is a fair description of the kind of comedy that Shakespeare was supplying at the Globe when Jonson's
new play opened there. Romantic comedies like *Twelfth Night*
and *As You Like It* may have delighted the audiences but they
represented every tendency that Ben Jonson deplored in the
Elizabethan theatre.

At the beginning of Shakespeare's career, long before Jonson
had known him, he had experimented with a strict Roman play
in *The Comedy of Errors*. Yet even this would not have won
Jonson's complete approval since it was based on identical twins.
Jonson had once considered using a similar situation himself and
then dismissed the idea as impractical, since he could not find
two actors who looked so much alike that they could "persuade
the spectators they were one." Jonson thought that the spectators had to be convinced through their intellects and satisfied
by their reason. Shakespeare knew that they could be persuaded
through their emotions, and that they would believe anything
so long as they were willing to believe it.

Jonson disapproved of Shakespeare's improbable plots and he
disapproved equally of his improbable settings. Jonson was so
insistent on the necessity for a realistic background that he not
only set his new comedy in London but at one point even went
so far as to specify the exact spot: "We must desire you to pre-
suppose the stage the middle aisle in Paul's . . . the west end of it."
He could not approve of a playwright who set one of his
comedies in a wood near Athens, complete with fairies, and another in the Forest of Arden, complete with lions. Jonson
wished to have nothing to do with either lions or fairies, and
since he was a firmly theoretical young man he felt that no
other playwright should have anything to do with them either.

When Shakespeare was writing romantic comedies in 1599

he found it easy enough to obey the first half of the classical
precept, "Delight and teach," but he took no interest in the second. He saw no reason to scold his characters or to make them
stand for moral qualities, and he had no wish to turn the stage
of the Globe into a mirror of the "time's deformity." In Jonson's eyes this meant that he was dodging his responsibilities as
a poet and the fact that Shakespeare's plays were so popular
only made matters worse.

In Jonson's eyes, Shakespeare was wrong even in his methods
of characterization. Falstaff, for instance, belonged to the ancient tradition of the braggart soldier, like Jonson's own Bobadilla, and to that extent Jonson would have approved of him.
But the braggart soldier was supposed to follow a definite pattern of behavior, and Falstaff refused to follow any pattern at
all. Shakespeare's *Henry V* was produced at the Globe at about
the same time as *Every Man out of his Humour*, and in it Falstaff dies. Neither Plautus nor Terence would have approved
of a braggart soldier who dies of a broken heart, and the wonderful piece of prose that reports his death is a mingling of
comedy and tragedy that Horace would have found deplorable.

As a playwright, Shakespeare represented every major tendency that Jonson was fighting against on the London stage. His
plays were not moral, orderly or realistic and they mirrored
nothing in contemporary London life. Sir Philip Sidney might
well have said of Shakespeare what he said of his predecessors,
that his plays were "neither right comedies nor right tragedies"
and that they mingled "kings and clowns" with a complete dis-
regard for the sacred laws of Greece and Rome. Shakespeare
had written one play with a Roman background, and his *Julius
Caesar* was playing at the Globe in 1599 at about the same time
that Jonson's "comical satire" was being presented there. But
even this was a play of which Jonson would not have altogether
approved. The subject was not approached with the learned
reverence that the occasion demanded and the play pleased
what Jonson had called "the fat judgments of the multitude."

What Jonson and the other learned Elizabethans failed to

understand about Shakespeare was the one thing that seems so obvious now. Shakespeare did not follow a set of rules, classical or otherwise, because his plays were shaped in obedience to a different kind of law. A play like *Julius Caesar* built itself up in his mind, scene by scene, in obedience to the same principle that keeps a plant moving in a certain direction and taking on a certain shape as it grows. The plant moves at the dictation of a force within the seed, not in conformity to anything imposed from the outside; and this force in Shakespeare, the creative drive of his imagination, was the one thing that Jonson consistently left out of his calculations. It is a lawless force in the sense that it cannot be logically formulated in advance, and anything that lacked logic was alien to Jonson. It was for this reason he said that Shakespeare lacked "art" and could still remember, years later, a line in *Julius Caesar* that he said was "ridiculous."

The Globe audiences welcomed Shakespeare's plays with uncritical enthusiasm, and Jonson himself admitted that Falstaff was getting "fat" on the applause he received. But if the uncultivated majority followed Shakespeare, there was a cultivated minority that was willing to listen to Jonson. Educated theatregoers could understand his learned references and approve of what he was trying to do. Moreover, if a play failed with the theatregoers there was always the book-buying public to turn to, and it was perhaps fitting that *Every Man out of his Humour* was the first of Jonson's plays to be put into print.

When the average Elizabethan play was printed, it was little more than a script set up in type, unacknowledged by the author and issued by some printer with a quick eye for profits. But Jonson hung over his manuscript like a mother since to him it was not merely a play but a poem. He wrote a long prose description to be printed in front of the text—really a series of little essays describing the characters—and he made up a composite motto from Horace to indicate to the reader that here, at last, was a new kind of play. He also put back the original ending, which the actors had changed because it displeased the audience. Jonson, firmly quoting Greek, felt the actors had made a great mistake. He listed five reasons why the original ending had been wholly justified and appealed to the "right-eyed and solid reader" to support him.

The bookshop of Jonson's publisher was strategically located near the law schools, at the gateway of Sergeants' Inn. The future lawyers who lived in the Inns of Court formed exactly the kind of audience that Jonson was looking for, moneyed, well educated and intelligent. Most of them came from well-to-do families, since legal training was expensive, and were the sons of "the best or better sort of gentlemen of all the shires of England." They had the artistic leanings suited to men of their station, and it had been two young gentlemen from the Inns of Court who wrote *Gorboduc*, a classical drama that drew praise even from Sidney.

The first edition of Jonson's play sold out within the year and a new edition had to be made; and when it was finally reissued in Jonson's collected works he dedicated it to those "noblest nurseries of humanity and liberty in the kingdom, the Inns of Court."

The common audience at the Globe may not have understood *Every Man out of his Humour*, but the men of learning at the Inns of Court had understood and approved. "When I wrote this poem, I had friendship with divers in your societies who . . . were great names in learning. . . . Of them . . . it was not despised."

# Chapter 9

THE WELL-EDUCATED YOUNG MEN of the Inns of Court were welcome customers at the Globe and the Rose, but they found the kind of plays there that could also be enjoyed by a butcher from East Cheap. The huge London amphitheatres accommodated thousands of playgoers and they could not be expected to concentrate on delicate and learned productions that would interest only a chosen few.

Some years earlier there had been two theatres in London that made a direct appeal to a cultivated and specialized audience. The singing boys of Paul's and the Children of the Chapel Royal rehearsed their elegant little plays under the supervision of their choirmasters for a final showing at Court and presented them in an indoor hall to the London public. During this brief, bright flowering in the 80's, John Lyly had written his charming plays for the boy actors and their skill and grace had delighted an appreciative public.

The hall in the Blackfriars that had been used by the child actors had long since reverted to tenements, but there was still a potential market for the kind of productions that would make a special appeal to an educated audience. Moreover, by 1600, a new and even better theatre had become available. Richard Burbage's father had remodeled some rooms in the Blackfriars and constructed an indoor playhouse out of them, hoping to open there with a company of men actors. James Burbage had put a great deal of money into the project; but the local residents had objected so bitterly to a common playhouse in their midst that he had never been able to open it and since his death it had stood vacant.

A Welshman named Henry Evans decided that the Black-friars residents would not object to a theatre if the actors were boys and if they did the kind of plays that had flourished in the 80's. Evans at one time had been manager of the original company at the Blackfriars, and he saw no reason why the success of the earlier Children of the Chapel could not be duplicated. On the second of September, 1600, Evans leased the Blackfriars theatre from the Burbages and opened it as a private theatre to be used by a company of boy actors called the Children of the Chapel Royal.

The new company had the same name as the old one, but there the resemblance ceased. The new company was no longer managed by its choirmaster but by a board of directors whose chief interest was in making money and who ran the theatre as a straight business proposition. As the father of one of the boys put it, they were concerned only with their "own corrupt gain and lucre." Since the choirmaster was a member of the board, the directors possessed a royal patent which enabled them to get "well-singing children" wherever they could find them, although the same embittered father pointed out that they were not really looking for singers but for talented children who could be turned into good actors. There is no doubt they found them, for two of the most brilliant young actors in London—Nathan Field and Solomon Pavy—were members of the boys' company at the Blackfriars.

It was easier to find actors than to find scripts, and for a short time the company tried to get along with the kind of plays that had been fashionable in the 80's. But Lyly's graceful little plays were hopelessly out of date by 1600, and Evans knew he would have to find modern scripts if he expected to keep his theatre filled. He needed something learned yet lively, aristocratic yet original, and the obvious person to write such a script for him was that promising young dramatist, Ben Jonson. It was for the

Children of the Chapel at the Blackfriars that Jonson wrote his second "comical satire" and he named it *Cynthia's Revels*.

Jonson was very willing to work for a smaller and more cultivated public. In the Prologue to his new play he assured himself that he would receive "gracious silence" and "sweet attention" from the Blackfriars audience, and he assured the audience in return that the play he gave them would be both learned and original.

Moreover, Jonson enjoyed working with the young actors, who apparently gave him the respectful attention that he found so difficult to command in the adult theatre. Young Nathan Field, who appeared in the cast of *Cynthia's Revels*, was adopted by Jonson as a kind of student and carefully educated in the works of Horace and Martial. Another member of the same cast, Solomon Pavy, died two years later when he was thirteen years old, and Jonson wrote one of the most famous and tender of epitaphs.

> Weep with me, all you that read
> This little story,
> And know, for whom a tear you shed,
> Death's self is sorry . . .

Jonson had a small boy of his own at home and he evidently loved children.

The play that Jonson wrote for the child actors was an ingenious attempt to combine modern satire with the mythological machinery that Lyly had used so successfully. Mercury and Cynthia move above a group of fantastic characters with Greek names who personify the various types of self-love that were current in London in 1600. They are Court types, rather than the city types that Jonson satirized in his two earlier plays, since the Blackfriars company was hoping to attract a Court audience.

The qualities that made Jonson's play interesting to his contemporaries have faded, but what gleams out of it, indestructible as pearl, are the songs. Jonson was a great lyric poet when he permitted himself to be and he could use the English lan-

guage with a cool, lovely grace that was more truly Greek than
all his laborious learning. His "Hymn to Cynthia" runs as
smoothly as moonlight on water:

> Queen and huntress, chaste and fair,
> Now the sun is laid to sleep,
> Seated in thy silver chair
> State in wonted manner keep.
> > Hesperus entreats thy light,
> > Goddess excellently bright . . .

Equally lovely is Echo's song, which must have been extremely effective on the Blackfriars stage. It was written as a
three-part madrigal, and the boy who played Echo took the
soprano part while two singers hidden backstage carried the
alto and the tenor. Behind the apparent simplicity of Jonson's
wording lies an intricate musical structure, and since he needed
two well-trained musicians offstage to give vocal balance he introduced them as "music from the spheres." Jonson's expert
manipulation of the musical background was not the result of
formal training, except for the little he received when he was a
schoolboy at Westminster. In this, as in everything else, he was
largely self-taught.

Jonson the poet could not supplant Jonson the reformer, and
the same character who was named Asper in *Every Man out of
his Humour* appears as Criticus in *Cynthia's Revels.* Criticus,
like Asper, is a castigator of vice, a virtuous and learned reformer who is admired by all the worthier members of the cast
and hated only by the base of heart. Like Asper, he rises above
the jealousy of these lesser men, and he ignores their plots "with
a careless smile." This is not a self-portrait of Jonson as he was,
but it is certainly a portrait of what he would have liked to be.

The two men who plot against Jonson's hero are named
Hedon and Anaides, a foppish courtier and a tavern swash-
buckler who resemble each other only in their mutual jealousy
of Criticus. They accuse him of being a "bookworm, a candle-
waster" whose long years of private study have left him with

no more learning "than a schoolboy," and Jonson makes it very clear to the audience that all this is the jealous talk of "impudent and arrogant" men who cannot appreciate true greatness.

Two London playwrights, Thomas Dekker and John Marston, thought they recognized themselves in the characterizations of Hedon and Anaides, in spite of the fact that Anaides was not a writer and Hedon had scribbled only a little Court poetry. But since Dekker and Marston were friends and had evidently been going around London attacking Jonson for his arrogance, the resemblance was close enough to look intentional.

Thomas Dekker had known Jonson fairly well for some time. They had collaborated on at least two plays for Henslowe, and Dekker represented the popular, competent kind of writing that Jonson was trying to soar above. Since Dekker was a fine poet in his own right, Jonson's assumption of superiority must have been profoundly irritating, especially since Jonson could not keep his theories to himself and had evidently been discussing them with more ardor than tact all over town.

Dekker's friend, John Marston, came from an altogether different background. He was a member of the Inns of Court, an Oxford graduate who had been sent to the Middle Temple to follow in his father's footsteps as a lawyer. Like many other young men of the Inns of Court, Marston began to write rhymed satires, and in a short time he was so enamored by the idea of a literary career that his father's hopes for him had to be abandoned.

Marston wrote two books of satire, dedicating the second to his "most esteemed and beloved self." Half Italian and very emotional, he was temperamentally suited to the current fashion of disillusioned mockery and enjoyed composing

sharp mustard rhyme
To purge the snottery of our slimy time.

Both books had the honor of being burned in the Archbishop of Canterbury's fire and Marston turned to a more lucrative career. He discovered that he had a talent for writing plays and began turning out scripts for Paul's Boys, a company of child actors that had been revived at about the same time as the Children of the Chapel.

Everything about John Marston must have irritated Jonson. Marston was ostensibly seeking the same goal, that of purging the follies and vices of mankind, but his sloppy, emotional way of writing was the exact opposite of the disciplined classic art that Jonson was trying to teach. Even Marston's vocabulary maddened Jonson, who felt that words like *glibbery* and *snottery* were not part of a poet's legitimate vocabulary.

In turn, Marston and Dekker were equally maddened by Jonson's conceit. Jonson might not approve of the plays of other men but he warmly admired his own, and the lively, colloquial Epilogue he wrote for *Cynthia's Revels* gives his considered opinion of his new play: "By God, 'tis good." Since this self-admiration was combined with an equally frank contempt for his fellow writers, the result was apparently too much for Dekker and he launched upon a play in which Jonson would be pilloried for the upstart he was.

Since Dekker was an experienced professional playwright, he probably did not write the script until he was sure he could get production for it. As a matter of fact, two companies produced it. It was presented by Paul's Boys, who counted Marston as one of their best playwrights, and it was also presented by the Chamberlain's company.

The men of the Chamberlain's company were not on good terms with Jonson at the moment. They had taken the risk of backing his first two experimental comedies and when he left them for a rival organization he had not done it very tactfully. He need not have emphasized the "gracious silence" that was now available to him at the Blackfriars.

Moreover the actors of Shakespeare's company had found, during the past winter, that the revival of the children's companies had cut into their profits. Many theatregoers had deserted the wintry, unheated interior of the Globe, which could only be reached by Londoners after a cold boat trip across the Thames or a detour by London bridge. Instead they were paying the extra prices that were being asked by the Children of the Chapel for the pleasure of sitting in the warm, lighted hall of the Blackfriars theatre while they listened to good music and lively, satiric dialogue. The actors at the Globe could not roof in their huge outdoor theatre or devote an hour to preliminary music, but at least they could take a leaf from the Children of the Chapel and capitalize on the current craze for satire.

All satire had drawing power, as the Archbishop of Canterbury could reluctantly testify; but personal satire, in which the Londoners delightedly recognized the target, was naturally the most successful. The London theatres had been using it for years, as openly as they dared, and it was naturally effective in a town of a quarter of a million where gossip spread quickly. If the Londoners heard that Thomas Dekker was planning a play that was a direct attack on Ben Jonson, the Globe could confidently expect a full house, for the average Elizabethan loved a fight whether it was between two gamecocks or two writers. Moreover, there was no danger that the feud would remain one-sided as long as it was Ben Jonson who was being baited.

Jonson rose so quickly to the bait that he had a script of his own finished and ready for production before Dekker's play could get on the boards. He called it *Poetaster, or The Arraignment* and packed into it a slashing attack on Dekker, on Marston and on the Chamberlain's Men. He finished it in a furious burst of speed, since he was determined to get it into production on the Blackfriars stage before Dekker's play could be presented at the Globe.

The "poetaster" of the title is John Marston. Jonson was convinced that Marston was his chief enemy and had been helping Dekker write his play, and the young dramatist is presented as a cringing, gabby, conceited rhymer. "We are a scholar, I assure thee . . . We are new turned poet, too, which is more; and a satirist too, which is more than that . . . We are a gentleman besides." At the end of the play the poetaster is cured of his bad literary habits. He is given an emetic and vomits into a basin some of the turgid words that Marston undeniably liked to use, after which he is put on a "strict and wholesome diet" of the classics.

Jonson characterizes Dekker as a more trivial figure, a mere "dresser of plays about the town" who has been hired by an actors' company to abuse a great writer because they need the money his script will bring in. "We have need on't; for this winter has made us all poorer than so many starved snakes." When he comes to the actors themselves, Jonson has a splendid time itemizing his former employers—the "eating player" with the belly, the "villainous out-of-tune fiddler," the "skipping swaggerer" and the "fat fool" with the goggle eyes.

The special crime of all these people, according to Jonson, is that they have dared to attack a man who is "poet and priest to the Muses." This noble, lofty and learned individual, who was called Asper and Criticus in Jonson's last two comedies, is now called Horace, and the play has an elaborate Roman setting to serve as a background for him. Horace is given the honor that is due him whenever he encounters any of the virtuous members of the cast, and in the end it is he who succeeds in reforming the poetaster.

Whether or not Jonson intended Horace as a portrait of himself, his delighted enemies naturally assumed that he did. Dekker promptly introduced Horace into his own play and called it *Satiromastix*, or the satirist whipped.

The chief interest of Dekker's play is that it gives a full-length portrait of what Jonson looked like in 1601. It is a malicious portrait, seen through the eyes of one of the more exasperated of his contemporaries, but it contains enough detail so that the Londoners who flocked to the Globe must have recognized it immediately.

Dekker brought in everything he could think of about his fellow playwright—Jonson's career as a bricklayer, his service in a road company, the *Isle of Dogs* affair and the killing of Gabriel Spencer. He brought in Jonson's bad complexion (he was pockmarked), his small size, his slowness in composition and the curious faces he used to make when he read his verses aloud. But above all, over and over again, he brought in Jonson's conceit. "Mr. Horace is ambition, and does conspire to be more high and tall as God a mighty made him."

An early scene in *Satiromastix* introduces Horace in his study, surrounded by books and deep in the self-conscious raptures of creation. When a friend of his arrives, Horace is able to give the glad news that yet another masterpiece has been born. "Damn me, if't be not the best that ever came from me." He reads it aloud, reverently drawing attention to the best bits, and when the friend makes an objection at one point Horace crushes him with the explanation that this happens to be a special "elegancy." He then pauses to ask his friend for criticism—"Deal plainly, do not flatter me"—but the friend hardly has time to open his mouth before Horace has swept on to describe the glory of his subsequent lines. "Oh, the end shall be admirable!"

Horace has deliberately entered into a campaign to draw attention to himself. When his plays are produced he has watched from the gallery and made so many faces that he drew attention away from the actors. When the play was over he has fraternized ostentatiously with the gallants in the expensive seats, "to make all the house rise up in arms and to cry, 'That's Horace, that's he, that's he, that's he that pens and purges humours.'" He has composed letters to important men, to "screw and wriggle himself" into their company, and he has kept a little packet of all the letters he has written and the replies he has received. Dekker spoils the full effect of this charge of sycophancy by also accusing Jonson of being impertinent to his "betters," and he is on safer ground when he concentrates on Jonson's arrogance. Horace says it is the will of the Muses

> That we to learned ears should sweetly sing,
> But to the vulgar and adulterate brain
> Should loath to prostitute our virgin strain.

This sounds like a parody but it is actually an echo of what Jonson himself had written in the Prologue to *Cynthia's Revels,* when he said of his lines that he was

> loath to prostitute their virgin strain
> To ev'ry vulgar and adulterate brain.

Dekker was apparently convinced that Jonson did not mean what he said. He characterizes him as a cheap showman who pretends to be a dedicated man but who is willing to do any sort of hack writing as long as he is paid for it. Dekker was wrong here, for Jonson was desperately in earnest. If only he could have been accorded the respect that was given the original Roman Horace, he could have been as wise and balanced as anyone. But when he felt this lack of respect, as in the case of Marston and Dekker, he lost his temper and his sense of proportion. When his fellow playwrights jeered at him he became a fury, and the more angry he became the more they jeered at him.

The actors at the Globe had reason to hope that a feud had been started which would rage long and prosperously on the London stage. The Epilogue to *Satiromastix* promised that if the audience applauded the play, "Horace will write against it and you may have more sport." But Jonson had written his last "comical satire" and the fight flickered out for lack of ammunition. It set off one final reverberation before it died, the good-natured reference in *Hamlet* to the warfare between the boy actors and the men. "There has been much to-do on both sides . . . There was, for a while, no money bid for argument, unless the poet and the player went to cuffs in the question."

Ben Jonson did not give up the fight because he wished to. The authorities had stepped in and muzzled him. The government did not approve of satire in any form, and in *Poetaster* Jonson had made the mistake of not confining his attack to playwrights and actors. He had also attacked the army and the law, and the law, in particular, was highly incensed. The matter was brought to the attention of the lord chief justice, and Jonson escaped only through the intervention of a friend of his named Richard Martin. Martin was one of the livelier wits of the Middle Temple and a lawyer who loved a joke. When *Poetaster* appeared in Jonson's collected works it was dedicated to Richard Martin, who had so successfully defended it against "the ignorance and malice of the times."

Since Jonson was not permitted to answer his enemies by writing another play, he thought he might do it by writing a kind of postscript to *Poetaster*, to be delivered by the boy actors from the stage of the Blackfriars. He wrote what he called an "apologetical dialogue" and it was presented once. Then it, too, was suppressed. Nor was Jonson allowed to include it in the printed version when *Poetaster* was published the following year.

Nevertheless Jonson did manage to insert a defiant note to his readers, informing them that all this suppression had been no fault of his. The reason the postscript was not available was because the reader had been "deprived of it by authority." He kept the text of his "apologetical dialogue" by him and finally, years later, he succeeded in getting it into print.

The postscript to *Poetaster* opens with the author being visited by two of his friends, who want to see "how he looks" after all the attacks that have been made on him. The author assures them that he is in his habitual state of dignified calm and quite indifferent to the "tongues of slaves."

The two friends want to know why his play stirred up so much excitement, and the author says he has no idea. His remarks about the law were adapted from Ovid, his satire against the military was not directed at true soldiers, and even his attack on the actors had not included the whole company.

> The rest might have sat still, unquestioned,
> Had they but had the wit or conscience
> To think well of themselves.

He admits that he made a direct attack on the two playwrights, but they had started the whole thing in the first place.

Ben Jonson had written three comical satires, and in them he had tried to transfer the "salt in the old comedy" to a more thin-skinned age. The venture had come to a disastrous end, but no one was to conclude from this that Jonson had lowered his banner and had been defeated in his attempt to adapt classical drama to the Elizabethan stage. If he could not succeed in comedy he would write a tragedy; and the two friends withdraw respectfully from the author's presence since he wishes to be left alone with his Muse.

> Leave me. There's something come into my thought
> That must, and shall, be sung high and aloof,
> Safe from the wolves' black jaw and the dull asses' hoof.

# Chapter 10

IT WAS RATHER HEROIC of Jonson to announce publicly that he intended to retire, "high and aloof," to write a classic tragedy. Although Henry Chettle was kind enough to call him "our English Horace," Jonson's hurried and difficult life had very little in common with Horace's placid existence and it did not give him much opportunity to retire and carve out a tragic masterpiece.

As a matter of fact, Jonson was still doing hack work for Philip Henslowe. The same year in which he was struggling to reform English comedy with the third of his "comical satires" he was also working for Henslowe and Alleyn, and it was the kind of work that must have been particularly galling to so ardent a classicist. For in September of 1601 Alleyn paid him forty shillings to write some additions to *The Spanish Tragedy*.

*The Spanish Tragedy* held about the same position on the Elizabethan stage that the dramatization of *Uncle Tom's Cabin* held in the affections of a later series of theatregoers. Kyd's bloody old play was a joke in intellectual circles and Jonson himself had made fun of it in two of his comedies, but the melodramatic vigor of the situations kept it alive on the stage. The famous scene in which Heironimo enters in his shirt to find his son's dead body waving in the wind aroused the same emotions in an audience as Eliza crossing the ice, and individual lines from the play had become household words.

In 1601, the type of revenge tragedy that Kyd had first made popular had again become the fashion in London and was making a great deal of money for Henslowe's competitors. The boy actors of Paul's were wading through the bloody plot of Marston's *Antonio's Revenge*, which Marston himself summarized as "Poison the father, butcher the son and marry the mother." The Globe was currently showing a very successful revenge tragedy written by one of its own actors—*Hamlet* by William Shakespeare—and Henslowe was not a man to delay while his competitors were making money. He commissioned revenge tragedies with his usual thoroughness, advancing five shillings to Henry Chettle (who specialized in comedy) to write *Hoffman, or Revenge for a Father* and setting Jonson to work on *The Spanish Tragedy.*

Jonson received his final payment in June of the following year, but even then he did not succeed in disentangling himself from hack writing. He was given an advance on a script "called Richard Crookback." The career of Richard the Third would have been suitable enough for a classical tragedy, and one had been produced on the subject at Cambridge in Jonson's boyhood, full of dignity and long speeches in Latin. But Henslowe was probably looking for something along the lines of Shakespeare's bloody and successful *Richard III,* and he would not have advanced the money to Jonson unless he was sure he could expect something equally melodramatic. However Jonson might feel about it, Henslowe had no interest whatever in pleasing Cicero and Horace.

By 1602 Ben Jonson had one consolation at least. He could arrange in front of him on his desk the printed texts of the four plays he had written not to please Henslowe but to please himself. The average Elizabethan dramatist had no interest in seeing his plays in print, since he was usually pinning his hopes of immortality on some narrative poem he had written or some collection of sonnets, and a man like George Chapman paid no attention whatever to the printing of his popular comedies. But Jonson thought of his plays as poems and gave each of them his devoted attention when it came out in book form. By now he had had dealings with three different publishers and he could eye his four little quarto volumes with the assurance that it was these, and not his work for Henslowe, that would go down triumphantly to posterity.

Jonson was apparently the first to write dedications for his comedies, a custom that was used for poetry but not for plays. In the case of *Cynthia's Revels*, he had two dedication sheets printed so that they could be inserted in the two gift copies he was planning, and the choice of recipients was characteristic of him. One was Lucy Harington, Countess of Bedford, and the other was his old teacher, William Camden.

Lady Bedford cultivated poets with the same interest she cultivated gardens, and in her long life she earned the gratitude of many poets, from George Chapman to John Donne. She was accustomed to receiving dedications, having been proffered her first when she was three years old, but she did not get many like Jonson's. Jonson saw no reason for crawling about on his knees where the nobility was concerned, and his verses to Lady Bedford have the graceful, courtly, almost teasing note of one equal to another.

> Go, little book, go, little fable,
>     unto the bright and amiable
> Lucy of Bedford . . .
> Tell her his Muse that did invent thee
>     to Cynthia's fairest nymph hath sent thee
> And sworn that he will quite discard thee
>     if any way she do reward thee
> But with a kiss . . .

The kiss is "of her white hand," but even so this was not the usual way for a bricklayer to address a countess. Ben Jonson became acquainted with many ladies of the Court before his long life was over, and he treated none of them with the frenzied humility that was considered correct in the relationship between poet and patron. He did not act humble because he did not feel humble, and the great ladies who were his friends had the good sense to like him for it. As Jonson said of Lady Bedford, they lacked "that solemn vice of greatness, pride."

The choice of William Camden for the other gift copy was inevitable, since Jonson never permitted himself to forget what Camden had done for him. It was more than twenty years since the undermaster at Westminster School had encountered the small schoolboy from Hartshorn Lane, but the passage of time had only strengthened the affection between them. In his long Latin dedication Jonson spoke what was no less than the truth: *Alumnus olim, aeternum amicus*. Once a pupil, forever a friend.

If Camden had been a touchy man his relations with Jonson might have become a little strained, since Jonson had chosen the Office of Heralds as one of his targets in *Every Man out of his Humour*. Camden had joined the office two years before the comedy was written and he was probably not amused by the scene in which Sogliardo, a "clown . . . enamoured of the name of a gentleman," buys a coat of arms from the Office of Heralds for thirty pounds. Jonson, with elaborate mischief, had worked out a detailed coat of arms for Sogliardo, complete with technical jargon and lacking only a frying pan for the crest; and a joke of this kind must have seemed to Camden somewhat lacking in humor, especially since he himself was being criticized for some of the grants he had recently approved.*

A more serious source of potential friction between Jonson and Camden was the fact that Jonson had recently become a Roman Catholic. Camden felt very strongly about the one "true religion," which for him was the Anglican, and part of the pride he felt over his long years of teaching lay in the fact that he had helped to strengthen the Anglican Church. Not only

---

* Nor would Jonson's joke have seemed very funny to the actors in the Chamberlain's company. Most of the major actors in the company—Phillips, Pope, Cowley, Heminges, Burbage and Shakespeare—acquired coats of arms through the Office of Heralds. Phillips and Pope (both of whom acted in *Every Man out of his Humour*) incurred criticism because they claimed ancestors to whom they were not entitled. Shakespeare's grant also was criticized, but chiefly because it was Camden who had given it. A fellow herald was jealous of Camden and was doing what he could to discredit his official conduct.

had three of his scholars become bishops but he had also succeeded in persuading some of his Irish students, "bred popishly," to see the error of their ways. He must have felt deep regret when Jonson turned Catholic, but even that could not disturb the close friendship between the two men.

Camden was interested in poets and he once made a list of writers "whom succeeding ages may justly admire." These included Sidney, Spenser, Shakespeare and his own Ben Jonson, and it must have been a source of pride to Camden to see his former student beginning to take his place among England's most important poets. As early as 1600 Jonson was receiving the honor of being quoted in the anthologies—those "choicest flowers of our modern poets" that supplied the London public with a short cut to current literature. Two popular anthologies were printed that year and Jonson's work was included in them both.

Robert Allot's pleasant little book, which he called *England's Parnassus*, was less an anthology than a kind of poetical dictionary. The verse was arranged under subject matter, and a browser in the C's could find quotations on Chastity, Cupid, Confusion of languages, Care of children, Courtier effeminate, Cruelty, Custom and Calm weather. Older poets like Shakespeare and Spenser were well represented, along with the newer writers like Marston and Jonson. Allot included fourteen quotations from Jonson, and the three that are untraceable probably came from some of the unpublished play scripts he did for Henslowe.

The other anthologist, John Bodenham, called his book *Belvedere, or the Garden of the Muses* and arranged it on much the same principle. Bodenham supplied a list of poets in the front, carefully dividing poetical members of the nobility like the Earl of Oxford and Sir Philip Sidney from the commoners. The commoners themselves are huddled together with no attempt at chronology, so that Shakespeare, for instance, appears between eighty-year-old Thomas Churchyard and twenty-eight-year-old Ben Jonson.

*Belvedere* attracted a certain amount of attention in literary circles and a school play that was produced at Cambridge the following year devoted one of its scenes to Bodenham's selection of modern poets. The discussion is interesting because it is probably a fair reflection of the kind of literary judgments that were fashionable at the universities the year that *Hamlet* and *Poetaster* were being shown in London. Shakespeare was still catalogued in the Cambridge mind as a love poet, on the strength of his two popular narrative poems, *Venus and Adonis* and *The Rape of Lucrece*, and the young gentlemen who discuss him on the Cambridge stage seem to feel that he has done very little of value since.

Ben Jonson had so vigorous a personality that the news of his temperament had penetrated even to academic circles and he is characterized in the play as "a bold whoreson, as confident now in making of a book as he was in times past in laying of a brick." He is dismissed however, as an unimaginative realist—"a mere empiric, one that gets what he hath by observation and makes only nature privy to what he indites." This was apparently the fashionable thing to say about Jonson at the moment, since the same charge is quoted against him in *Poetaster*. "He is a mere sponge, nothing but humours and observation; he goes up and down sucking from every society, and when he comes home squeezes himself dry again." It was a curious judgment to make on Jonson's comedies, which are so firmly and laboriously grounded on his reading, but no more curious than to dismiss Shakespeare as a love poet.

Jonson and Shakespeare are mentioned again towards the end of the same play. Two Cambridge boys impersonating Richard Burbage and Will Kempe come onstage to discuss the famous fight that had recently taken place between Jonson and the Chamberlain's Men, and Kempe says, "That Ben Jonson is a pestilent fellow; he brought up Horace giving the poets a pill; but our fellow Shakespeare hath given him a purge that made him bewray his credit."

This is usually interpreted to mean that Shakespeare must

have attacked Jonson in one of his plays but, if so, the attack
has never been traced. It is conceivable that the reference is to
some role that Shakespeare, as an actor, took in the company's
production of *Satiromastix*. Or it may even be that the Cambridge boys thought that Shakespeare was the author of *Satiromastix*, since it was produced by his company and Dekker's
name had not yet been identified with it in print. They evidently did not know very much about the Globe company,
since they were misinformed about Will Kempe. Kempe was no
"fellow" of Shakespeare's when *Satiromastix* was produced,
since he had left the Chamberlain's Men shortly after the Globe
was built and was currently working for a rival company.

In the same year that the Cambridge play was presented,
Jonson also made a literary appearance in a curious little book
called *Love's Martyr*. This long allegorical poem had a kind of
appendix on the subject of the phoenix and the turtle dove,
with a series of poems contributed "by the best and chiefest of
our modern writers." Two of these poems were anonymous
and the remaining ones were by Shakespeare, Chapman, Marston and Jonson.

Marston might be a fellow contributor, but Johnson was certainly not on speaking terms with him in 1601. This was the
year in which *Poetaster* was written, and the war was not confined to the stage. Jonson once told a friend of his, with some
pride, that he had had "many quarrels with Marston" and one
of them was so violent that Jonson "beat him and took his pis-
tol from him." On the other hand, the feud was not a permanent one. Three years after *Poetaster* was written, Marston
dedicated one of his plays to that "most elegant and weighty
poet, his sincere and hearty friend, Ben Jonson." The year after
that, Marston contributed a commendatory poem to Jonson's
latest play and the two men were peacefully writing a script
together.

George Chapman, who also contributed to "The Phoenix and
Turtle," was one of Jonson's closest friends. They had both
entered the theatre as hack writers and Chapman was working

on "Benjamin's plot" for Henslowe the same year he published
his magnificent translation of the first seven books of the *Iliad*.
Like Jonson, Chapman was a scholar and a violently self-
conscious one, quick to see criticism where none was intended.
Jonson said he "loved" Chapman and it must have been true,
since otherwise they were too much alike to remain close
friends for a quarter of a century. After Chapman's death there
was found among his papers "An Invective written by Mr.
George Chapman against Mr. Ben Jonson" in which he had
evidently worked off a good deal of private irritation against
his illustrious friend. But nearly everyone was angry with Jonson at least once, and it is to Chapman's credit that he never
published the attack.

The other contributor to "The Phoenix and Turtle" was
William Shakespeare, and as far as the records go Jonson never
managed to quarrel with that easy-going man at all. Although
Jonson quarreled with the Globe actors, Shakespeare cannot be
identified with any of the individuals that Jonson singled out
for ridicule, and in his "apologetical dialogue" he specifically
states that some "better natures" in the company had permitted
themselves to be misled. Long after Shakespeare's death, when
Jonson himself was an old man, he wrote of his friend: "I loved
the man and do honor his memory (on this side idolatry) as
much as any. He was indeed honest and of an open and free
nature." Earlier, when Jonson had written of Shakespeare, he
called him "my beloved," and it was Jonson who gave him his
most famous title—"gentle Shakespeare."

Some of this gentleness in Shakespeare came from his natural
courtesy of mind, the quality that Henry Chettle had noticed
in him back in 1592. But a little of it, perhaps, came from the
fact that Shakespeare was not subjected to any sense of strain
in his work. Men like Chapman and Jonson were trying to
make a living with their pens, striking a precarious balance between their pride and their purses, and Chapman even went so
far in 1602 as to permit himself to be hired to write a play for
a man who wanted to use it to blackmail a woman into marry-

ing him. Chapman did not want to enter the area of cheap journalism but he was forced into it through his need for money; and, like most Elizabethan writers, his position was one that helped neither his temper nor his self-respect.

Shakespeare, on the other hand, could please himself. He earned his living as an actor, not as a writer, and when he wrote a play it was not because he needed the money. Shakespeare wrote an average of two plays a year, which was an abnormally low output by Elizabethan standards, and there was no financial pressure on him to force him to write more quickly or in a different way. The income from two scripts a year was a comparatively small matter to a man who was one of the leading shareholders in a prosperous theatre like the Globe.

Since Shakespeare did not make his living by his pen he was freed from the basic dilemma of his fellow playwrights. He did not need to do hack work to support himself, and he did not have to look for a patron. He was not isolated from the healthy, lively atmosphere of the practical world of the theatre, but he was freed from the worst of its pressures, the necessity of writing for money.

Jonson knew that pressure well and he must have been feeling increasingly desperate in the summer of 1602. He had promised himself the year before that he would retire, "high and aloof," to write a classical tragedy, but obviously he could not do it while he went on writing melodramas for Henslowe.

What Jonson needed was a patron and within the year he had found one. In February, 1603, a gossipy young lawyer named John Manningham noted in his diary: "Ben Johnson the poet now lives upon one Townsend and scorns the world." This was apparently Sir Robert Townshend, who became the first of many hospitable gentlemen who welcomed Ben Jonson into their homes, and it was here that Ben Jonson found the leisure at last to write his Roman tragedy.

When the play was put into print Jonson autographed a copy for his former host, as a "testimony of my affection . . . which I desire may remain with him and last beyond marble."

Jonson evidently felt that Sir Robert was rather fortunate to have had some part in a play that was going to last "beyond marble," and the tone of the dedication is both characteristic of him and very unlike the usual one of the period. The year Jonson wrote it, Sir Francis Bacon was sending out special copies of his *Advancement of Learning* to a selected list of influential gentlemen. Bacon was not a humble man, yet he used the word three times in his covering note to the Lord Treasurer. "I humbly present one of the books to your Lordship . . . Humbly desiring your acceptation thereof, with signification of humble duty, I remain . . ." Jonson, however, saw no reason to pretend to a humility he did not feel. As he once said, in a general dedication to the whole Court, he was its "servant but not slave."

Jonson was convinced that his Roman tragedy would "last beyond marble" because it would bring back the high principles of antiquity and show his detractors, once and for all, the glory of a more ancient and disciplined way of writing. The subject, of course, had to come from Roman history and Jonson chose the career of Sejanus, a favorite of the Emperor Tiberius who rose to be "co-partner of the empire" until his evil and his insolence brought about his fall.

Jonson was determined that his play should be solidly based on historical fact and he consulted only the best authorities. Shakespeare had been content with the gossipy and rather inaccurate Plutarch when he wrote *Julius Caesar*, but Jonson turned to Tacitus since that great Roman historian was interested only in carefully sifted facts. Moreover Jonson used Tacitus in the best and most recent of scholarly editions, that of Justus Lipsius, Professor of History at Leyden, in the Antwerp edition of 1600. He also had Dion's Greek text at his elbow, backed by Juvenal and Suetonius, and out of all these resources he slowly built up his careful, solid mosaic of historical fact.

In a way it was Jonson's devotion that betrayed him. It was the act of a conscientious scholar to include a whole oration from Tacitus in the body of the play but it was not the act of

a playwright. The Elizabethans went to the theatre to see recognizable human beings in action, not to watch a series of
Roman statues who might be accurately carved down to the
last known detail but who altogether lacked the breath of life.

Jonson was further betrayed by the fact that only one model
of classical tragedy was available to him. Of the vast body of
Roman tragedy only Seneca's had survived, and with his glittering rhetoric and his lack of interest in characterization he made
a poor model for Jonson to follow. The Seneca that Jonson
used was not, of course, the badly translated Seneca whose
melodramatic situations were seized upon by popular writers
like Kyd. It was the true and original Seneca that Jonson took
as his model, bound about by Latin dignity and moral aphorisms. The authority of Seneca was so unquestioned among the
learned that when Sidney praised *Gorboduc* he based his admiration on the fact that it was full of "stately speeches and
well-sounding phrases, climbing to the height of Seneca his
style and as full of notable morality."

Jonson was trying to achieve the same goal in his tragedy of
*Sejanus*, although he found, as the authors of *Gorboduc* had
found before him, that he could not achieve the final classical
gesture and maintain the unities of time and place. Jonson,
apologizing for this, explained that it was impossible, in the current state of the theatre, "to observe the old state and splendor
of dramatic poems." Nevertheless he felt that he had fulfilled
all the "other offices of a tragic writer," which he listed as
"truth of argument, dignity of persons, gravity and height of
elocution," and insofar as this was his ideal he achieved it. The
historical background of *Sejanus* is sound, the people are of exalted rank, the blank verse is measured and solid. But the play is
motionless because the people are not real. Jonson's Roman play
has the truth of archaeology, but Shakespeare's Roman play has
the truth of life.

When Jonson finished *Sejanus*, after what had apparently
been months of slow, intense labor, he offered it to the Chamberlain's Men at the Globe. His well-publicized scuffle with

them was now a thing of the past, and no company was better equipped to give his masterpiece the production it deserved.

The cast of *Sejanus* is available and shows that the production of Jonson's play must have been an excellent one.

The principal tragedians were

| | |
|---|---|
| Ric. Burbage | Will. Shakespeare |
| Aug. Phillips | Joh. Heminges |
| Will. Sly | Hen. Condell |
| Joh. Lowin | Alex. Cooke |

Many of these men had been the "principal comedians" in Jonson's first humour comedy, but as the experienced members of a repertory company they were able to assume a very wide range of parts.

The Globe actors knew their audience, which was large, opinionated, excitable and impatient, and they probably had grave doubts about the wisdom of trying to present a pure Senecan drama in their huge amphitheatre. It was perhaps at their suggestion that Jonson accepted a collaborator, and with great tact they chose one whom Jonson admired. In his introduction to the play Jonson speaks of this collaborator; and while he does not identify him, he calls him a "genius" and speaks warmly of his contribution and the best guess is that he was George Chapman. Whoever he was, he came in with his contribution after Jonson had finished the play. For it is not included in the printed version and could be removed so cleanly that there was not the slightest trace it had ever existed.

The actors at the Globe must have given *Sejanus* an excellent production, since they were by now the best company in London. But it was fatally apparent that the audience was becoming bored, and a bored audience, in a great public theatre like the Globe, could be a savage one.

Sejanus, the Roman, had been torn apart by a mob, and Jonson said later that his play had "suffered no less violence from our people here, than the subject of it did from the rage of the people of Rome." William Fennor described the debacle of the play in bad poetry but with much sympathy:

> With more than human art it was bedewed,
> Yet to the multitude it nothing shewed.
> They screwed their scurvy jaw and look't awry,
> Like hissing snakes adjudging it to die.

Once more Jonson had appealed to the general public to support his crusade and once more he had found himself beneath "the dull asses' hoof." Yet if the play failed with the general public it did not fail with the educated men who were Sidney's successors and who realized what Jonson was trying to do. Men like the cultivated Lord Aubigny approved of it, and it may have been because of *Sejanus* that Jonson was a guest in his house for five years.

Jonson valued what he called "the love of good men" but he was determined to reach the general public in one way or another, and two years after the stage failure of *Sejanus* he brought it out in book form. His friends rallied round with commendatory poems to point out to the reading public that it was being offered a masterpiece. George Chapman contributed nearly two hundred lines in praise of Jonson's "chaste Muse," John Marston rallied to the support of his onetime enemy, and various other poets joined them in deploring

> the people's beastly rage,
> Bent to confound thy grave and learned toil.

Chapman and Marston both signed their names in Latin— *Georgius Chapmannus* and *Johannes Marstonius*—since it was generally agreed that Latin was a much more impressive language than English could ever be.

To supplement this array of learning, Jonson did something that had never been done before with the text of a contemporary play; he printed in the margin a full list of all his sources.

Jonson admitted that no one but scholars could use his notes, since they were "all in the learned tongues, save one," but he was determined to prove what he called the "integrity of the story" and his readers could gaze reverently at all the Latin abbreviations even if they could not understand them. There are three hundred and eighteen of these marginal notes, furiously complete and furiously accurate. The bricklayer was showing the world that he could compete with the greatest scholars in their own field, and the playwright whose work had been hissed out of the theatre was making his appeal to a longer and slower judgment.

After *Poetaster* failed, Jonson had formally announced that he was abandoning comedy for tragedy.

> Since the Comic Muse
> Hath proved so ominous to me, I will try
> If Tragedy have a more kind aspect.

In tragedy he met disaster also, and no doubt a lesser man would have stopped trying. But Jonson did not stop trying and he would not concede defeat. He came of a fighting race, and the men of Annandale should have been proud of their son.

# Chapter 11

WHEN *Sejanus* WAS ACTED at the Globe, England had a new ruler. Queen Elizabeth had died in March, old and weary and very lonely, and since she had never married there was no direct heir to the throne. Many people in the suburbs were afraid of civil war and rushed their valuables into the walled city of London for safety, but Elizabeth had knit together a sober and orderly kingdom and the crown passed quietly to the son of her cousin, Mary Queen of Scots. Thirty-seven-year-old James the Sixth of Scotland became James the First of England, and after half a century England had a man for a ruler again.

The event stirred the Londoners to a flood of poetry. Everyone from Lord Burghley's elder son to the least of Henslowe's hacks rushed into print with combined wails for the death of the Queen and shouts of joy for the advent of the King, and if they had done nothing but read each other's work they would almost have had a sufficient number of customers.

The new king was both a scholar and a poet, and everyone hoped that a new day was dawning for the needy writers of England. It was true that Elizabeth had also been a scholar and a poet, a translator of Latin classics and one who excelled in "ode, epigram, or any other kind of poem heroic or lyric, wherein it shall please her Majesty to employ her pen." But the Queen of England was what might be called an elegant amateur, while the King of Scotland was a very conscientious professional.

King James started his writing career when he was eighteen years old with a little book called *Essays of a Prentice in the Divine Art of Poesie*. His advice on the art of writing had the commonplace earnestness of the second-rate schoolmaster that he always was at heart: "If you call the sun Titan at a time . . . call him Phoebus or Apollo the other time." James explained anxiously in his next book that his royal duties interfered with the time he had hoped to give to his writing. "Beloved reader . . . in case thou find . . . many incorrect errors . . . I must pray thee to accept this reasonable excuse . . . Scarcely but at stolen moments have I the leisure to blenk upon any paper." Like a true author he ended his apology with an advertisement for his third book, addressing his "beloved reader" with an anxious humility that sounds odd in so conceited a man. But James had a desire for affection and approval that amounted almost to a craving, and he was in complete contrast to that arrogant, independent spirit who had preceded him on the throne of England.

Part of James' longing to be loved came from his lonely and difficult boyhood, when he had been surrounded by books and by the cold theologians of the North. When he was four he was put under the tutelage of George Buchanan, who may have been the greatest scholar of his age but who was not well equipped to handle a small child. Buchanan was old and harsh and hated the very idea of royalty; and James was so frightened of him that half a century later he had a nightmare in which he dreamed he was trying to pacify "his master Buchanan, who seemed to check him severely, as he used to do." Ben Jonson once told King James to his face that he did not read poetry well. "Buchanan had corrupted his ear when young and learned him to sing verses, when he should have read them." This was an open piece of impertinence, but James, unlike Elizabeth, did not object to impertinence, and in any case the remark was chiefly directed against the bleak old scholar who had darkened his boyhood.

The most cruel thing that Buchanan did to James was to turn

him into a pedant. The young king was stuffed with Latin and Greek and philosophy and theology until his natural good sense and a broad streak of comedy were nearly choked out by the load of self-conscious erudition he carried about with him. Sir John Harington, who met the new monarch shortly after he came to London, wrote an unkind but truthful sketch of an interview that King James vouchsafed him. Harington said that the King behaved throughout like "my examiner at Cambridge" and insisted on quoting from "Aristotle and such like writers, which I had never read and which some are bold to say others do not understand." James inquired anxiously if England "did not entertain a good opinion of his learning" and finally permitted the amused Harington to escape after promising to take his education personally in hand. "I will not fail to add to your understanding in such points as I may find you lack amendment."

Still, James had never had an easy life and in some ways it was surprising that he turned out as well as he did. His father was a weak and vicious fool who was murdered less than two months after James' baptism; his mother was forced to abdicate and he grew up under a succession of regents. His wet nurse was a drunkard and as a result he was so weakened he could not walk until he was six, and even then he was condemned to a shamble that for the rest of his life forced him to lean on a courtier or hold a wall for support. If he worked at his desk for a week he became ill, and the only place his ungainly body was really comfortable was on horseback. He could sit a horse for hours without tiring, and his English subjects found they had a king who spent most of his time in the hunting field.

One of the chief merits of hunting in James' eyes was that it protected him from petitions. It was impossible for him to be asked a favor without immediately wanting to grant it—a serious fault in a king as James himself was penitently aware. But his desire for love and approval was so strong that he could not check it, and if he had not enjoyed hunting, with its comparative seclusion, the English treasury would have emptied even more rapidly than it did.

James' pedantry and his spendthrift nature were both warmly approved by his contemporaries. His subjects rejoiced in his learning and it was left to an ecclesiastic to bestow the final accolade: "Had he been born to a private fortune, he might have deserved to be a bishop." As for the money he spent, a king was supposed to spend money. Lavishness was the duty of all persons of high rank, and when the late Lord Burghley was accused of parsimony a friend defended him hotly against the charge. "I can prove he spent liberally. . . . He spent infinite sums."

What really embarrassed James' subjects was his ardent desire to keep the peace, and when he was called *Jacobus Pacificus* it was a term not of admiration but of contempt. The interminable wars that were the curse of the century were, in the eyes of most of his subjects, merely a healthy way of avoiding the cankers of peace, although they had no wish to be taxed for them or to risk their own necks in an outright war with Spain.

James had two other cherished projects: union with Scotland and religious toleration. His subjects disapproved of these also and he succeeded in neither of them. But in general he was a well-liked king, viewed with complacence both by his subjects and by himself, and the poets of seventeenth-century England never found any reason to withdraw the eulogies with which they greeted him when he arrived in England in 1603.

As James drew nearer London the crowds thickened. By the time he reached Theobalds, the country home that Lord Burghley had left to Robert Cecil, his clever younger son, so many people had gathered to see the new ruler "that it was incredible to tell of." Although Theobalds was twelve miles from London the crowds started forming at four in the morning, and when the King finally reached his capital city the people were packed between Enfield and the city walls. James was met by the mayor and an "unspeakable number of citizens," who jostled each other so violently that the orderly little blue-coat boys of Christ's Hospital, drawn up neatly to welcome their monarch, were "all displaced" by the multitude.

The new king's wife, Queen Anne, came south more quietly in June, bringing with her the two older children, Henry and Elizabeth. Yet even in her case suitable entertainments had to be planned for every step of the way, since it was inconceivable in the Renaissance for royalty to be treated otherwise. A whole series of country gentlemen employed a whole series of poets in composing suitable, rhymed welcomes, and when Queen Anne came to Althorp on the twenty-fifth of June her entertainment was designed by Ben Jonson.

The owner of Althorp was Sir John Spencer, a steady, honorable, rather old-fashioned man who lived the quiet life of a country squire and took his local responsibilities seriously. Just before the Queen's arrival he had finished setting out a plantation of oaks, to continue a tradition that had been observed by his father and his grandfather before him, with a stone marker to commemorate the event. His wife had died in childbirth, after giving him seven sons and daughters, and unlike most men of the period he did not marry again. Ben Jonson referred to this in his script, as he did to Sir John's casual clothes and sturdy independence, using the same light touch with which, two years earlier, he had simultaneously teased and flattered Lady Bedford. For Jonson felt at home among the nobility and brought a note of relaxed good humor into his dealings with them that they evidently liked.

Jonson designed his entertainment to take advantage of the grounds at Althorp. He had a satyr hidden in a tree, waiting for the flourish of trumpets which was the cue that the Queen and her nine-year-old son were approaching, and he gave the satyr some charming lyrics in which he trades insults with the Queen of the Fairies. A great many poets, from Sir Philip Sidney down, had written these little combinations of playacting and dancing that were offered whenever royalty came to visit, and Jonson's "Entertainment at Althorp" is one of a long line. But it is one of the liveliest and loveliest of them all and shows what a charming fairy tale Jonson could invent when he permitted himself a vacation from learning.

Queen Anne enjoyed herself at Althorp, for Scotland had been too poor a country to give her the festivities she loved. When she left her native Denmark at fifteen in a burst of farewell pageantry, her new husband had written ahead imploring his subjects to spruce up for her arrival. "A king of Scotland with a new married wife will not come hame every day." Scotland had done its best and Edinburgh dressed up the nine Muses in cloth of gold to sing psalms to the new Queen as she passed along the streets; but there had not been enough money to keep it up and Anne, for lack of other amusement, had turned to meddling in politics. The French minister prophesied that she would be a great force in English politics, but for once the astute Duc de Sully was wrong. As soon as Anne arrived in England she found a much more interesting occupation in spending money on festivities, and the great flowering of the English masque in the seventeenth century was the direct result of the new Queen's craving to be amused.

Since Althorp was only about sixty-five miles from London, it was soon enveloped in a crowd of noble ladies jockeying for position in the new Court. Jonson's little fairy tale was given on Saturday, and by Sunday "an infinite number of lords and ladies" had arrived at the quiet country estate. The speech that Jonson had prepared to be given on Monday could not be heard "by reason of the throng" and the same thing was true of another speech he had written for Anne's departure.

All England was flocking to London for the coronation and each shop, tavern, theatre and lodginghouse was preparing for a mighty harvest. So much money was tied up in the coming event that the authorities tried to avert their eyes from a plague that had crept into the suburbs in March. In July the Privy Council awoke to the danger, but by that time the damage had been done. Plague orders were sent to all the parish churches by the middle of the month, and London knew that its great enemy was upon it once again.

The crowds dwindled and then vanished, and the new king was hurriedly crowned in a service at Westminster Abbey to which the general public was not admitted. By that time fifteen hundred people were dying each week and many doctors and clergymen were hastily leaving town. The brave men who remained could do little except pray for a change of wind, since it was believed that a steady south wind had tainted the air and brought the infection. A few intelligent doctors advised the Londoners to get rid of the bed linen of the dead, and by the end of August piles of old bedding and rags were "thrown so thick in the highway as a man can neither come in nor go forth of the City." But no one knew that the plague was rat-borne, and the Dean of Westminster, attempting valiantly to keep the streets clean, offered a penny apiece for the killing of all stray dogs—the dogs that might otherwise have destroyed the flea-infested rats.

The Court left town as soon as the coronation was over, but it brought the plague along with it and carried it about the countryside. At Hampton Court, which was so crowded with courtiers that they had to be housed in tents, "they died two or three in a day of the plague." Many people felt that the plague was a sign from heaven that James' reign would be a violent one. "Their wisdoms failed, for he was a king of mercy . . . yet surely it had some moral." John Stow, who was writing a history of London, believed that the thirty thousand deaths within the city were God's judgment upon it for "gluttony and other sins." The mind of England, still medieval, searched for some logical connection in the moral sphere and did not look for physical causes. Yet when the black rat of medieval England was driven out by the brown rat, which harbored a different kind of flea, the great series of plagues that had shadowed English history disappeared forever.

During the plague Jonson stayed for a time at a country house in Huntingdonshire. One night, while he was asleep, his seven-year-old son appeared to him in a dream, his forehead slashed with a bloody cross. He was not the little Benjamin that Jonson had left behind in London, but full grown as his father believed he might be on the Day of Resurrection. Jonson prayed all night and as soon as it was morning he went to the room of William Camden, who was also a house guest, and told him what had happened. All Jonson's friends knew he had a vivid imagination and Camden succeeded in persuading him that the vision was the product of his own mind. Then a letter came from Jonson's wife in London, telling him the boy had died of the plague, and Jonson, like hosts of his fellow Christians, was left searching his heart for the crime he must have committed.

My sin was too much hope of thee, loved boy . . .

Some years later, a friend of Jonson's died of the plague in his arms and he was able to tender the final service he could not give his own son.

Jonson was at least among friends when the news came. Camden was his fellow guest and their host was that considerate and loving man, Robert Cotton. Cotton was nearly the same age as Jonson and had once been his schoolmate—one of the rich little boys who had entered Westminster School to share Camden's teachings with the boys from the slums. Like Jonson, he was of Scotch descent, but Cotton could trace his ancestry back to Robert Bruce and had been knighted that September by King James, who called him cousin. Cotton's chief interest in money was that it made it possible for him to amass his wonderful library, which he shared so lavishly. He had the wit to know that books were meant to be used and was unlike some of the antiquarians of the period, who were as "jealous of their books as if every hand which toucheth them would ravish them." Jonson was not the only scholar of the period who was deeply indebted to Cotton; and when he died all England was in his debt since his collection ultimately formed the basis of the British Museum. He was very close to William Camden, who called him the "dearest of all my friends," and the two of them had recently been north on an antiquarian trip, looking for old coins and carvings to "the sweet food and contentment of our minds."

King James kept his Christmas at Hampton Court during the plague year, but otherwise the season was celebrated in the usual way with plays, dances and dinners for the ambassadors. Queen Anne felt a special interest in the masques since she was presenting one of her own, and her ladies ransacked Queen Elizabeth's wardrobe to find material for their costumes.

A successful masque was a complicated affair, with its intricate dances and long hours of rehearsing. Even the question of which Court ladies to use out of anxious hundreds was a delicate problem, and the production required the services of a tactful and energetic general manager. The post was filled, this year at least, by Lady Bedford, who had gone up to Scotland to salute the new queen and was firmly established in her good graces before the entourage reached Althorp. Every poet in England must have looked longingly in Lady Bedford's direction as Christmas drew near, and Ben Jonson had some reason to believe that the lady he called "Cynthia's fairest nymph" might choose him for the honor of writing the Queen's first masque.

Instead, Lady Bedford chose Samuel Daniel. He was a grave, innocent, learned poet who had tutored in various noble houses and had always given satisfaction. King James had stopped at the house of Lady Bedford's father on his way south from Scotland and Daniel had been commissioned to write the welcoming speeches, supplying seventy-three dull but worthy stanzas for the occasion. He was, said Ben Jonson coldly, ignoring some of the lovely lines that Daniel had written, "a good honest man . . . but no poet."

Daniel gratefully dedicated his masque to Lady Bedford, and on the whole his work gave complete satisfaction. Queen Anne enjoyed herself as Pallas, in a blue mantle and jeweled buskins, and Daniel reported the occasion proudly. "By the impartial judgment of all the beholders . . . it was not inferior to the best that ever was presented in Christendom . . . And for the captious censurers, I regard not what they say."

The chief among the "captious censurers" seems to have been

Ben Jonson, who created such a disturbance during a masque that Christmas at Hampton Court that he had to be forcibly ejected. He was thrust out by Lord Suffolk, who, as Lord Chamberlain, was responsible for keeping order, and with him was removed a sympathetic friend and fellow poet named Sir John Roe. Roe even went so far as to compose a "moral epistle" on the episode.

> Forget we were thrust out. It is but thus:
> God threatens kings, kings lords, as lords do us . . .

Jonson never lacked at least one helpful friend, whatever the occasion.

A month or two later, the poets of London began to look hopefully towards another sort of commission. The King's formal procession through London, which had been postponed because of the plague, was scheduled for March, and by the first of February sixteen committees had been organized to make the necessary arrangements. Every city in Christendom had been presenting these triumphal processions for centuries and they had been growing increasingly ornate. The great wooden archways under which royalty passed were intricately carved and painted and then crowded with living figures. They were so expensive to construct that some of the European cities mortgaged their income for years to rear them and so beautifully designed that a series of artists from Holbein to Rubens had a hand in them. London had not been able to welcome a new monarch since 1558, and the sixteen committees worked valiantly to make the occasion a memorable one. They hired a hundred and forty carpenters, under the supervision of the brilliant Stephen Harrison, to build the arches, and seven master painters to decorate them.

Seven series of speeches were to be given, one at each of the seven arches, and the greater part of the assignment went to Thomas Dekker. In Jonson's eyes the choice must have seemed indefensible. Jonson disapproved of the author of *Satiromastix* much more than he disapproved of Daniel, who was at least a learned man and knew something of courtly matters. But Jonson could afford to ignore this unfortunate choice on the part of the city fathers, since he himself was given the commission for the first and last of the gates, those at Fenchurch and Temple Bar.

Jonson hurled himself into the task with the devotion of a man who was designing a memorial for posterity rather than working on a fugitive structure which would be pulled down as soon as the parade was over. He wished to produce something that would be as soldily designed as any classical play, "with that general harmony so connexed and disposed, as no one little part can be missing to the illustration of the whole." He searched all the available books for information on classical symbolism and supported himself with Tacitus and Martial and a whole parade of the ancients.

Dekker permitted himself a jeer at anyone who would "carve up the whole mess of the poets" and make "a false flourish here with the borrowed weapons of all the old masters." But, whatever Dekker might think, Jonson was not trying to show off. He was trying to rear a memorial worthy of himself, his city and his king, and everything about it had to be exactly right no matter how much labor it cost him. To get one piece of information correct he turned to Camden, whom he called "the glory and light of our kingdom," but for nearly everything else he turned to Continental authorities. In the published account of the work, the text travels through a stream of marginal notes and Jonson cites his authorities with the same relentless thoroughness he showed in *Sejanus*.

Jonson's design for the arch at Fenchurch was almost incredibly intricate. It was crowded with figures and with Latin quotations, and the whole city of London was reproduced in accurate detail across the top. The costumes were worked out with a careful regard for their symbolism, and the property department must have been kept busy supplying all the supplementary devices, from a squirrel to a bundle of Roman rods, that the determined poet required.

There were twelve living figures on the Fenchurch arch, not counting the musicians, and each of them had to climb to a precarious perch and remain motionless until the King arrived. Two of the symbolic figures, the River Thames and the Genius of the City, were played by professional actors since they had to deliver speeches. The Genius of the City was Edward Alleyn, glorious in purple, and below him reclined one of the boy actors from the Blackfriars, representing the Thames "in a skincoat made like flesh, naked and blue . . . a crown of sedge and reed upon his head, mixed with water-lilies . . . his arm upon an earthen pot, out of which water, mixed with live fishes, are seen to run forth and play about him." The boy from the Blackfriars had ten lines of blank verse to remember, a very cool costume for the middle of March, and a rather uncomfortable position on one elbow. Whatever the classical requirements may have been it seems almost too much to have expected him to deal with live fish also.

The crowds gathered beneath the motionless actors until the streets were "paved" with people. The glass windows along the line of march had been taken down and railings put up, and the crowd was "glued together" for a long wait. The procession finally came into sight, with the King under his canopy as the climax, and when Jonson's arch was reached a curtain "painted like a thick cloud" was pulled back to show Jonson's learned devices in all their glory. Alleyn delivered his two long speeches "with excellent action and a well-tuned, audible voice" and it is to be hoped that the little boy with the fishes did equally well. A great many of the speeches along the route had to be left undelivered and James probably did not hear the oration that Jonson had planned for him at Temple Bar. The actors could not make themselves heard over the shouting of the crowd, and in any case it was clear that the King was getting bored.

If speeches were to be made, King James preferred to make

them himself; and four days later he had his opportunity, arriving in his chariot of state, with his lords spiritual and temporal, to make his first speech before Parliament. In private James had a low opinion of Parliaments and once remarked to an ambassador, "I am surprised that my ancestors should ever have permitted such an institution to come into existence." Nevertheless he knew what was expected of him, and he knew enough about rhetoric to compose an excellent speech that touched his hearers deeply. "I will never be ashamed to confess it as my principal honor, to be the great servant of the commonwealth." James did not really picture himself as a servant of the commonwealth. He saw himself as a wise teacher watching over a group of rather quarrelsome infants and he understood nothing whatever about the country he had come to rule. But he sounded well and the speech was a great success.

With praiseworthy alertness, Jonson wrote a long poem celebrating the King's first appearance before Parliament. Most of it consisted of the routine compliments to royalty that were considered indispensable in the seventeenth century, but Jonson was something of a schoolmaster himself and he included a little lecture on the duties of a king. He hoped that James would not take too much pride in "vain stirs," such as the show the Londoners had just put on for him, and he further suggested that James would be a good king only if he were first a good man.

Jonson struck something of the same note again when Sir William Cornwallis invited the King and Queen to dinner on the first of May and commissioned Jonson to write the entertainment. Jonson wrote a pretty little May-day welcome, ending with a scene in the garden after dinner while Pan offered drinks from a fountain that ran wine. Pan's comments to the assembled guests have the cheerful impertinence that Johnson knew so well how to write and the parting wish to King James has almost the friendliness of an equal. "That your loves be ever flourishing as May and your house as fruitful . . . That no bad fortune touch you nor good change you . . . That you triumph . . . over the ridiculous pride of other princes and forever live safe in the love rather than the fear of your subjects."

Ben Jonson was not by nature a courtier. He once said of himself that "he would not flatter though he saw Death" and although the remark was exaggerated it was not altogether untrue. Yet no writer made such a success at the Court of King James as Ben Jonson. Although James firmly believed that a king was God's lieutenant on earth he did not let this exalted view of his station interfere with his liking for ordinary, comfortable behavior in those about him. He was as "pleasant and fellow-like" with his servants as with the highest nobility, and one of his favorites in England was an old park keeper named Robin whom he liked for "his plain, honest and bold speech . . . The King would be more familiar with this Robin than with any man." Moreover, James liked a quick wit and was willing to laugh at a joke even when it was directed at himself; and it is altogether fitting that he should have become the patron of that hero of the joke books, Ben Jonson.

The two men were curiously alike in some ways, if allowance is made for Jonson's greater intelligence. James longed to be the perfect king in the same way that Jonson longed to be the perfect poet, and the nobility of the ideal only made it harder for them both when they encountered criticism. Both of them pictured an ideal state of affairs in which they would impart wisdom to respectful and sympathetic listeners, and when James described himself as "the great schoolmaster of the nation" he was expressing a wistful hope with which Jonson would have sympathized. Their chief difficulty was in finding the proper listeners, for no one would sit quietly and attend to what they said. But, in some better-designed universe, Jonson would have made an ideal headmaster with King James operating learnedly and conscientiously as his assistant.

# Chapter 12

B EN JONSON RECEIVED HIS FIRST sign of royal favor in
1604. Queen Anne commissioned him to write her
Christmas masque and he was given the chance he had
missed the previous year.

Queen Anne knew what she wished the masque to be; she
wanted something in which she and her ladies could be disguised as "blackamoors." Jonson also knew what he wished the
masque to be, and it was a much more complicated assignment.
He wanted to link the English Court with ancient Greece and
Rome and to use the masque as a vehicle for the moral wisdom
that the classical writers had expressed allegorically in their
mythology.

To a lesser degree, all the European poets who wrote Court
shows were aiming for this same goal. The Renaissance was an
age of allegory, just as the Middle Ages had been, but now it
was an allegory jeweled and feathered and curled, in which
Court ladies and gentlemen acted out moral precepts and qualities. If a lady masquer appeared with frogs embroidered on her
gown, any well-trained observer was supposed to know at once
that she stood for Curiosity, and the poets operated under a
well-established series of conventions which had made the
masque a kind of aristocratic equivalent of the old morality show.

Like nearly everything else in the Renaissance, these conventions had originated in Italy. The Italians worked out a set of
elaborate symbols in their academies and then spread the gospel

through a series of books that were widely used by poets and designers. One of the most popular of these manuals was the *Iconologia* of Cesare Ripa, which had been reissued in an illustrated edition just in time for Jonson to use it in planning the costumes of the allegorical figures on his city arches. It was through Ripa that Jonson knew Liberty should have white robes and a cat, Safety a serpent at her feet and Promptitude a squirrel. Ripa's book was easy to use, with its careful pictures and thorough table of contents, and it was obviously reliable since the symbolism was based on standard classical authors like Cicero, Horace, Vergil and Seneca. Jonson could use the *Iconologia* with the knowledge that his work would be grounded on the best authorities and at the same time could spare himself a great deal of laborious research.

The Italians had supplied another useful short cut to Renaissance writers by turning out mythological dictionaries. These told a Court poet everything he needed to know about Mercury, Diana, Neptune or any of the other deities that kept appearing and reappearing in Court shows all over Europe. The exact details of these gods and goddesses were so complicated that even the original Greeks and Romans had difficulty in keeping them apart in their minds, and the Italian dictionaries filled a real need. The most popular of these was one by Natale Conti, who wrote with the liveliness of a novelist and who had been considerate enough to translate all his Greek quotations into Latin.

Jonson had neither the money nor the time to collect a large library and he used short cuts to learning wherever he could. He quotes Ovid in a marginal note in his first masque, but it is really Ovid as quoted by Conti. Nevertheless, Jonson used his sources with great care. He would not permit Queen Anne's lady blackamoors to show reverence to the moon until he had checked this Ethiopian custom in the Greek text of Stephanus of Byzantium in the 1568 edition.

In spite of his book learning, Jonson was a practical man of the theatre with a long experience in stagecraft. He knew that he had not been commissioned to write a masque in order to show off his own erudition. The chief aim of the masque was to show off the Queen and her eleven fellow dancers in an effective setting, and to give a restless, sophisticated audience something new.

When Daniel wrote the Court masque of the previous year he had made no effort to be original. He followed the old tradition of the masque and cluttered up the hall with portable scenery, putting a mountain at one end of it, a Cave of Sleep and a Temple of Peace at the other. As a result there was not enough room for the spectators, and, what was worse, no way of focusing and holding their attention.

What was clearly required was the same sort of contrivance that Jonson had used when he designed the arch at Fenchurch —a single set which could be concealed by a curtain until the last possible moment. This simple and obvious solution had never occurred to anyone, and Ben Jonson was the first to use it in a royal masque in England.

So sweeping an innovation would not have been possible if the stage designer had been an old-fashioned conservative left over from the previous reign. But Jonson's stage designer was as young as Jonson himself, and, like him, was doing his first masque. The two men worked together as though they had been made for each other, and it was largely through their combined efforts that the masque flowered into the magnificence it achieved in the Jacobean Age.

The stage designer was named Inigo Jones and he had been trained in Italy. Italy was not only the home of the emblem books and the dictionaries of mythology but it was also the home of the most brilliant and expensive theatre staging in Europe. The theatre in Italy was limited to a single set, owing to the Italian reverence for the unities, and to offset this scenic disadvantage the Italian showmen had formed the habit of inserting elaborate stage shows into the intermissions. As many as three hundred stagehands were used on a single show, and a theatre in Florence had no difficulty in bringing onstage a sea full of waves, a ship full of sailors, and a watchman singing madrigals in the mast while Aphrodite, accompanied by a dolphin, rode her shell on the waves below. If Ben Jonson required a sea scene for his twelve lady blackamoors, no one was better equipped to supply it than an Italian-trained designer like Inigo Jones.

Jones had been born in London, the son of a clothworker in West Smithfield. He was introduced to Queen Anne through her brother, the King of Denmark, and had been working at the Danish Court before he came to England to design masques. Nevertheless his heart was still in Italy, and although his enthusiasm was that of a convert rather than of one born to the faith, it was on that account all the more intense. In time Jones became an architect, one of the greatest in England, and he taught the doctrine of neoclassic Italian architecture as intensely as Jonson tried to teach the precepts of Horace.

Jones and Jonson were rather alike in temperament. They were both brilliant, arrogant, dictatorial men, full of theories and crusading zeal. It is not so remarkable that they finally quarreled as that they worked together in harmony as long as they did.

The chief source of friction between Jones and Jonson was the fact that Jonson considered the script writer the dominant figure in the masque and Jones felt this position belonged to the designer. When Samuel Daniel worked with Jones he made himself respectfully subordinate and even went so far as to say so in print. "The art and invention of the architect gives the greatest grace and is of the most importance; ours, the least part and of least note." To Jonson such a remark was flat heresy. Far from being "of least note," Jonson felt that his contribution was the soul of the masque and that Inigo Jones merely supplied the body.

Jones and Jonson collaborated on thirteen masques and raised that delicate art to glory between them, but in the end they were not on speaking terms. This was not so much a matter of temperament as a basic difference of opinion, since Jones was trying to build a spectacle and Jonson was trying to create a poem.

Jonson embarked on the writing of his first masque with the same sense of dedication that he felt when he started to write a play. He had to use as his basis Queen Anne's determination to be a blackamoor, and with some ingenuity he built the fabric of the action around it. Searching through his authorities he found that three ancient writers and one modern one testified to an Ethiopian river called the Niger that flowed into the western ocean. Since this was a masque, the ocean became Neptune, gray-haired and tridented, and the river became an Ethiop, his curled hair blue-black and his wrists twisted about with pearls. Since twelve ladies were to appear in the masque, the river Niger has twelve daughters, and they go voyaging with their father to find a land where their beauty will be no longer scorched to blackness. The land they find is England, ruled by the benign sun of a great king, and there they disembark and give their dance.

Once Jonson had sketched in the general outline of the action, Inigo Jones could begin work on the designs. They had agreed upon a single set, which was to be a seascape, and Jones tackled the problem of giving the illusion of an ocean on the stage of the Banqueting Hall. The platform was only forty feet square, set on wheels and raised about four feet above floor level to accommodate the machinery beneath, and Jones obviously could not achieve the elaborate effects of the Italian showmen. But he had the waves skillfully painted and operated by cranks, and they looked realistic enough when they were set in motion against a rear frame painted to look like a distant sea. Jonson was especially impressed by the way Inigo Jones handled the perspective, with "the whole work shooting downwards from the eye" to give an illusion of distance.

Jones was also in charge of the costuming and two of his sketches have survived. One shows the light-bearers who accompanied the lady blackamoors, dressed all alike in knee-length kirtles of sea-green. (Sir Francis Bacon, who was something of an expert on masques, made the point that "sea-water-green" showed up extremely well by candlelight.) The other drawing shows the costume for Queen Anne and the other daughters of Niger, glorious in bright blue gowns and golden shoes. Their hairdresses were intricate to the point of imbecility—"thick, and curled upright in tresses like pyramids, but returned on the top with a scroll and antique dressing of feathers and jewels interlaced with ropes of pearl." They also had pearls about their necks and wrists, to contrast with the "blackness" that Queen Anne had insisted upon.

There was some difficulty over the casting, since there were only eleven parts available and every woman in Court was competing for the honor of appearing with the Queen. The choice of Lady Bedford, that "fine dancing dame," was probably automatic; so was that of the wife and daughter of the Earl of Suffolk, since he was Lord Chamberlain and the whole masque was under his direct supervision. Lady Hatton used all her influence to get a part, and failed, but the Pembroke family, which was becoming powerful at Court, was well represented.

Jonson knew most of the women who took part in his first masque, but his special favorite was perhaps Lady Wroth. She was a niece of Sir Philip Sidney and, according to Jonson, a "lady most deserving her name." She hoped to become a writer herself and was apparently very kind to Jonson. In turn he dedicated one of his best plays to her and wrote two epigrams and a sonnet in her praise.

The ladies rehearsed strenuously for about six weeks, learning the steps of the complicated dances in which they were to appear, and in the meantime Jonson worked with the musical director on the songs. Unlike the dances, the songs were all performed by professionals and Jonson had the full resources of the Court, with its brilliant array of singers and instrumentalists, at his disposal. When Thomas Campion did a masque the following year he used what almost amounted to a full orchestra, balancing the lutes and the harpsichord with nine violins and forming a kind of musical triangle of which the cornets were the apex. Campion, who was an excellent musician, over-emphasized the songs at the expense of the story, but Jonson managed to keep the music an integral part of the action. He assigned the first song to a tenor dressed as a blue-haired Triton and balanced it with the treble voices of two boy singers who were appearing as sea-maids.

Sir Francis Bacon did not approve of a delicate use of music at masques. "Let the songs be loud and cheerful, and not chirpings or pulings. Let the music likewise be sharp and loud and well placed." He might not have approved of Jonson's delicate echo song, "Daughters of the subtle flood," but it is a remarkable piece of work, with the effect of a diminuendo achieved not only through the music but also through a gradual shortening of the syllables. Jonson many times expressed the warmest admiration for the Court musicians, and they had good reason to return his praise.

Meanwhile about a hundred men were at work preparing the Banqueting Hall for the great event. A state seat was put up for King James and scaffoldings erected for the rest of the audience. A carpet was laid, ready for the lady blackamoors to descend upon when they began their dance. The Office of the Revels sent their men over to set up the complicated arrangement of wires and plates that held up the candles that lit the hall, and the painters started "painting the roof overhead with clouds and other devices." The Banqueting Hall had a canvas roof, and it was already thick with layers of paint from all the preceding shows that had been held in it.

Jonson's masque was to be given on Twelfth Night, the climax of the Christmas season and the chief masquing night of the year. Since there was no system of reserved seats, the Lord Chamberlain and his staff of ushers had to use their white wands forcibly to maintain order and some ladies complained bitterly of the way they were treated. The crowd was so great that some of the would-be spectators were trapped in the galleries "in several heaps betwixt doors" and never saw the spectacle at all. Those who were fortunate enough to get seats had to endure the long wait that was inevitable on these occasions, but they could always look at each other's clothes and at the curtain. The curtain had a landscape painted on it and behind it was the usual last-minute hysteria that attends any dramatic production, a final struggle over costumes and lights with the royal Grooms of the Chamber hovering in anxious attendance.

Then, at last, the curtain was drawn and "an artificial sea was seen to shoot forth as if it flowed to the land." In front of the sea were Tritons and sea-maids, while the actors who played Ocean and Niger were carried by sea horses "as big as the life." Behind them came the twelve lady masquers, seated in a great shell of simulated mother-of-pearl set about with lights. To illuminate their azure costumes still further, they were attended by twelve light-bearers standing on sea monsters and holding torches made of shell. Everything was a moving glory of gold and blue and pearl, and even a spectator who objected strongly to having Court ladies painted black had to admit grudgingly that the opening scene was "very fair."

Another effective moment came when "the Moon was discovered in the upper part of the house, triumphant in a silver throne." It was the duty of the Moon to welcome the lady masquers to the shores of England, and they then disembarked from their shell to present their long-rehearsed dance. Each lady carried a fan, and Jonson had caused the fans to be painted with emblems suited to the couples that carried them. Lady Rich and the Countess of Suffolk, for instance, were supposed to symbolize swiftness and spotlessness, and so their fans were decorated with a pair of naked feet in the river.

These little symbolic emblems, which served as a kind of miniature guessing game, were extremely popular in Court circles all through the Renaissance. The knights carried them on their shields when they went into tournaments, and even William Shakespeare, who had comparatively little to do with the Court, was hired by a nobleman to make one such design. Jonson worked out the series of emblems on his fans with the help of a standard Italian encyclopedia on the subject, Piero's *Hiero-*

*glyphica*, and he even accidentally copied one of Piero's misspellings from the Greek. The careful labor that Jonson expended on these little painted toys was characteristic of the solid and conscientious scholarship he put into his masque, which was even more evanescent than the little fans and vanished as completely by daybreak as though it had never been.

What remained was the bills. A great many people had contributed their services, and Jones and Jonson headed a long list of musicians, actors, carpenters, painters and property makers who had all supplied their expensive assistance. The bill for the costuming was especially large, since the lady blackamoors had been hung with "most choice and orient pearl," and the whole masque cost the Exchequer about three thousand pounds.

This preposterous sum was fully justified in the eyes of the Renaissance, since a Court show of that kind played its part in the intricate game of foreign diplomacy. Ambassadors were always invited to attend as honored guests, and the more lavish the spectacle the more obvious was the power and prestige of the nation. Moreover, if Queen Anne could spend three thousand pounds on a single night's entertainment it was clear that she was a true queen. "The more money that is spent on things of this sort, the more deserving they are of praise, for, in truth, they are to be associated with magnanimous princes . . . to whom ugly parsimony is an evil stranger."

Jonson's first masque was a complete success and it launched him on his long and successful career as a Court poet. The stepson of a bricklayer was now an associate of royalty, and the palace he used to pass each morning on his way to school was now a kind of second office to him.

During the rest of his long life Ben Jonson was a familiar figure at Whitehall and he came to know most of the courtiers well. Some of them he liked and admired, but on the whole he did not find them very impressive. A man who was at home among the Romans was not likely to be affected by a few extra jewels and laces, and Jonson spoke the truth when he once remarked that "he never esteemed a man for the name of a lord."

# Chapter 13

Jonson's *Masque of Blackness* was only part of a magnificent series of entertainments held at Court that year. The honor of opening the season went to Shakespeare's company, which had been taken under royal patronage and was now known as the King's Men, and they ushered in the Christmas revels with "a play in the Banqueting House at Whitehall called The Moor of Venice." This was *Othello,* with Richard Burbage playing the title role, and the dark violence of Shakespeare's Moorish hero must have made a curious introduction to Jonson's "lady-Moors" with their fans and their elegant dancing.

Fourteen plays were presented at Court during the Christmas season, and either eleven or twelve were produced by the King's Men. Seven of these were Shakespeare's, with his *Merchant of Venice* repeated because it had been "again commanded by the King's Majesty." Two of the remaining plays were Jonson's, and both *Every Man in his Humour* and *Every Man out of his Humour* were presented at Whitehall that Christmas.

The King's Men owned a third play of Jonson's, but *Sejanus* would not have been a good choice for a Court production. It had been a failure with the general public and moreover it had been accused of containing seditious material.

In its search for sedition, the Privy Council under James was just as nervously alert as the Privy Council under Elizabeth. Even so inoffensive and respectable a dramatist as Samuel Daniel got into trouble because a play of his named *Philotas* suggested a vague parallel to the Essex conspiracy. Any play that dealt with a conspiracy was automatically suspect in the eyes of the Privy Council, and in Jonson's case he was a known satirist and had a prison record in connection with *The Isle of Dogs*.

Jonson himself believed that he was "called before the Council for his *Sejanus*" because of the personal animosity of the Earl of Northampton. One April day Jonson was involved in a brawl with a member of the Earl's retinue and he was convinced that Northampton had become his mortal enemy. But even if that learned and unscrupulous intriguer had not accused Jonson before the Council, a play like *Sejanus* might well have fallen under suspicion. The Archbishop of Canterbury would not have liked the remarks on the burning of books, and it contained a very cynical speech on the subject of obedience to kings.

But the chief difficulty with *Sejanus* was that it pictured a conspiracy. It showed a monarch who was plotted against by one of his own subjects, and although this subject was clearly a villain, Renaissance monarchs did not wish to see any conspiracy against royalty enacted on the stage. Jonson made amends when *Sejanus* was printed by adding a postscript in which he explained that the play was really a warning to traitors; for if the heavens brought down vengeance on those who plotted against evil princes, how much more dreadful God's punishment would be on those who conspired against a good monarch. This bit of medieval Christian moralizing makes an odd introduction to a Roman tragedy, but it must have satisfied the authorities or the play would not have been allowed to appear in print.

The misfortunes that dogged *Sejanus* were not the fault of the King's Men, and Jonson let them have the script of his next play. It was a comedy called *Volpone*, written in the incredibly short time of five weeks, and it was produced at the Globe with Burbage, Heminges and Condell in the leading parts.

After his recent disasters Jonson might reasonably have been expected to lower his standards a little, but the Globe audience discovered immediately that he was as determined as ever to reform the English stage. The actor who came out to speak the Prologue told the waiting audience that "our poet" intended to "mix profit" with pleasure. He had also planned a scrupulous observance of the unities:

> The laws of time, place, persons he observeth,
> From no needful rule he swerveth.

There was to be no "monstrous and forced action" and the whole comedy would be constructed according to the rules that the "best critics" had laid down.

After this dictatorial opening, some of the theatregoers may have shuffled their feet and feared they were in for another bout of cultural instruction. But the first act of *Volpone* had hardly begun before they discovered they were wrong; in his five energetic weeks Jonson had written a masterpiece.

The story of the evil Venetian grandee who baited his hook with gold had the sense of theatre that all Jonson's earlier plays had lacked, and the stupidest butcher of East Cheap would have sat with his eyes riveted on the stage, watching Volpone spin the web into which his gold-crazed neighbors fall. For the first time in Jonson's career his learning fused with his knowledge of stagecraft and he achieved the classic comedy of which he had dreamed. Even the doctrine of the unities is Jonson's servant, not his master. The action takes place in a single day, not because the Italian schoolmen had thus interpreted Aristotle, but because the plot needed to be concentrated on a hard, tight, brilliant center. It was as though Jonson had at last assimilated the rules so thoroughly that he was able to forget them.

Moreover, for the first time Jonson gave free rein to his ability to write poetry. The subject of the play is love of money, but by moving the setting to Venice and out of everyday England Jonson was able to give it a sheen as glittering and magnificent as gold itself. The play opens with Volpone's invocation, in a kind of morning song, to his wealth.

> Open the shrine that I may see my saint.
> Hail, the world's soul and mine.

And when Volpone's servant is describing to him the beauty of the heroine, the catalogue rises to an inevitable climax.

> . . . a beauty ripe as harvest!
> Whose skin is whiter than a swan, all over,
> Than silver, snow or lilies! a soft lip
> Would tempt you to eternity of kissing!
> And flesh that melteth in the touch to blood!
> Bright as your gold! and lovely as your gold!

Blind in the glitter of gold, one Venetian is willing to betray his wife and another his son. Volpone pulls them in with a rising hysteria of delight at the glorious strength of money, and in the end he goes down to ruin along with the men he has corrupted. The play has all the evil splendor that Englishmen attributed to the Italians of the Renaissance, packed into a smooth, brilliant plot and illuminated by some of the most magnificent lines Jonson ever wrote. The scene in which Volpone attempts to seduce the heroine can only be matched, in the sensuous, glittering texture of the poetry, by the brush of some of the Italian painters.

Jonson's interest in realistic comedy found a place for itself even in the glory of Venice with a deft introduction of two of his fellow countrymen, a pair of visiting tourists named Sir Politic Would-Be and his lady. Sir Politic was so successful a characterization that he became a kind of byword for the English political amateur who traveled in Europe seeing secret documents concealed in every cabbage and triumphantly detecting a code in the special handling of a toothpick. His lady is one of the earliest and most horrifying examples of a special species of tourist. She talks so steadily that even Volpone cannot stand it and she is obliged to recommend a cordial so that he can get his strength back. The unhappy man cannot even mention a dream but she has had a better one, and she knows all the latest patter on books and art. In fact, she is even an expert on applied psychology.

This portrait is of course taken from life, and Jonson must have seen the sisters of Lady Would-Be many times at White-hall. Yet the general outline of the portrait comes from a fourth-century Greek writer named Libanius, and Jonson merely modernized the original sketch. The whole play, as a matter of fact, is a network of Greek, Roman and later European sources, and even the songs have their roots in Jonson's scholarship. The song about fools is an adaptation of the Latin prose of Erasmus; and the famous song in the seduction scene,

> Come, my Celia, let us prove
> While we can the sports of love . . .

is in part an almost direct translation from Catullus.

Jonson the poet was never parted from Jonson the scholar, and although his Venice is a fabled city of crime and wealth it is firmly planted in an accurate use of local detail. When Shakespeare used Venice as the background for Shylock and Othello he was content with a few general facts he had picked up about the city, but Jonson was incapable of being so casual. Before he started his play he had to have the whole city of Venice clear in his mind, from the arcade that ran on the north side of the Piazza di San Marco to the fishmarket on the Grand Canal. He had to know the coins the Venetians used, the clothes they wore, the wines they drank, and even the exact technique of the *commedia dell' arte* or the name of a local ball game.

Jonson had never been to Italy, and he got his information either from books or from friends who knew the country. One of Jonson's close friends at this period was an Anglo-Italian named John Florio, who had been devoting most of his life to making the Italian language better known in England. Florio had issued two textbooks on the subject, as well as the excellent dictionary that Jonson had used when he was searching for Italian names for the characters in his second humour comedy.

Florio had the warmest admiration for his "exquisite" dictionary and dedicated it to two earls and a countess. The countess was Lady Bedford, whom Florio called, in his excitable way, his "most-most honored because best-best adorned Madame" and it was at her house that Florio labored over his famous translation of Montaigne's *Essays*. Apart from the sale of his books, Florio made his living by teaching Italian, and there is still in existence his mock-magnificent letter to Jonson's friend Cotton, asking that *"molto magnifico signior"* to please pay his bill. By the time Jonson was writing *Volpone*, Florio was safely tucked into a Court position and getting a hundred pounds a year from Queen Anne as her reader in Italian. He had also just become a grandfather and the Queen sent a cup to the baby's christening.

When *Volpone* was printed, Jonson presented a specially inscribed copy to Florio. "To his loving father and worthy friend, Mr. John Florio, the aid of his Muses, Ben Jonson seals this testimony of friendship and love." The use of the word "father" was a graceful tribute from a younger man to an older one who had helped him, and when Jonson himself became an old man many of the younger poets called him father also.

Jonson published *Volpone* with great pride in 1607 and wrote a long, exultant dedication in which he presented the play to Oxford and Cambridge: "To the most noble . . . sisters, the two famous universities, for their love and acceptance shown to his poem in the presentation." The King's Men were especially well liked at Oxford, where, during this period, they were performing four summers out of six, and they had apparently had a great success at both universities with *Volpone*. It meant a great deal to Jonson to have his play received so warmly at the two great centers of learning, and he was deeply grateful for their "love and acceptance."

Twenty years earlier Jonson had hoped to enter one of the universities and instead he had been apprenticed to a bricklayer.

He never laid aside his dedication to the ideals of scholarship, but he had been obliged to struggle alone and without assistance. Moreover his efforts had met with a good deal of hostility, and even Jonson himself had to admit that it was not easy to go on writing with no one to support him. As he said in his dedication to *Volpone,* a writer's art cannot "raise itself" unless there are "commenders and favorers to it." Jonson was at last beginning to find commenders and favorers and he was especially proud to find them among university groups.

The dedication to *Volpone* is a long and eloquent reiteration of Jonson's consecrated sense of a poet's mission. The true poet must first of all be a good man, since "so divine a skill . . . should not be attempted with unclean hands." Jonson could still hear Sidney's defense of poets ringing in his mind; and all the writers he had studied since, Strabo and Minturno and the rest, only confirmed what Jonson had already decided long before. The poet was an "interpreter and arbiter of nature, a teacher of things divine . . . a master in manners." Therefore, in his latest play, he had labored to follow "not only the ancient forms" but especially that "doctrine which is the principal end of poesy, to inform men in the best reason of living."

At the end of the dedication, Jonson rose to the loftiest statement he ever made of his ambition as a poet. "If my Muses be true to me, I shall raise the despised head of poetry again and, stripping her out of those rotten and base rags wherewith the times have adulterated her form, restore her to her primitive habit, feature and majesty, and render her worthy to be embraced and kissed of all the great and master-spirits of our world."

They are noble words. And yet the "times" of which Jonson spoke so scornfully were the ones in which Shakespeare was writing *Antony and Cleopatra* and *King Lear.*

Shakespeare's plays were not obedient to classical laws and therefore Jonson could not accept them as serious poetry. Like may other learned men of his generation, he could not believe that a man who wrote so casually and with so little apparent effort could be a true artist, especially since his work pleased the ordinary London public and aroused what Jonson persisted in calling the "rude and beastly claps" of the multitude.

Jonson looked at Shakespeare's plays in the white light of his own ideal. It was an heroic ideal and it served him well in *Volpone;* but its light was too single and too strong to make him a reliable critic and sometimes it glowed so brightly that it blinded him altogether.

# Chapter 14

THE BOY ACTORS at the Blackfriars were given a new patent when King James came to the throne. They also acquired a new licenser, for the special right to license their scripts went to Samuel Daniel instead of remaining vested in the Master of the Revels. The new post brought Daniel ten pounds a year and he must have needed it badly, since a member of the board later complained that Daniel was continually asking for advances.

Driven by his need of money, Daniel sold a play of his own to the same company. Like many poets, he believed that it was a kind of degradation to write for the stage and he assured the Earl of Devonshire that he would never have consented to the production "had not my necessities overmastered me." If Daniel felt he lowered himself by letting his work be staged in a comparatively aristocratic indoor theatre like the Blackfriars, it is fortunate that he never had to submit to the ultimate indignity of having it appear in a great outdoor amphitheatre like the Globe.

The average Jacobean writer could not afford to share Daniel's lofty point of view. George Chapman was writing plays for the boys at the Blackfriars. So was John Marston, who ultimately became a shareholder. And so was Ben Jonson, who joined forces with Chapman and Marston in 1605 and collaborated with them in writing a comedy for the Blackfriars company.

Since Chapman, Marston and Jonson were all highly opinionated men, it did not look on the surface like a very promising
venture. But they were professional writers and knew how to
get into a co-operative frame of mind, and among them they
managed to produce one of the most charming comedies of the
Jacobean age.

The title of the play, *Eastward Ho*, was an echo of the cry
of the London boatmen looking for customers to take down
the Thames. The rival company of Paul's Boys had just produced a comedy called *Westward Ho*, written by the hardy
Thomas Dekker and a newcomer named John Webster, and
the Blackfriars company chose the title to supply a little necessary competition. But the three playwrights paid no attention
to the rival comedy once they sat down to write their own.
They were parodying an older point of view and they evidently
had a delightful time doing it.

In the previous decade a great many Londoners had flocked
to see a series of plays that hymned the virtues of prominent
London citizens or the noble thrift and impossible achievements
of idealized London apprentices. Thomas Heywood made his
initial reputation with *The Four Prentices of London*, in which
he stroked the conceit of the average Londoner until it purred,
and when he finally put the play into print he defended it as
characteristic of the period. "As plays were then, some fifteen
or sixteen years ago, it was in the fashion." The point of view
that is fashionable in one period is ready to be parodied in the
next, and Chapman, Marston and Jonson settled down to the
delicate and delightful mockery of *Eastward Ho*.

The hero of the play is everything a London apprentice
should be—pure-minded, industrious and willing to keep his
place. Even the books he reads are the kind that improve his
character. "As for my place and life, thus I have read:

> Whate'er some vainer youth may term disgrace,
> The gain of honest pains is never base."

This repulsively virtuous youth works for a goldsmith named Touchstone, who has risen to wealth because he was armed with moral maxims—"good, wholesome, thrifty sentences, as 'Touchstone, keep thy shop and thy shop will keep thee.' " The goldsmith has a virtuous daughter who plights her troth to the apprentice in a stately array of aphorisms, and that side of the family comes to a good end.

The goldsmith has a second daughter who wants to become a lady, and since London was full of hopeful girls eying the Court the three playwrights have a fine time with their Gertrude. She earnestly practices the "Court-amble" and the fashionable way of holding her hands, and she even tries to be gracious to her plebeian relatives. "I'll . . . call thee Sister Mil still, for though thou art not like to be a lady, as I am, yet sure thou art a creature of God's making, and mayest peradventure to be saved as soon as I."

The plot of *Eastward Ho* gave the three playwrights a wicked opportunity to pillory both the Court and the City and they made the most of it. Unfortunately they chose one target too many, and again Jonson found himself in trouble with the authorities.

One of the standard jokes in London at the moment was the flood of new knighthoods that James had granted as soon as he came to the throne. Another was the horde of hungry Scots who had followed their ruler to the fat pastures of England, and in *Eastward Ho* the two jokes were combined. One of the boy actors at the Blackfriars had no trouble getting a laugh when he put on a Scotch accent and remarked, "I ken the man weel, he's one of my thirty-pound knights."

King James was in a sensitive frame of mind on both subjects. He had publicly apologized to Parliament for his "infirmity" in granting so many knighthoods, and he had been deeply disappointed in his optimistic expectation that the English and the Scots would get on well together. "The ane country has wealth and the other has multitude of men, sae ye may pairt the gifts and every one do as they may to help other." James was correct about the multitude of men but wrong about the sharing. Any man less theoretical than James would have known that the English courtiers, desperately angling for Court positions themselves, would not welcome the strenuous competition of the Northerners.

The Scots, in their turn, were touchy about the multitude of English jokes on the subject and a gentleman named Sir James Murray decided that the authors of *Eastward Ho* had deliberately set out to insult him. He went to the King and stated his case, successfully arousing the King's very quick temper, and the startled playwrights found themselves in prison.

In the case of *The Isle of Dogs* everything had at least been done in a formal and official manner by the proper authorities. In the case of *Eastward Ho* the prisoners were given no kind of examination and the only way to get out was the way they had got in—by political pressure.

Both Chapman and Jonson sat down and wrote letters, on what they called "prison-polluted paper," to every influential personage they knew. It was Chapman who wrote the King, imploring him "to take merciful notice of the submissive . . . sorrows of your two most humble and prostrated subjects." Both men sent petitions to the Earl of Suffolk, who, as Lord Chamberlain, wielded a great deal of influence, and Jonson sent a long letter to the newly created Earl of Salisbury.

The Earl of Salisbury was Robert Cecil, Burghley's younger son, who was chief secretary of state under King James as his father had been under Queen Elizabeth. He tried to run England as intelligently as his father had done, but he was handicapped by working for a monarch who was politically a fool. The crippled, solitary little man was obliged to develop a cautious, underground way of working, masked by a courtesy so unfailing that it unnerved many of his associates in that boisterous and assertive age.

Jonson was fortunate enough to be on good terms wth the Secretary of State, and he spoke in his letter of the "former benefits" he had received from Salisbury. He insisted that all he wanted was a hearing, since he had, "unexamined," been "committed to a vile prison, and with me . . . one Mr. George Chapman, a learned and honest man." Jonson admitted he had a reputation as a satirist, but he insisted that he had never attacked individuals but only general abuses. "I may be otherwise reported, but if all that be accused should be presently guilty, there are few men would stand in the state of innocence." He added that he had never given offense to "any person of honor or authority" and had always "labored to keep their dignity . . . safe," and here he reached what was certainly the heart of the matter. It was the dignity of a "person of honor" that had been insulted, and in the delicately balanced world of Court life that was a serious offense.

Jonson sowed his letters broadcast through the Court, since the more people he could get to intercede for him against "his Majesty's high displeasure" the better his chances would be. He wrote to at least two lords who cannot be identified and to one lady, hoping they would "inform his Majesty that I never in thought, word or act had purpose to offend or grieve him." One of these lords was probably Aubigny, whose brother was a close friend of the King's and who became one of Jonson's most useful patrons.

Jonson also wrote to William Herbert, Earl of Pembroke. The Earl was a nephew of Sir Philip Sidney and was doing his best to follow in his uncle's illustrious footsteps as a patron of poets. He was very kind to Jonson, and his habit of giving him twenty pounds every Christmas season to "buy books" was a gesture as generous as it was imaginative. The letter Jonson wrote him from prison was that of a grateful man. "You have ever been free and noble to me." It was also that of an anxious man. "The anger of the King is death (saith the wise man) and in truth it is little less with me and my friend, for it hath buried us. . . . Most honored Earl, be hasty to our succour."

The Earl of Pembroke had a brother, the Earl of Montgomery, and Jonson sent a letter to him also. The Earl of Montgomery had no special interest in writers, but he was very popular with James and had married the niece of the Secretary of State just before she danced in Jonson's *Masque of Blackness*. Montgomery's chief claim to literary fame is an accidental one; many years later the editors of Shakespeare's plays dedicated the First Folio to him and to his brother. At the moment he was merely a handsome young man, interested in horses, who might conceivably be willing to put in a good word for the imprisoned playwrights.

All these hopeful letters to so many distinguished people may have had some effect, but in any case James was never angry long. As his physician remarked, "He is very wrathful but the fit soon passes off." The fit passed off, to the profound relief of Jonson and Chapman, and they were released from prison.

To celebrate, Jonson gave a party and "banqueted" all his friends. Included among the guests was William Camden, currently revising the sixth edition of his *Britannia*, and a six-foot young lawyer named John Selden. In time Selden became a greater scholar even than Camden, as well as one of England's most influential parliamentarians, and his friendship with Jonson never wavered. Jonson taught him to enjoy Horace, and Selden in return developed a profound respect for Jonson's powers. In a rather ponderous prose style that was very unlike the liveliness of his conversation, Selden gave testimony of his affection for his "beloved friend, that singular poet Mr. Ben Jonson, whose special worth in literature, accurate judgment and performance, known only to that few which are truly able to know him, hath had from me, ever since I began to learn, an increasing admiration."

Jonson's banquet must have been a fine affair throughout, but the highest point occurred "in the midst of the feast." Jonson's old mother was still living, and she got up to propose a toast to her son and to make a speech. There had been a rumor abroad that the punishment for the erring playwrights was to be mutilation, to have "their ears cut and noses," and it is not impossible that King James had actually threatened something of the sort in the first heat of the moment. Jonson had once been branded, and his mother was not willing to have him endure a worse disgrace. She showed the people at the banquet a piece of paper, in which had been wrapped the poison she planned to bring her son in prison if the sentence had gone into effect, and since she was no coward she intended "first to have drunk of it herself." If all England had been searched to find a suitable mother for Ben Jonson, a better one could not have been found than this magnificent and spirited old lady.

In October of this same year of 1605, Jonson was himself a guest at a small supper party in the Strand. His host was one of the most handsome and delightful men in England, Robert Catesby—"dear Robin" to his admiring friends. Catesby was a member of an old Catholic landed family, and his guests that evening were all Catholics too. The distinguished little group that Jonson had been invited to join included Lord Mordaunt, Sir Jocelyn Percy, and two cousins of their host named Francis Tresham and Thomas Winter.

It must have been a pleasant evening, for Catesby was a brilliant conversationalist. His kinsman, Lord Monteagle, said that his conversation gave "such warmth as we need no other to maintain our health." Catesby had reason to be in especially high spirits that evening, for a plan which he had helped conceive the previous year was progressing excellently and there was every reason to believe that it would succeed.

Catesby's plan was to blow up Parliament, so that the entire government of England—King, Lords and Commons—would be liquidated at a single blow. Thomas Winter, who was eating his supper so pleasantly near Ben Jonson, had spent most of the previous month working with a colleague named Guy Fawkes, bringing in fresh gunpowder to a cellar under Parliament House in case any of the old supply had been injured by the damp.

The most curious aspect of the Gunpowder Plot was the innocent good cheer and the wholehearted idealism of the men who took part in it. They seemed to feel they had embarked on a project which was not only worthy but wholly practical; and as they worked together like brothers, earnestly digging a tunnel under Parliament House and sharing their little supply of baked meats, they were sustained by the thought that "justice and punishment" would be combined as soon as the gunpowder exploded.

It is true that the conspirators were all devout Catholics and that the pressure on Catholics was growing increasingly heavy in spite of James' efforts at religious toleration. It is also true that the conspirators were bankrupts, and that it was usually the bankrupts who plotted against the existing order. Both Catesby and Tresham had beeen involved in the Essex conspiracy, that other revolt of the bankrupts at the end of the preceding reign; but the Essex conspiracy had aimed at nothing more than the destruction of a single Court faction while the men of the Gunpowder Plot were blandly contemplating wholesale and indiscriminate murder.

The original group kept expanding, chiefly because Catesby did not have enough money to go on buying ammunition and renting rooms. But his enthusiasm was so infectious and his charming manner so difficult to resist that it was easy enough to find converts. Sir Everard Digby, an otherwise normal and admirable young man, contributed fifteen hundred pounds to the venture, partly for religious reasons but chiefly because "the friendship and love he bare to Catesby . . . was so powerful with him, that for his sake he was even contented and ready to hazard himself and his estate."

Francis Tresham, Jonson's fellow guest, came in with two thousand pounds, and it was Tresham who brought the plan to disaster. His brother-in-law, Lord Monteagle, was a member of Parliament and as such was scheduled to be blown up on November the fifth when Parliament convened. Tresham could not bear the thought of murdering his sister's husband and wrote him an anonymous letter. "Devise some excuse to shift of your attendance at the Parliament, for God and man hath concurred to punish the wickedness of this time."

Lord Monteagle promptly took the letter to the Secretary of State and the plot was uncovered; Guy Fawkes was arrested just before midnight on the fourth of November as he stood guard over the gunpowder in the vault. But Fawkes steadfastly refused to give any testimony, beyond claiming that his name was John Johnson, and for the next few days no one in the government knew the names of the chief conspirators or how many Catholics were involved.

On the seventh of November, Ben Jonson appeared before the Privy Council. There was no question of his loyalty, in spite of his prison record and the fact that he had been seven years a Catholic; but since he was a Catholic the Privy Council hoped he might put them in touch with a priest who had volunteered some information. The priest needed a safe conduct, and the Privy Council issued a warrant "unto Benjamin Johnson to let a certain priest know, that offered to do good service to the State, that he should securely come and go to and from the Lordships."

The next day Jonson reported to the Secretary of State that so far he had had no success. He had approached the chaplain of the Venetian ambassador (who had a right to be in England, in spite of the fact that he was a priest, because he was in the retinue of a foreign diplomat) and the chaplain had apparently been soothing but unhelpful. Someone suggested that Jonson approach the chief English ecclesiastic, the Archpriest, Dr. George Blackwell, and there were "other such like suspensions." The man Jonson had hoped to communicate with had either left town or gone into hiding, although Jonson said that if he himself "had been a priest" he would have welcomed the opportunity to serve his king and his country.

The Secretary of State did not really need Jonson's priest. Salisbury had an excellent spy system, inherited from his father, and most of the members of the plot had been under observation long before the Monteagle letter. The leaders of the conspiracy were rounded up quickly and efficiently and most of them were executed. Jonson's onetime host, Robert Catesby, was fortunate enough to die fighting, but his severed head was affixed over the Parliament House and a Mr. Dobbinson charged the Privy

Council about twenty-four shillings for the ironwork that had to be used. William Camden wrote an official account of the trial of the chief conspirators, in Latin, so that it could be used as Protestant propaganda on the Continent, and English school-boys for years afterwards were assigned the subject for their verse compositions. Guy Fawkes, the "devil of the vault," was burned in effigy once a year thereafter, and the instinctive English mistrust of Catholicism deepened.

It was inevitable that the Gunpowder Plot should increase the persecution of English Catholics, and equally inevitable that Ben Jonson should be involved along with the rest. His attempt to assist the Privy Council did not alter the fact that he was a recusant—one who failed to conform to the established religion of England.

On the seventh of January, less than two months after Jonson tried to get in touch with the priest at the request of the Secretary of State, his name was presented to a London jury as that of a suspected recusant. Two days later, at the Old Bailey, the jury brought in a true bill, sustaining the charge, and Jonson was faced with two choices. Either he could present himself and stand trial, or he could stay away and be automatically convicted. He stayed away.

Jonson's name was one of twenty on a long and distinguished list that included even the wife of an Exchequer official. The arts were well represented on this particular list of recusants, for Dr. Thomas Lodge, physician and former playwright, was on it; so were Hugh Holland, who had written some complimentary verses to *Sejanus* the year before, and Edmund Bolton, who wrote equally warm words of praise to *Volpone* the year following. Music was represented on the list by Martin Peerson, whom Jonson must also have known since Peerson wrote the setting for Jonson's May-day song at Highgate.

Twenty recusants were accused and only one appeared at Old Bailey to answer the indictment. The rest, along with Jonson, stayed away. This put them automatically under the jurisdiction of the Court of Exchequer, which handled the fining of recusants, and what happened to Jonson there has not been traced.

The government did not share the emotional hysteria against Catholics; its own attitude was frankly financial. A convicted recusant could be fined twenty pounds for each month he stayed away from services at the Anglican church, with the forfeiture of all his goods and two-thirds of his lands if he could not pay the mounting fine. Jonson possessed neither goods nor lands, and the Exchequer probably made no attempt to prosecute him. The kind of recusant that really interested the government was someone like Francis Beaumont's brother John, who was cited as a recusant this same year, just after he had inherited the family estate, and who consequently lost most of it.

In Queen Elizabeth's day the government was able to count on a revenue of about eighteen thousand pounds a year from fines levied on Catholics, but under James this revenue dropped to about ten. Parliament started an investigation into the comparative collapse of this ancient and honorable form of income and discovered that James had been handing out individual Catholics to his subjects as their special financial property— "to one man two recusants; to another four recusants; to others twenty recusants; and to others fifty recusants." A gift of this kind to a needy courtier was as good as a pension, and the only risk run by the recipient was that his investment might die or, worse still, become a Protestant.

The fines against the Catholics were not hard to enforce, but in general the penal act that followed the Gunpowder Plot was too savage to be effective. It demanded, for instance, that anyone who made a convert to Catholicism should be put to death, and in that case Ben Jonson would once more have stood in the shadow of the gallows. For in this same year of 1606 he was formally accused of being "a seducer of youth to the popish religion."

This charge was made one day after his name was proclaimed in Old Bailey, but it had been set in motion by a wholly different set of authorities. Jonson was living in the Blackfriars at the time, and by law he was required to go each Sunday to the local parish church, that of St. Anne's, to take communion there. The local churchwardens and the parish constables were supposed to keep a list of anyone who failed in this elementary political duty of all true Englishmen and report it to the ecclesiastical court in London. The new penal act had a provision that was designed to stimulate their enthusiasm still further; if they failed to turn in a complete list of names they would themselves be fined, but a reward of forty shillings went with every conviction they managed to obtain.

Jonson appeared in the Consistory Court of London to answer the churchwardens' charges against him, and he fought back vigorously. His wife's name had been linked with his on the presentment, and he maintained that they had both been going to St. Anne's regularly. Moreover, his wife had been taking communion, although he admitted that he himself had not.

As for the charge that he was "seducer of youth to the popish religion," Jonson denied it categorically and demanded that his accusers be obliged to bring proof. It was not an uncommon charge in such cases. The previous year, for instance, the musician William Byrd and his wife Ellen were up on a similar charge, and the chief accusation against Mrs. Byrd was that she had tried to convert her maid, who went by the awesome name of Thoda Pigbone. Jonson was attractive to young people and congenitally unable to resist teaching them, and it may be that the charge had some truth in it. Nevertheless, the churchwardens could not substantiate it, although the judge set several court days in May at which they could have put in an appearance.

The Consistory Court was willing to concede that Jonson could not take communion against the dictates of his conscience, but on the other hand it was clear to the Court that Jonson's conscience was entirely mistaken. To rectify this situation Jonson was given, at his own suggestion, a list of prominent people which included the Dean of St. Paul's and the chaplain of the Archbishop of Canterbury. From this list he was to choose one.

He was then to discuss the chief points of religious doctrine with this expert twice a week, reporting the results to the Consistory Court on the final court day of the next term.

Whatever the arguments may have been that were marshaled by this august theologian, they apparently made no difference to Jonson. For the next four years he endured the difficulties and risks of his position and remained a Catholic. Then he suddenly returned to the Anglican fold, with such enthusiasm that he drank all the wine in the cup when he attended his first communion.

Such a gesture was very characteristic of Ben Jonson. And it was equally characteristic of him to have become a Protestant again just as the penal laws against Catholics in England were finally beginning to relax.

# Chapter 15

I N SPITE OF JONSON'S STRUGGLES with the authorities, he continued on his triumphant way as a Court poet. During the next five years he composed three masques for the Queen, one masque for the Prince of Wales, three entertainments for the King, and two masques for Court weddings.

The first of Jonson's wedding masques was presented at Whitehall in January of 1606, only a few days before his name was read out as a recusant in the Old Bailey. The Lord Chamberlain's daughter was being married to the Earl of Essex, and the talents of Ben Jonson and Inigo Jones were again combined to produce a show splendid enough to be worthy of such a union.

Inigo Jones worked out a new scenic device for this wedding masque of *Hymenaei*—a globe of the world which turned to display eight gentleman masquers sitting inside, all glorious with jewels. The lady masquers descended from a framework of clouds, even more laden with jewels, and as one spectator remarked, "I think they hired and borrowed all the principal jewels and ropes of pearls both in Court or City." Even the shoes of Lady Bedford and her fellow performers were "set with rubies and diamonds," and the ladies must have glittered magnificently as Jones' careful cloud structure brought them "gently sloping down" to the stage level.

It was generally agreed that "Inigo, Ben and the actors . . . did their parts with great commendation" and Jonson thought so too. He warmly praised the dance master, Thomas Giles, and was so impressed by the work of Alphonso Ferrabosco, who composed the music and superintended the musicians, that he wrote a long paragraph in his praise. "Virtuous friend, take well this abrupt testimony and think whose it is. It cannot be flattery in me, who never did it to great ones; and less than love and truth it is not." Ferrabosco was about the same age as Jonson, and the two men had formed a close friendship. Like John Florio, the musician came from an Italian family, and Jonson wrote two poems to his "loved Alphonso."

When Jonson published his masque, he reinserted a section of the marriage song which had been omitted in the actual performance, and added a characteristically lofty notation. "I have here set it down whole and do heartily forgive their ignorance whom it chanceth not to please." The song was in part an adaptation of Catullus, and the masque as a whole shows Jonson's determined scholarship even more clearly than the *Masque of Blackness*. Jonson was convinced that *Hymenaei* should be "grounded upon antiquity and solid learnings" and he had made an extensive and accurate survey of Roman marriage customs before he began. He was equally resolved that his masque should have a moral base, without which the best of scholarship was useless in the eyes of the Renaissance, and he composed a sober and eloquent plea for dignity and good sense in married life.

The marriage for which the masque was written was a cold-blooded affair which had been engineered by Court politicians to unite two ancient houses. The thirteen-year-old daughter of the Earl of Suffolk, Frances Howard, was being married to the fourteen-year-old Earl of Essex, and the union ultimately ended in a divorce even more contrived and cold-blooded than the marriage had been. Frances Howard was determined to rid herself of a husband she hated, and if she had not succeeded in getting a divorce she might well have murdered him as she did the next man who stood in her way.

Frances Howard might never have become a murderess if

she had lived in a normal environment. But she was a violently emotional woman brought up entirely at Court and living in a conniving, silly atmosphere in which there was too much money and not enough to do. Jonson's noble masque was presented in an atmosphere that offered very little in the way of either standards or morals, and while Queen Anne was a highly respectable woman she had no influence on the behavior of the men and women who crowded into Whitehall.

Even Queen Elizabeth, who was something of a martinet, had found it extremely difficult to enforce a reasonable standard of behavior, and towards the end of her reign one observer remarked gloomily that to call a man "a chaste courtier" was an insult "almost asking a stab." Queen Elizabeth tried to be especially strict with her maids of honor, since she was responsible to the girls' families for their welfare at Court; and yet the young Earl of Pembroke felt he had been most unfairly treated when she exiled him to the country merely because he had made Mary Fitton pregnant.

In the Jacobean Court the Queen had much less control and money was being spent much more lavishly. More and more people were drawn to Whitehall, and the process that had begun under Elizabeth was accelerated. When Lady Rich appeared as one of the masquers in the *Masque of Blackness* she was living in open adultery with Lord Mountjoy. And at this same masque, when various jewels and purses were lost in the crowd, one lady lost that unimportant trifle, "her honesty . . . being surprised at her business on the top of the tarras."

The most pathetic victims were the country girls of good family who came to Court to serve in Queen Anne's household and who were half-drunk in the heady new atmosphere of freedom and sophistication. One of these was a relative of Lady Bedford's named Cecily Bulstrode, who had a brief but violent career at Court and who went down to posterity chiefly because she managed to infuriate Ben Jonson. He wrote an epigram about her, which was the normal way during this period of showing one's disapproval.* But Jonson was incautious enough to let his manuscript get into the wrong hands. It was "stolen out of his pocket by a gentleman who drank him drowsy and given Mistress Bulstrode, which brought him great displeasure."

Cecily died in her twenties and the news was brought to Jonson by the servant of a mutual friend. Jonson was shocked and depressed by the information: "Would God I had seen her before." He made amends as well as he could, writing a fourteen-line epitaph in which he gave her the wisdom of Pallas and the modesty of Cynthia and finishing it with such speed that he was able to send it to his friend immediately. The epitaph did not give Jonson's full opinion of Cecily Bulstrode, but no one expected the unvarnished truth in Jacobean memorial verse.

It is only fair to say, in defense of the morals of the English Court, that it was no worse than any other Court in Europe and better than some. When the King of Denmark arrived for a visit he was able to give the English a liberal education in the matter of "carousal and sports." Queen Anne's brother was a hard-drinking, vigorous monarch who embraced women and the arts with equal enthusiasm and who had been filling Denmark with his beautiful buildings and illegitimate children. "Now will drunkards be in request," wrote a prophetic resident of Paris to an English friend when he heard of the Danish visit.

King Christian was an expensive guest, and James spent nearly the whole of the subsidy that had been voted by an emotional Parliament after the Gunpowder Plot in an effort to entertain his flamboyant brother-in-law. No one could have been less pleased than the Earl of Salisbury, who was trying to keep down government expenses. Moreover, since he was Secretary

---

* When a clerk in the Exchequer Office quarreled with one of the young girls in his master's household, he promptly "writ some verses on her," and when Sir John Harington was irritated by a peer he comforted himself with the reflection that he could "write a damnable story" about him "and put it in goodly verse."

of State he knew that he would have to entertain both kings in his house at Theobalds, and he had been uncomfortable enough when he opened his house to James just before the coronation. "Too much crowding doth not well for a cripple." Even a single king had put a strain on his housekeeping arrangements and he had been obliged to borrow some extra dishes from the Lord Keeper.

It was of course necessary to arrange an entertainment for the occasion and the Earl of Salisbury turned to Ben Jonson. Jonson wrote the greeting that was delivered to the two Kings, and the farewell that was spoken when they left; and Salisbury's copy of the manuscript is still in existence, along with some slight alterations made in the Secretary of State's own handwriting.

The two royal guests enjoyed themselves at Theobalds but the occasion was not as dignified as the Earl of Salisbury may have hoped. A show had been planned in which the Queen of Sheba presented a casket filled with wine, cakes and jelly to his Danish Majesty. Being half-drunk, she deposited it in his lap and he, being wholly drunk, collapsed on the floor and had to be taken away to sleep it off, smearing the bed of state with cake and jelly. Sir John Harington was among the guests and the occasion appealed to his strong sense of the ridiculous. "Now did appear, in rich dress, Hope, Faith and Charity. Hope did essay to speak, but wine rendered her endeavors so feeble that she withdrew . . . Faith . . . left the Court in a staggering condition . . . Charity came to the King's feet and . . . in some sort she made obeisance. . . . She then returned to Hope and Faith, who were both sick and spewing in the lower hall. Next came Victory in bright armor and . . . by a strange medley of versification did endeavor to make suit to the King. After much lamentable utterance she was led away . . . and laid to sleep in the outer steps of the antechamber."

The house that served as a background for all this activity was one of the show places of England. It had been built by Lord Burghley, who lavished a special love on the gardens, and it incorporated all the Renaissance notions of true magnificence with its twenty towers and its great halls. It might almost have been designed as part of one of Inigo Jones' masques, for its main hall was decorated with a roof of stars and "by some ingenious mechanism the sun was made to pursue its course across them." In one of the galleries were fifty-two trees, representing the fifty-two shires of England, and from the branches hung all the coats of arms in the realm so that each visitor could pick out his own. The trees were painted so realistically that it was said the birds sometimes came in through the open windows and perched among them. There was a billiard table at Theobalds, there was a canal winding through the garden so that guests could go "rowing between the shrubs" and there was a semicircle of Roman emperors carved in white marble around the summerhouse.

There was also a very fine deer park, and this was the attraction that especially appealed to King James. He had plenty of royal residences near London, but none on the north side of town, and after the entertainment for King Christian had been successfully concluded James set his heart on owning Theobalds. Next year the Secretary of State presented it to him, with a deed of conveyance made out for the fourteenth of May, 1607, and Ben Jonson wrote the script that formally welcomed the King to his new house.

By this time Jonson's services as a writer were in constant demand. A month after his second welcome to the King at Theobalds he was approached by Sir John Swinnerton on behalf of the Company of Merchant Tailors, who were planning a July banquet for King James and needed professional assistance. Normally the boys of the Merchant Tailors' school would have provided the script and the performers, but a new standard in Court shows had been set and the company feared "that their schoolmaster and scholars be not acquainted with such kind of entertainments."

Jonson had written a similar show for the Haberdashers' Company three years earlier, and he had no difficulty turning out a highly successful speech of eighteen verses. It was delivered by a professional actor, little John Rice of the King's Men, who was coached in his part by John Heminges and dressed as the spirit of gladness with a taper in his hand. The services of many other professionals were required also, from Dr. Bull, who brought his own organ and charged for the freighting, to John Allen, the great Court tenor, who sat in a ship suspended from the rafters and sang unheard over the din below.

The harassed committee that superintended the affair found it was no easy matter to entertain royalty. Like the Earl of Salisbury they had to descend to borrowing and dispatched one of the company wardens to the Lord Chamberlain to get the loan of some royal silver for the occasion. They also had to hire extra chairs. They were fortunate in possessing "the biggest hall in town," but it was next door to a tavern which had fitted up a place of recreation for its customers on the roof. The roof directly overlooked the hall garden, and the company of Merchant Tailors had to raise the height of its own brick wall in order to get privacy for the King's visit.

In the end the royal dinner cost the company more than a thousand pounds, including a hundred pounds in gold presented to the King and eight shillings that went for "driblets." The affair went down in London history as a "hearty and cheerful welcome" and the expense could be written off to the good will that was needed by all London businessmen in their extensive dealings with Whitehall and the King.

King James was "marvelously well" pleased with Jonson's verses, and in the autumn of this same year Jonson was given another opportunity to please the royal family. Queen Anne was planning a new masque, her first in three years, and she commissioned Jonson to follow her last show, the *Masque of Blackness*, with a suitable sequel.

Anne wanted the daughters of Niger to be used again, but with four more ladies and no blackening; and Jonson solved the story problem with the ease of long experience in his *Masque of Beauty*. The daughters of Niger have been delayed three years by a search for their missing sisters, until the East Wind, resplendent in colored wings and gold-embroidered buskins, arrives with the glad report that all the nymphs have been found safe on an island, completely transformed. Then the curtain at Whitehall went up to disclose the Queen, the Countess of Bedford and fourteen other ladies on their floating isle, surrounded by youngsters of the Court as light-bearing cupids. The musicians were dressed as the spirits of ancient poets, in garments of crimson and purple and crowned with laurel, and they sang the opening lyric with two voices echoing from the fountain.

> It was for beauty that the world was made,
> And where she reigns, love's lights admit no shade.

Jonson wrote another masque for this same Christmas season, to celebrate the marriage, a month later, of young Viscount Haddington, one of the King's favorites, to the beautiful daughter of the Earl of Sussex. The bride's family name was Radcliffe, and Jonson felt justified, on Camden's authority, in opening his masque with a red cliff. In due time the cliff parted, with a "loud and full music" that drowned out the noise of Inigo Jones' machinery, and the twelve gentleman masquers were displayed in an effectively delayed entrance. Since Viscount Haddington was Scotch, the gentlemen were a tactful mixture taken from both countries, all gloriously arrayed in lace and embroideries with jewels and feathers on their heads. The scholarship of the masque is as exact as ever; but Jonson was beginning to feel that his audience needed a little relief from spectacle and splendor and he supplied a comic dance of twelve little boys with a "variety of ridiculous gesture, which gave much occasion of mirth and delight to the spectators."

Both masques were presented in the new Banqueting Hall that James had just erected to replace the old Elizabethan structure—"very strong and stately" and in "every way larger than the first." Both were very successful and the Venetian ambassador sent a respectful report to his home government on the *Masque of Beauty*. "The apparatus and the cunning of the stage machinery was a miracle, the abundance and beauty of the lights immense, the music and the dance most sumptuous." Queen Anne was determined to equal its success the following year and Jonson was commissioned to write the finest masque she ever attempted, the *Masque of Queens*.

In theory the new masque was to cost only a thousand pounds, but the bill for the fabrics alone came to nearly two thousand. The King gave a blank check to the masque officials since "our dearest wife hath resolved for our greater honor and contentment to make us a masque this Christmas." The Queen took a special interest in the complicated machinery that Jones had contrived for the occasion, with its "divers wheels and devices," and towards the end she was holding "daily rehearsals and trials of the machinery."

Each masque was an international event and the King of France sent a special message to his ambassador to hold firm on the matter of precedence. Since Queen Anne was pro-Spanish, the Spanish ambassador had been given a seat of honor at her last masque and the French ambassador had not put in his appearance at all. Now, with a veiled threat from the King of France in his pocket, La Boderie stood firm, and there was nothing for the Court officials to do but pray that the Spanish envoy would go home before the masque was presented.

The day that was scheduled for the masque arrived and the Envoy Extraordinary from Spain was still in London. Day after day he lingered, while Queen Anne and her ladies went on practicing their dances, the scenery waited, and all Court affairs came more or less to a standstill. Finally, a month later, the Spaniard left London and the *Masque of Queens* could be presented. The French ambassador attended in triumph, along with his wife and daughter, and Ben Jonson's long-delayed show was finally unveiled.

After so long a wait, the assembled audience had a right to expect something out of the ordinary. When the curtain was drawn the audience, "in full expectation," looked to see what Jonson had arranged for them; and they saw Hell.

Inigo Jones had designed a cavern, "flaming beneath" and smoking to the top of the roof, and out of it, "with a kind of hollow and infernal music," came a troop of witches. The smoky violence of this first scene was to give dramatic contrast to the radiance that surrounded the Queen and her ladies and it was Jonson's first use of what he called the "antimasque," although the principle had been foreshadowed in the comic dance of the little boys. The witches were also there to serve a moral purpose and stood for the various forces of ignorance and superstition that threatened Good Fame.

But Jonson's witches could be enjoyed for their own sake. He had combined his reading of the classics and of European authorities with the stories he had heard as a boy, and out of his vigor as a writer he managed to cast a magic spell of his own over the Whitehall audience. The verses he wrote for his witches were echoed in the whirling beat of the dances that Jeremy Hearne designed for them, and Jonson's lines have the leap and gallop of the ancient folk rhythms from whose dark soil they came.

The King must have watched this part of the masque with special interest, for witchcraft was a living issue in Scotland. It was the remnant of the old fertility cult, driven underground by Christianity but still flourishing with well-organized vigor. When James had sailed to Denmark to get his bride, three of the witches' covens had banded together to raise a storm at sea, acting under the leadership of a man who could hope to claim the throne if James had no heirs. Whatever future generations might think, the North Berwick witches were fully convinced of their own powers and, as Camden said, "openly confessed that they had raised those storms." When Jonson's witches at Whitehall attempted to raise a storm in a mutter of rhythmical incantation, most of the audience must have watched with uneasy interest, especially since the masque happened to fall on the night of February the second, which was one of the four great yearly witchcraft festivals. There were a few rationalists in England who believed that the witches were self-deceived and that it was not possible to enter into a personal league with the Devil; but if any such skeptics were present they could always enjoy Jonson's magical poetry—second only to the witches' lines in *Macbeth*—and his astonishing array of learning.

The second scene in the masque also displayed Jonson's learning, for the Queen and her ladies were seated aloft over Chaucer's House of Fame. Inigo Jones had outdone himself, for the structure had "great gates and turning doors below, and a globe and sundry seats above for the Queen and ladies to sit on and be turned round about," and the lady masquers then descended in triumphal chariots to which the witches were bound as a symbol of the triumph of virtue over ignorance and malice.

Jonson gave Inigo Jones full credit for the ingenuity of the machinery, "since it is a virtue, planted in good natures, that what respects they wish to obtain . . . from others, they will give . . . themselves." Jonson wished it to be clear that his praise of Jones was the result of his own generous nature, but he spoke with real warmth of the work of his "excellent friend," Ferrabosco, in the same masque.

In spite of Jonson's efforts to keep him in his place, Inigo Jones was assuming an increasingly important position and his drawings were beginning to be reverently preserved. His costume designs were as magnificent as ever, and the Countess of Bedford was glorious in pink, with a helmet, as the Queen of the Amazons. The costume of Lady Guildford, the daughter of one of the masque officials, deserves special comment for its Renaissance combination of ingenuity and lack of humor. She was supposed to represent the Queen of Caria, whose dubious claim to fame was the fact she had made herself her husband's "tomb" by swallowing his ashes, and Inigo Jones dressed the lady, very suitably, in orange tawny, yellow and "ash-color."

Jonson was a little shaky in his scholarship where this same Queen of Caria was concerned and confused two women with the same name, but in general his *Masque of Queens* is a monument to his impassioned and accurate scholarship. Prince Henry asked him for a personal copy of the masque, annotated to show all the sources, and Jonson had difficulty in tracking some of them down since he had drawn so largely on his fabulous memory of his "former readings." Nevertheless he managed to produce a complete documentation of the whole masque, from the white wings of Good Fame "as she is described in Inconolog. di Cesare Ripa" to the "elegant arguments" of Remigius in his *Daemonolatria*. The manuscript is still in existence, the text and annotations arranged on the page in Jonson's beautiful handwriting with the neatness and precision of a Renaissance flower garden.

The King's elder son was fifteen years old when he asked Jonson to copy out the *Masque of Queens*, a gentle and learned young man who had already proved himself to be a good friend to poets. George Chapman had found a longed-for haven in Prince Henry, a "dear and heroical patron" who had promised him three hundred pounds when he finished his translation of Homer. Jonson felt an equal gratitude to him for being capable of reading poetry intelligently. "Poetry, my lord, is not born with every man, nor every day. And in her general right it is now my minute to thank your Highness, who not only do honor her with your ear but are curious to examine her with your eye and inquire into her beauties and strengths."

Jonson had first met Prince Henry at Althorp, when the sober and handsome little nine-year-old had arrived from Scotland with his mother. Since then Henry had grown into a broad-shouldered young man who was so unlike his parents that James must have sometimes felt he was almost ostentatiously so. The prince ran his three establishments at St. James, Richmond and Nonesuch so economically that he never spent beyond his income. He even kept a budget of his expenses, and he never let any entertainment be accompanied by disorder. King James was notorious for his habit of laughing and talking at divine service, but Prince Henry sat alert and attentive through the longest sermons; and he was so opposed to his father's habit of swearing that he set up little boxes throughout his own households to receive the fines of anyone who indulged in an oath. Henry was, in fact, the very model of a virtuous Renaissance prince, and neither his father nor his mother liked him very much.

Henry's own ideal was Henry of Navarre, the brilliant and vigorous King of France, and he tried hard to model himself on the French King. He worked industriously at swordplay and tilting, and the year after the *Masque of Queens* he decided that he would give a tournament. The medieval tournament had degenerated into a stylized Court show called the Barriers, but the old forms of fighting had been kept up and Prince Henry wanted his tournament to be a real test of arms.

Ben Jonson was commissioned to write the preliminary speeches and he set the Barriers against an Arthurian background. King Arthur appeared as a star, Merlin rose from his tomb, and the Lady of the Lake presented an apostrophe to the young prince. Then Henry and six of his friends issued from a pavilion at one end of the Banqueting Hall and battled fifty-eight defendants with pike and sword, "giving and receiving that night 32 pushes of pike and about 360 strokes of swords."

The following June, Henry was invested as Prince of Wales and by Christmas he was ready to present a holiday masque of his own. Jonson wrote *Oberon* at his request, and the masque of the fairy prince is one of the most charming shows of his career. He gave it a fairy-tale background, with a moonlit rock and porters dressed in leaves, and the satyrs sing a charm full of the nursery nonsense that Jonson could do so delightfully.

> Buzz, quoth the blue fly.
> 　Hum, quoth the bee.
> Buzz and hum they cry,
> 　And so do we.
> In his ear, in his nose,
> 　Thus, do you see?
> He eat the dormouse,
> 　Else it was he.

The kingdom of the fairies was made of "countless lights and colors all shifting, a lovely thing to see," and the Prince and his fellow masquers were dressed alike in white and scarlet, with jackets of gold and silver, white and scarlet plumes and black masks. The Prince wore a scarlet band across his body to distinguish him from the other gentlemen, but he might have been detected equally well by the quality of his dancing. For Prince Henry did nothing that he did not do superbly.

Queen Anne presented a masque of her own the month after *Oberon,* and again Jonson was commissioned to write the script. Since the Court was making a determined effort to economize, *Love Freed* cost only a little over seven hundred pounds. Yet even this was more than the government should have spent in the current state of its finances.

The Earl of Salisbury was now Lord Treasurer as well as Secretary of State, but he could have found small pleasure in his extra office. The Exchequer was in a "chaos of confusion," and the best Salisbury could do was to keep a kind of precarious balance between a decreasing income and a steadily increasing expenditure.

The root of the problem lay in the fact that there was no regular tax system; the country was still operating on the medieval theory that a king should live off his own income. If he needed extra money for some special purpose he had to ask Parliament to vote him a subsidy, and even Queen Elizabeth, for all her experience and tact, had found subsidies difficult to get. By a system of rigid government economy she had managed to maintain her unique position as the only solvent monarch in Christendom, but James had inherited her poverty without inheriting either her thrift or her skill in managing the House of Commons. Moreover, the inflationary rise in prices that had commenced during her reign was increasing, and even if James had been a model of economy it is doubtful if the old feudal device of crown revenues could have been stretched to cover the cost of running the government of seventeenth-century England.

James had the best of intentions where money was concerned. He sent a special letter to the Privy Council to ask their
advice, "since there are so many gapers and so little to be
spared." He even went so far as to sign a document in which he
solemnly promised not to give away any more Crown lands to
his eager courtiers; but the only result was that the courtiers
subsequently asked for money instead of land and King James
gave them money instead. After his poverty-stricken reign in
Scotland he could not resist the impulse to be equally lavish in
his own household, spending twelve hundred pounds on new
furnishings for Theobalds or nearly six thousand to welcome
his Danish brother-in-law, and he squandered money himself as
freely as he gave it away to his needy courtiers.

According to Renaissance theory, King James was right in
spending so much money. "A magnificent mind is inseparable
from the majesty of a king. If he did not give, his subjects and
servants would live in a miserable climate." Certainly there was
nothing miserable about the climate of the Jacobean Court,
with its silks and its jewels and the glory of its masques, and it
could always be left to the weary and ailing little Lord Treasurer to find the money somehow to pay for all this splendor.

# Chapter 16

J ONSON'S EMPLOYMENT AT COURT interfered for a time with
his work in the theatre, and it was not until four years
after *Volpone* that he was ready with a new play.

The play was produced by Jonson's good friends, the boy
actors, but not in their usual theatre. After a series of legal difficulties they had given up the lease on the Blackfriars theatre,
which reverted to the Burbage family. The Burbages had
"placed men players, which were Heminges, Condell, Shakespeare, etc." on its stage, and the King's Men were using the
Blackfriars as an indoor winter theatre to supplement the Globe.

West of the Blackfriars was an area known as the Whitefriars, where a shaky theatre company had been attempting to
operate until it was finally evicted for failing to pay the rent.
The company which had formerly been known as the Children
of the Blackfriars moved into the empty theatre and reorgan-
ized as the Children of the Whitefriars, and it was under this
new name that they presented Jonson's latest comedy.

The leading player of the company was still Nat Field. He
was no longer the little boy who had headed the cast of *Cynthia's Revels*, but a grown man in his twenties. His respect for
Jonson, however, was undiminished. Field was hoping to make
a career for himself as a writer and Jonson, with considerable
kindliness, had asked him to contribute some verses to the published version of *Volpone*. It was Field's first appearance in
print and he found himself in the company of men like George

Chapman, Francis Beaumont and John Donne. But what chiefly impressed young Field about being in the book was his own "damnable presumption" in attempting to praise a play by the great Ben Jonson.

Jonson called his new comedy *Epicoene or The Silent Woman* and it was well suited to an acting company made up mostly of boys. The play is one long, lively practical joke, with the ruthlessness and high spirits indispensable to this form of amusement. Jonson himself took a small-boy delight in practical jokes, such as the elaborate one he once played on "a lady." She wanted to consult an astrologer and a friend of Jonson's led her in elaborate secrecy to a house in the suburbs. She mounted a ladder into the hiding place where the astrologer was to be found, in his flowing robe and long white beard. The only light in the room was a "dim-burning candle," which was just as well since it was Ben Jonson behind the whiskers.

It was in somewhat the same spirit that Jonson wrote his brilliant and lively *Epicoene* and devised the tale of an old man named Morose who could not endure noise. Morose lives on a street too narrow for the creak of carts and makes his servant go about the house in woolen "tennis-court socks." When he goes for a walk he wears "a huge turban of night-caps on his head, buckled over his ears" and he has spent six months looking for a quiet woman to take as his wife. The play opens when his nephew finds him a wife, a gentle lady who can hardly raise her voice above a whisper. But as soon as they are married she turns into a violent shrew and the rest of the play records the old man's struggle to get a divorce. There is an outrageous and lively scene in which Jonson parodies the whole subject of canon law, but in spite of his best legal efforts Morose cannot rid himself of his wife. His nephew, who would have been disinherited by his uncle's marriage, offers to get him out of his difficulty in return for a strict financial guarantee and the play ends when he walks over to the bride and removes her wig. "She" is a boy whom the nephew has deliberately planted to protect his inheritance.

The action of the comedy covers a single day, and the structure is as rigidly classical as it was in *Volpone*. The plot is an interweaving of two classical sources, Libanius and Plautus, and the earnest young reformer who wrote *Cynthia's Revels* would have approved of it wholly.

Nevertheless Jonson was in a more relaxed frame of mind than he had been in the days of his early comedies for the Blackfriars boys, and he no longer clung quite so tightly to his early position as the sole defender of classicism. He was as delighted as Shakespeare might have been with one of the characters in *Epicoene* who makes a mistake about the word *corpus* and announces proudly that he once knew "both the Corpusses . . . they were very corpulent authors." Even the Prologue Jonson supplied for his new comedy was unlike his earlier ones.

> Of old, the art of writing plays
> Was to content the people.

A sect of writers has appeared who care for "nothing that is popular" and Jonson says he does not approve of this attitude. He wishes to please the guests at his dinner and not the cook.

The younger Jonson might have interpreted a remark like this as unfaithfulness to the classic Muse. But by this time Jonson was no longer wooing the Muse. He was, as it were, married to her, and so happily that he felt safe in teasing her a little.

Jonson was in the same cheerful and somewhat irresponsible mood when he wrote his mock-heroic verses, "On the Famous Voyage." In this he marshals an indecorous accumulation of detail on a rowdily indecent subject and blandly calls on classic lore to assist him.

> 'Tis odd
> That all this while I have forgot some god
> Or goddess to invoke, to stuff my verse.

He rhymes "Pollux" with "the worst of all lucks" and in general behaves like a relaxed and happy man who is so sure of himself and his art that he no longer feels obliged to take it seriously on all occasions.

Yet in his heart Jonson took it seriously enough. This is the period of his finest writing, of his highest and most disciplined intensity, and the following year he produced another play that is worthy to be ranked beside *Volpone*.

Jonson called his new play *The Alchemist* and it proves his complete mastery of classical comedy. It takes a great deal of vigor in a writer to maintain that sort of control, to work out a plot that can be wound as tight as a spring without becoming rigid and characters that remain true to type without becoming mannered or unreal. Even in *Volpone* there had been an occasional wavering and a sense of contrivance, but *The Alchemist* is exactly what the great critic inside Jonson intended it to be—a vast, brilliant portrait of his own times set within the strictest limits of classical requirements. Jonson even succeeded in obeying the nearly impossible Italian theory that "the time of the representation and that of the action represented must be exactly coincident," for the action of *The Alchemist* takes place in the same two hours that are required to show it on the stage.

Jonson's plot is a simple one. Three crooks take over an empty house in London during its owner's absence and fish for loose change with every bait they know. Like every large town, London was full of people who were convinced they could get something for nothing, and a procession of eager dupes fall into the hands of those three experienced operators, Subtle, Face and Doll.

Out of this flat and uncomplicated base, Jonson wove and rewove a glittering fabric, rich in detail and illuminated with some of his most vigorous poetry. When Face offers Doll a promising new prospect, the business deal with the prostitute is lifted by the splendor of the lines into something quite different.

> He shall be brought here, fettered
> With thy fair looks, before he sees thee, and thrown

In a down bed as dark as any dungeon;
Where thou shalt keep him waking with thy drum,
Thy drum, my Doll, thy drum, till he be tame
As the poor blackbirds were i' the great frost
Or bees are with a basin; and so hive him
I' the swanskin coverlid and cambric sheets
Till he work honey and wax, my little God's gift.

*The Alchemist* is a realistic play, rooted in the Jacobean London of Jonson's own day. But the town had a kind of idiotic splendor all its own, and some of the touches in the play that sound like a poet's fantastic imagination are actually an echo of sober civic records. The case of Dapper, who gives his money to the gang because they have promised to let him see the Queen of the Fairies, could be duplicated in the records in the London courts. A short time after Jonson wrote his play, John and Alice West were arraigned in Old Bailey for dressing up as the King and Queen of the Fairies and promising fairy gold in exchange for coin of the realm; and four years earlier a young gentleman from Dorset paid six pounds to a crook who had promised him an introduction to the same Queen. The men of the Middle Ages believed that she would lavish fairy gold on anyone she loved, and the theory still had sufficient standing to lead "to the impoverishing of many simple people."

The Jacobean world stood halfway between the medieval and the modern, and a confidence man of Jonson's day consequently had many advantages. He could play on the hopes of a medievalist like Dapper, with his fairies, and with equal success on a modern businessman like Drugger, who had opened a tobacco shop and felt that a proper understanding of astrology would bring him more customers. Jonson's crooks are well versed in the necessary astrological patter and can tell Drugger the best way to have his shelves face and which days are unlucky for a Libra man to do business.

They are equally well versed in the trade that gives the play its title, and Subtle is in fact a practicing alchemist. Alchemy was just at the point of turning into modern chemistry—an ancient and still highly respected art that was the same lode-stone to crooks it had been in Chaucer's day. It had an intricate vocabulary which Jonson, in his thorough way, had completely mastered; and although he knew, like any intelligent Jacobean, that it was used by charlatans, he could not help sympathizing with the dream of turning base metals into gold. Jonson's knight, Sir Epicure Mammon, walks about in a kind of sensu-ous, drugged trance in which he can look at a whore like Doll and see her worthy to be hung with diamonds.

> You were created, lady, for the light.

The knight's sin is not exactly greed. It is the "itch of mind" that made Faustus barter everything he had for knowledge and Tamburlaine for power, the Renaissance lust to be a colossus and bestride the world. When his dream shatters, he is shattered with it.

> I will go mount a turnip cart and preach
> The end of the world.

But while it lasted it had a kind of evil magnificence.

In direct contrast to Sir Epicure Mammon are those de-stroyers of poetry, Tribulation the pastor and Ananias the deacon. They have been sent by a congregation in Amsterdam to make a great deal of money as quickly as possible, and Jon-son dislikes them both exceedingly. He dislikes their sanctimo-nious jargon, their greed, their grayness and their disapproval of everything unlike themselves. They eye a pair of Spanish breeches with deep mistrust as being "superstitious and idola-trous" and they are outspoken on the subject of millinery. "Thou lookest like Antichrist in that lewd hat."

The intensity of the Puritan's hate of worldly show was an-other legacy from the Middle Ages. It was a continuation of the medieval doctrine that all the sons of Adam must fix their gaze intently on the world to come, with any enjoyment of the things of this world to be rejected as sin. A medieval Christian could confess and be forgiven, but the Protestant had no one to whom he could confess. He stood before an unbending judge at the tribunal of his own conscience, and the longer he wrestled for the safety of his soul the greater became his fear that he might fail. Whatever was happy and natural and loving seemed to the Puritan a snare of the devil. When Katherine Stubbes, the young wife of the reformer, lay dying, she drove away the little pet dog that had come to lie at her feet. For she believed that she had "offended God grievously" for having loved the little dog and shown her love, and she prayed her Maker to forgive her for such a sin.

The Puritans were people of independent spirit and frequently disagreed among themselves but they were united on one thing at least. They were all convinced that the theatre was one of the snares of the Devil to drag unwary souls to hell and they fought it with every weapon at their command. The London playwrights, in their turn, recognized a common enemy and did everything in their power to discredit the new movement. They united in showing the Puritan as a bleak, sanctimonious, psalm-singing hypocrite, stalking about with his eyes lifted ostentatiously to heaven while he clutched at every chance to make money on earth.

There was a certain amount of truth in this caricature and a great deal of untruth. It did not take into account the virtues of the Puritan—his idealism, his political independence and his lonely courage. Puritanism would not have swept over England, growing stronger every year, if there had not been a streak of heroic iron in that great, if narrow-minded, engine of reform. The playwrights did not see the heroism; they saw only the iron. And it is difficult to blame them, since if the Puritans had had their way a play like *The Alchemist* would never have been permitted to come into existence.

Jonson's new play was produced by his old friends, the King's Men, now acting at both the Blackfriars and the Globe. A comedy like Jonson's, with its single set and the use of only one level, was very well suited to an indoor hall like the Black-friars and as a matter of fact Jonson had never made any use of the architectural freedom that was available at the Globe. He always semed to work mentally for an indoor stage, although a successful play like *The Alchemist* would have been presented in both theatres. It was also presented on the road, and in 1610 the King's Men took it along with them in their yearly tour of the provinces. It was especially well received at Oxford, where it was presented at the same time as Shakespeare's *Othello*.

The cast of *The Alchemist* was full of familiar names. Bur-bage, Heminges and Condell all performed in it, as they had in *Volpone, Sejanus* and Jonson's two Humour comedies. Another member of the cast was John Underwood, who had played in *Cynthia's Revels* and was now a grown man with a son. An-other former boy actor who had joined the King's Men was William Ostler, who played in *The Alchemist* as he had once played in *Poetaster*.

The King's Men had no trouble recruiting brilliant young actors to replace the older ones, and these young men did not merely join a business organization but became members of a closely-knit group of friends. Ostler, for instance, married John Heminges' daughter shortly after *The Alchemist* opened. Nicho-las Tooley, another young member of the cast, took special and grateful care to mention in his will the "motherly care" that Mrs. Cuthbert Burbage had given him; and when John Under-wood died he left the care of his five orphaned children to his "loving and kind fellows," the King's Men.

It was at about this time that one of the original members of the company retired and left London for his native Warwick-shire. William Shakespeare had taken part in the original in-corporation in 1594, and only Heminges and Burbage had been sharers as long as he. All his plays were owned by the King's Men and he had spent nearly the whole of his life in the theatre in their company.

Shakespeare had written many kinds of plays during his long career in the theatre. He had done history plays, revenge tragedies, satires, light comedies and farce, and in fact he had produced almost everything except a script that dealt realistically with the current London scene. He had never attempted the classical and orderly approach of which Ben Jonson approved, and the final comedies he wrote just before his retirement were a complete denial of everything that Jonson was trying to achieve in the theatre.

Plays like *The Tempest* and *The Winter's Tale* possessed all the romantic qualities that Jonson had disliked in Shakespeare's comedies of the late 90's, in addition to a special fairy-tale atmosphere that Jonson disliked even more. *The Tempest* was a kind of modified masque, with its magic and its dances, and Jonson deplored the current tendency to transfer the spirit of the Court masque to the London stage, "wherein, now, the concupiscence of dances and antics so reigneth, as to run away from Nature and be afraid of her." Jonson was a strong advocate of the natural and the realistic in art, and it could not be denied that in his final group of plays Shakespeare had paid very little attention to realism.

A play like *The Winter's Tale* was even more irritating to Jonson than *The Tempest* because the whole approach of the playwright was so casual. The unities are ignored, and the action covers sixteen years while the locale leaps from Sicilia to Bohemia and back again. Shakespeare had taken the plot from a cheap popular novel that Robert Greene had written more than twenty years earlier and which had recently been reprinted, and although he took the names of some of the characters from Sidney's *Arcadia* the play itself would have horrified Sidney. It was exactly the sort of thing he had been protesting against when he attacked the loose-jointed, casual, unclassical plays of the early Elizabethans in his essay which had so delighted the young Ben Jonson. When Jonson dedicated his latest play to Sidney's niece, he could be safe in the knowledge that he, at least, had written a play of which the author of *An Apology for Poetry* would have thoroughly approved.

In Jonson's opinion, as in Sidney's, a conscientious artist had no right to play about with impossible fairy tales set in remote countries. The function of a playwright was to mirror the life he saw around him. He should do what Prince Hamlet advised —"hold, as 'twere, the mirror up to nature; to show virtue her own feature, scorn her own image, and the very age and body of the time his form and pressure." Hamlet, as a university man, knew the correct way to write a play, and Jonson would have agreed with him unreservedly. In *The Alchemist* he showed the "form and pressure" of his age, and the play is a brilliant picture of one aspect of London life in 1610.

It is the risk of Jonson's way of writing that the colors of what was once modern fade in a few years, so that in the end nothing is left but an antiquarian interest. *The Alchemist* escapes this fate because Jonson was a great artist, and in the hands of an artist any theory will serve. But Shakespeare was a great artist also, a greater than Jonson, and he was served as well by his lack of theories as Jonson was served by the abundance of his.

As a matter of fact, even Jonson could not always keep to the narrow path he had laid out for himself. He meant *The Alchemist* to serve as a lesson in morality and he emphasized in the Prologue the "wholesome remedies" and "fair correctives" that would be administered to the audience through his lines. But Jonson's delight in color and vitality overcame his theoretical insistence on classic morality, and the outrageous but ingenious Face emerges unscathed at the end of the play, his cheerful impudence intact. The moral of the play, if any, is that it is better to be a knave than a fool. Jonson had a strong moral sense and a gift for social indignation, but his heart was drawn towards liveliness and vigor even when he knew that by Renaissance standards they were both unclassical and undesirable.

# Chapter 17

B EN JONSON HAD DONE what he set out to do. He had mastered the severe and exacting art of classical comedy and had made it at home on the London stage. But what he had done for comedy he had been unable to do for tragedy, and his one attempt at classical tragedy had been a failure.

A less determined man might have been content to leave matters there, but Jonson was incapable of admitting defeat. He set to work with furious ardor and with all the resources of his disciplined, intelligent mind to produce a tragedy that would reform the English stage and bring it back to the greatness that was Rome, and the year after *The Alchemist* he presented the King's Men with the script of *Catiline*.

The subject of Catiline's conspiracy was a favorite with Elizabethan playwrights. Henslowe, for instance, had made an advance to two of his hack writers for a play he called "cattelanes consperesey" and the investment had probably paid him well, since Catiline's plan to seize Rome was as violent and theatrical as the Gunpowder Plot.

Jonson, however, was not looking for violent theatre material. He was looking for a classical subject from which he could build what he called a "true poem." His first tragedy, that of *Sejanus*, had not come under this heading, as Jonson admitted at the time, since it had not obeyed "the strict laws of time" and did not have a "proper Chorus." Jonson said he did not believe it was possible to achieve a strict classicism on the modern stage, but by the time he wrote *Catiline* he had changed his mind. *Catiline*, he stated proudly in his dedication to the Earl of Pembroke, was "a legitimate poem."

This time Jonson did not or would not accept a collaborator. His new script was going to represent a heavy investment for the King's Men, since there were more than thirty name-characters in the cast and this meant a large number of hired actors as well as the services of Burbage, Heminges, Condell and the other sharers. Moreover, *Sejanus* had been a financial failure when the King's Men had presented it eight years earlier, and the success of Jonson's later comedies could not quite erase the memory of his spectacular failure to enlist public support for his Roman tragedy. The King's Men did not claim to be an educational organization, and it is a credit to their sense of responsibility as men of the theatre that they were willing to invest heavily in Jonson's new play.

Jonson's chief information about Catiline's conspiracy came from a folio edition of Sallust, which he lavishly marked with pencil as he worked. Nevertheless he parted company with the Roman historian on one aspect of the story, for Sallust had been a lieutenant of Caesar's and his account of the conspiracy was naturally slanted in Caesar's direction. Jonson, on the other hand, was convinced that Cicero had been the hero of the occasion and he made Cicero the focus of his play.

Cicero was a great man in Jonson's eyes, and his whole career was a kind of vindication of Jonson's theory of the dignity of the writer. For Cicero was not only a great name in politics but in letters, a disciplined, intelligent, devoted artist who created a prose style that had revolutionized literary history. Jonson, no doubt unconsciously, read a little of himself into Cicero. Throughout the play he keeps emphasizing the fact that his hero is of comparatively low birth; the patricians who surround him in the Senate consider him "a mere upstart that has no pedigree." Moreover he is jeered at by his enemies because he has the gift of expressing himself well. He is the "talker," the "tongue man," and is accused of forgetting his place.

> Why should he presume
> To be more learned or more eloquent
> Than the nobility?

Jonson followed Sallust, however, in his portrait of Catiline, and here he made a mistake. Since Sallust was on Caesar's side, he blackened the conspirator's character in a way that was not historically justified, and Jonson (being on Cicero's side) went even further and made Catiline a monster. One of the weaknesses of the play is a tendency to array Virtue against Vice, a tendency that Shakespeare had succeeded in avoiding in his Roman plays. Unlike Jonson, Shakespeare was no scholar. He merely picked up Roman history and used it for his own purposes, searching behind the stately speeches and the ancient togas for the reality of human nature.

Jonson was not particularly interested in human nature in his tragedies. He wanted something clearer, stronger and more consistent as the basis for his art. He wanted to touch the mind, not the heart, and in this he succeeded. *Catiline* is a packed, intelligent, and very well-written piece of work, solidly and carefully put together from the best available authorities. But there is no reality in it and no heart, and not all the excellent acting of the King's Men could save it from the disapproval of the audience.

The play apparently did fairly well for the first two acts and then came to disaster. From Jonson's point of view the climax of the play was Cicero's great oration against Catiline in the Senate, and he presented it in nearly three hundred lines of "prodigious rhetoric." The people of London had been subjected to Cicero's oration when they went to grammar school and they had no intention of paying their good money to hear it again in the theatre, no matter how skillful Ben Jonson might be in translating Latin rhetoric into English blank verse. By the time Jonson reached the familiar "*O tempora, O mores!*" he had lost his audience, and he never got it back again.

*Catiline* was published the same year, and Jonson wrote a

furious preface addressed to what he called the "reader in ordinary." "Though you commend the first two acts, with the
people, because they are the worst, and dislike the oration of
Cicero, in regard you read some pieces of it at school and
understand them not yet, I shall find the way to forgive you."
Jonson's way of forgiving the ordinary reader was to ignore
him, and he turned instead to address himself to what he called
"the reader extraordinary."

> To you I submit myself and work. Farewell.
> Ben Jonson.

Two of the most popular playwrights of the day wrote commendatory verses for *Catiline,* assuring Jonson that his great
work was not understood by the commonplace minds of the
period. John Fletcher informed his "dear friend" that his labors
would outlive him, and Francis Beaumont gave him praise
because he had not

> itched after the wild applause
> Of common people.

Beaumont and Fletcher were both well-educated young men
who came from literary families, and they had both undergone
the discomfort of writing carefully designed plays that had
been rejected by the general public. Fletcher had tried to
domesticate the classical pastoral on the English stage, and when
*The Faithful Shepherdess* collapsed Jonson had risen in public
defense of his friend's "murdered poem." Meanwhile Beaumont
and Fletcher had collaborated on some highly successful plays
for the King's Men, and while they condoled with Jonson on
the stupidity of the theatre-going public they had already
scored an enormous success with *Philaster* and *The Maid's
Tragedy* and were embarking on the equally popular *A King
and No King.* Jonson himself, in spite of his expressed contempt
for the kind of plays "these fools admire," had done very well
with *The Alchemist.* But there was a kind of unwritten law in
Jonson's circle that if a play failed it was invariably because of

the stupidity of the general public and never because there might be some lack in the play itself.

Jonson called Fletcher his "dear friend" but Beaumont also had a special place in Jonson's heart. Francis Beaumont was then in his late twenties, and like many young writers he was irresistibly drawn to the strength, the authority and the delightful mind of Ben Jonson. When Beaumont was in the country with Fletcher, trying to finish a script, he sent Jonson a letter in verse from the place of his enforced exile. He sat in the sun, which was good for little but drying the hay, and dreamed of the delightful times they had had together at the Mermaid Tavern. It seemed to Beaumont that none of them had ever been so clever or witty as they were then.

> What things have we seen
> Done at the Mermaid? heard words that have been
> So nimble, and so full of subtle flame,
> As if that everyone from whom they came
> Had meant to put his whole wit in a jest
> And had resolved to live a fool the rest
> Of his dull life . . .

In fact, said Beaumont with a straight face, there was so much wit abroad when Jonson and his friends were at the Mermaid that it infected the next two companies to use the room.

In Beaumont's eyes the soul and center of the gathering, the source of both light and learning, was Ben Jonson himself, and the letter from the country closes on a note of honest gratitude.

> Destiny . . .
> Bring me to thee, who wilt make smooth and plain
> The way of knowledge for me; and then I
> Who have no good in me but simplicity,
> Know that it will my greatest comfort be
> T' acknowledge all the rest to come from thee.

Beaumont was only one of many young writers to say this, and as Jonson grew older their numbers increased. The arrogance he showed to the general public he did not show to them, and when Jonson wrote some verses of his own to Beaumont he said he was "not worthy" of such respect.

The Mermaid Tavern in which Jonson held court was in Bread Street, a well-run house famous for its fish dinners and its excellent wine. It had already outlasted three reigns when Jonson and his friends began to meet there, and the fact that it succeeded in pleasing writers finally gave it immortality. Taverns like the Mermaid were the Jacobean equivalent of the eighteenth-century coffee houses, and they satisfied the ingrained London passion for getting together and talking. Jonson delighted in conversation, especially his own, and he brought to the Mermaid much of the glory that Beaumont remembered as he lay drowsing in the country sun.

Wine at the Mermaid cost twopence a quart more than ordinary tavern wines, but it was evidently worth it. Jonson, who was an experienced drinker, sent out to the tavern when he had a guest to dinner in his own house, and he once wrote a charming set of verses on the menu he would offer a friend. There would be salad with the mutton and a hen with wine sauce, ending up with cheese and fruit and

> a pure cup of rich Canary wine
> Which is the Mermaid's now but shall be mine.

There would also be, at Jonson's table, a great deal of cheerful, free, unguarded conversation, which belonged with good wine and was equally important.

Like his beloved Horace, Jonson had an enormous capacity for enjoyment and he seized upon each day delightedly as it came along. He had found somewhere a bit of doggerel which he "scorned" as poetry but which accurately expressed his opinion in the matter.

> So long as we may, let us enjoy this breath,
> For naught doth kill a man so soon as death.

Jonson might be a grave and ardent classicist but he liked doggerel, and he was a true Englishman in his enjoyment of nonsense. He was fond of repeating, with perfect cheerfulness,
another doggerel rhyme of which he was the hero.

> Here lies Benjamin Johnson dead
> And hath no more wit than a goose in his head . . .

It is not surprising that the joke books at the end of the century included a great many anecdotes of which Jonson was the
central figure. No doubt they are all apocryphal, but they are
suited to a man who had a weakness for silly jokes and made a
large collection of them. He liked, for instance, the story of the
man who let his hair grow long in the hope that it would go to
seed and he could "sow of it on bald pates." He also had a large
collection of riddles with which to plague his unwary friends.
"What is it, that the more you cut of it, groweth still the
longer?" The answer was "a ditch," as every schoolboy knows.

There was still a good deal of the small boy in Jonson, with
his delight in nonsense and in practical jokes, and like any industrious small boy he would go to an infinite amount of trouble to rear a lofty edifice on a foundation of silliness. One of
the most elaborate was the helpful assistance he gave Coryat's
*Crudities*, which was published the same year as his own *Catiline*.

Thomas Coryat was an Oxford scholar who had specialized
in Greek and who was in some ways a very learned man. But
he looked like a buffoon, with his head shaped "like a sugar loaf
inverted," and he found it profitable to behave like one. Like
many Englishmen he was a determined traveler, but after he
had written a long and careful account of his journeys he
dressed it up in mock rhetoric to make it entertaining. Then he
enlisted Jonson's help in getting the book before the public, and
Jonson embarked on the project with glee.

Coryat's *Crudities* emerged as a cheerful parody on the solemn folio publications of the period. The average folio had half
a dozen commendatory verses in front of it and so Coryat's

book had about eighty, written "in the best and most learned languages" and excluding only Irish and Welsh. The long roll call of names included most of Jonson's fellow drinkers at the Mermaid and elsewhere, men like Richard Martin, Thomas Campion, Inigo Jones and John Donne. Most of the humor was frankly collegiate, and the author was the butt of a great many "free and merry jests."

Jonson's own contribution was more elaborate. He wrote a series of couplets to expound the pictures on the title page, which show Coryat at various embarrassing moments in his travels, and he also wrote a "character" of the author which consists of a series of affectionate insults. He then finished with an acrostic on Coryat's name and a message of welcome:

Come forth, thou bonny, bouncing book . . .

Ben Jonson was enjoying himself but there was a real kindness under all the nonsense. For it is reported that all this activity "did very much advantage the sale."

John Donne was one of the host of poets who contributed verses to the *Crudities*. He had also contributed commendatory verses to *Volpone* when it was published four years earlier, and he and Jonson were close friends.

Donne was about the same age as Jonson, but he had started life in very different circumstances. His father, a London businessman, had married a relative of the great Sir Thomas More and Donne was brought up a Roman Catholic. He went to Oxford when he was eleven and was serving as a volunteer on the Essex expeditions to Cadiz and the Azores at about the time Jonson was beginning to do hack work for Henslowe. A fellow volunteer to the Azores, the son of Lord Keeper Egerton, recommended him to his father and Donne became the great man's secretary. But the intensity that made him one of the greatest of love poets wrecked his career; he ran away with the niece of Egerton's second wife and lost the Lord Keeper's favor. When Donne emerged from prison in 1601 he was without any prospects, and he spent his next years leading the difficult life of a poet looking for a patron.

Donne was one of the few writers for whom Jonson had a profound admiration. He regretted the obscurity of Donne's style, which he feared would make him unreadable in future generations, and he deplored his experiments with rhythm. But he considered him "the first poet in the world in some things" and in spite of Jonson's independence as a writer he paid Donne the compliment of sending him his own work for criticism.

Donne once attempted to act as peacemaker during a quarrel in which Jonson was involved. Jonson believed he had been maligned by someone and was in a warlike mood, and Donne urged his friend not to answer back. Jonson wrote a letter in which he apologized for not heeding the advice. "You cannot but believe how dear and reverend your friendship is to me (though all testimony on my part hath been too short to express me) and therefore would I meet it with all obedience." But he cannot be obedient if it means enduring with meekness an unjust charge, and he urges Donne to withdraw from the fray, "lest yourself may undergo some hazard, for my questioned reputation, and draw jealousies or hatred upon you." Jonson would risk himself but he would not risk a friend, and it is easy to see why so many people loved him.

The same year that *Catiline* and Coryat's *Crudities* were published, Donne brought out a poem in praise of fifteen-year-old Elizabeth Drury, who had just died. Jonson protested that the poem was "profane and full of blasphemies" and that Donne had written of the girl in terms that should have been reserved for the Virgin Mary. Many people agreed with Jonson, and Donne defended himself by saying "that he described the idea of a woman and not as she was." He might have added that he was a middle-aged man with a family to support, and that, since Sir Robert Drury was mourning the loss of his daughter, a poet who was looking for a patron had a right to use somewhat extravagant language. At any rate, the poem was a success from the financial point of view, for Donne was made welcome at

Drury House and was able to live rent-free until he took orders in the Anglican Church.

In the case of a proud and sensitive man like John Donne, the degrading atmosphere of the Jacobean system of patronage must have sometimes seemed intolerable. Yet he had to endure it, just as George Chapman did, if he expected to make a living by his pen. The only writer who seems to have remained impervious to the whole atmosphere is Ben Jonson, who had a family of his own to support but nevertheless showed very little respect either for money or for lords.

Jonson had a calm conviction that the rich men who supported him as a poet were honoring themselves, not him, and he strode through that slavish atmosphere with the happy certainty that he was supplying something of much more value than money. No story is more characteristic of Jonson than one which was told to Robert Boyle by one of Jonson's friends. Jonson was complaining to this friend that some great man had treated him very badly, in the face of the fact that Jonson had once done him a special favor. "The ungrateful wretch knows very well that before he came to preferment I was the man that made him relish Horace."

The story may be apocryphal, but it is very like Ben Jonson. He was convinced that what he had to offer was more valuable than either position or wealth and on one occasion when he was dining with Lord Salisbury, the Secretary of State, he announced publicly at table that he did not think his host was treating him with sufficient honor. From Jonson's point of view there was no loftier position than that of poet, and he saw no reason to be unnecessarily abject in his dealings with courtiers.

Even in the Court masques, which by their very nature had to be flattering to the titled performers, Jonson had begun to show a kind of cheerful familiarity. The next masque to follow *Love Freed* was *Love Restored*, which was presented in January of 1612, and Jonson opened it with a scene in prose that barely skirted impudence. After the glittering audience had gathered, an actor appears onstage to announce that there will be no masque that evening after all. The poet will not be paid, of course, but "it's no matter; his wit costs him nothing." A country goblin is much shocked by the news for he has spent hours trying to work his way into the Banqueting Hall. The goblin has considered using Coryat's method (he was once carried to a masque in a trunk) but naturally scorned to stoop as low as Coryat. He has tried to smuggle himself in as a tire-woman, a musician, the man who helped to hang the lights and as various members of the audience, and his lines give Jonson a notable opportunity to insult the whole paraphernalia of the masque. He then reverts to his own shape as Robin Goodfellow, complete with broom and candles, and is hoping to take part in the show.

But the show will not go on, for such things are vanity and the "ruin of states." It would be far better if the lady spectators in Whitehall were "housewifely employed . . . i' their chambers at home and their old nightgowns . . . rather than to wake here in their flaunting wires and tires, laced gowns, embroidered petticoats and other taken-up braveries."

All this is nothing but friendly teasing, and Jonson promptly redeems himself with the ladies. For the speaker quoted above is unmasked and found to be the god of Money. Then the god of Love makes his entrance, accompanied by ten masquers symbolizing the various qualities that exist in a Court where Love reigns, and their dance shows the harmony that can exist anywhere if money is not worshiped as a god.

In real life money was the god of the Jacobean Court, in spite of the graceful conclusion of Jonson's masque. It was also, in general, the god of Jacobean London. But it was no idol of Jonson's. He had chosen a better master, which he identified in his masque as "the spirit of Poetry," and part of his unshakable self-confidence came from that fact. For the god of money demanded fear of his servants, and the god of poetry asked only for love.

# Chapter 18

AMONG JONSON'S MANY ACQUAINTANCES in London was Sir
Walter Raleigh. It was almost inevitable that the two
men should know each other, since Raleigh was not
only a scholar and an omniverous reader but was currently engaged on a book of so monumental a nature that he welcomed
the assistance of every man of letters who knew anything about
the subject.

Raleigh, like Jonson, was incapable of admitting defeat. He
was now in his fifties and had been a prisoner in the Tower
since 1603 on a charge of conspiracy. But he refused to admit
that his mind could be in prison, and it seemed quite reasonable
to him to embark on a history of the world, beginning with
the Creation and continuing down through the ages. Although
many of Raleigh's contemporaries considered him a dangerous
freethinker, he nevertheless designed the book to show that
"this ridiculous world" can trace in its history the will of God
in human affairs. Prince Henry, that great patron of letters, encouraged him; Sir Robert Cotton, that gentle and generous col-
lector, lent him books a dozen at a time; and Ben Jonson wrote
out a "piece" on the Punic Wars which Raleigh incorporated
in his pages.

When the first and what proved to be the only installment
of Raleigh's *History of the World* was published, Jonson wrote
some verses to appear opposite the elaborately engraved title
page to explain the symbolism of the various figures. History

stands on a skeleton and on a drooping figure labeled Oblivion, to raise in her arms a globe of the world that reaches up to two winged figures that represent Good and Evil Fame. Jonson, as an accomplished symbolist and moralist, had no difficulty explaining Raleigh's idea in rhyme:

> From death and dark oblivion, near the same,
> The mistress of man's life, grave History,
> Raising the world to good or evil fame,
> Doth vindicate it to eternity.

Jonson and Raleigh were both men of the Renaissance, brought up on symbols, and almost by instinct they translated ideas into images. They had also been brought up on Cicero, who believed that the chief purpose of history was to teach virtuous action; and Raleigh in his *History*, like Jonson in his plays, was trying to bring back what Camden called "ancient virtue" and which somehow managed to be both Roman and Christian.

Raleigh and Jonson were alike in their learning and in their heroic ideals, as well as in their frequent inability to live up to them, and it was natural that when Raleigh needed a tutor for his son he should think of Jonson. Young Walter Raleigh, whom his father called Wat, was going abroad for a year or so to finish his education and he needed an older man to keep an eye on him and help him with his studies. Europe was full of young Englishmen under the guidance of similar tutors, polishing their French and their manners and seeing a little of the world.

Wat was an unmanageable youngster with a quick temper, and there had been trouble over one of his tutors already. The learned Dr. Daniel Featley had been teaching him divinity and the classics at Oxford and doing his best to curb Wat's restless spirit, while the boy's regular Devonshire tutor wrote letters of complaint to Lady Raleigh in which he described Featley as a tyrant. In Lady Raleigh's eyes her son could do no wrong, but

Wat was obviously at the point where he needed a strong hand to guide him. Possibly Sir Walter hoped that Jonson would supply the strong hand. At any rate, it was arranged in 1612 that he should go abroad as Wat's tutor.

Jonson had not been abroad, so far as is known, since he went as a soldier to the Netherlands, and on that occasion he had been shunted about by the authorities with no responsibilities and no freedom of action. On this occasion he had both, but especially the first, for traveling was a complicated matter in the seventeenth century and Jonson was in charge of a headstrong young man.

The one complication that Jonson escaped was a financial one, since Raleigh was paying for the trip. A traveler was allowed to take a limited sum of money out of England, usually not more than twenty pounds, and an Englishman who wanted to stay abroad for any length of time was obliged to make complicated financial arrangements with friends at the Royal Exchange or on the Continent. Jonson's trip was financed by bills of exchange, with a European agent of Sir Walter's doling out an allowance in set amounts at set times of the year. Since the rate of exchange fluctuated wildly, he and Wat might get more or less than they expected and they naturally hoped for more. In one case the Antwerp agent reported that he had given Mr. Raleigh and Mr. Jonson ten pounds more than they were entitled to, but that they had importuned him "so earnestly" that he could not refuse. In defense of the two travelers it might be said that prices had been rising in France ever since the civil war, and that in any case a tourist had to expect to "pay somewhat more than one that is born in the country."

Fortunately, Paris lodgings could still be had for about twelve shillings a month and Paris was the Mecca of every rightminded Englishman. It was the home of learning and the arts, and the late King Henry had greatly increased its wealth and splendor through his "politic and peaceable government." The most patriotic Englishman had to admit that Paris was in many ways finer than London, with its tall white buildings, its fourteen gates and its five bridges over the Seine. It could be pointed out that Paris had her faults too. There were so many coaches and carts that they sometimes caused a traffic tie-up of "an hour or two before they can disentangle." The police system was inadequate, so that hardly a night went by without a robbery or a murder, and the streets were so dirty that a kind of black oil settled on the traveler's garments and could not be washed out of some colors at all.

The English sometimes accused the French of eating too much, talking too fast and being too demonstrative. They lacked, the English felt, a sense of dignity. But Jonson would have liked them for that, just as he would have liked the old French women, with "more toes than teeth," who danced so vigorously that their few remaining teeth clattered like the keys of a virginal. Nor would Jonson have disapproved of a love of games so intense that even the French workmen and the small children played tennis.

In theory, young Raleigh was spending his time abroad in an effort to improve his mind and his manners. When young Mr. Puckering had been in Paris two years before, his days were carefully subdivided by his tutor so that horsemanship, dancing and fencing could be alternated with the more sober accomplishment of translating Latin authors into French. It may be that Wat followed this exemplary program but the only activity that history records is of a somewhat different kind. He got Jonson "dead drunk" and then had him drawn through the streets on a cart, "at every corner showing his governor stretched out and telling them that was a more lively image of the crucifix than any they had." Lady Raleigh considered this a very amusing escapade and just the sort of thing his father would have done at that age, but Sir Walter thought otherwise.

Jonson apparently bore his charge no particular ill will, but it was a dangerous joke to play in a town like Paris whose official religion was Roman Catholic. The only Protestant who had managed to hold an influential position for any length of time was the Duc de Sully, and he could hardly be judged by ordinary standards. He was like "a great furnace which, out of a strong and vigorous heat of understanding and courage, casts also a great smoke of vaunting and rigorous arrogancy." This is a description that some of his contemporaries might well have applied to Ben Jonson, and it probably pleased Jonson that the Duc de Sully was said to be "of Scottish extraction." The great Cardinal DuPerron, who had converted Henry of Navarre to the Catholic religion, also tried to convert Sully, but he never succeeded.

When Jonson was in France he met Cardinal DuPerron and, like Sully, he was not impressed. The Cardinal was at the height of his prestige, a man of formidable brilliance and great mental powers. He showed Jonson some translations he had made from Vergil, and Jonson told him candidly that they were "naught." They were admittedly not very literal translations, but it would be interesting to know what the Cardinal said in reply.

DuPerron was one of the leaders on the Continent in a verbal battle between the Catholics and Protestants that was occupying all Christendom from King James down. Various small skirmishes eddied about the leaders, and Jonson assisted in one of these while he was in Paris. Dr. Daniel Featley, Wat's Oxford tutor and a prominent theologian, was invited to debate his position with a prominent Catholic in a meeting held at the lodgings of a Paris gentleman. Ben Jonson, who was one of the guests, served as a kind of witness to the formal Latin debate and afterwards signed a certificate testifying to the accuracy of a written report of the meeting. Jonson had only recently turned Protestant, and as one who had been argued with by a prominent Protestant divine under a court order he must have been thoroughly familiar with both sides of the discussion.

The following year Jonson and young Raleigh left Paris to visit Brussels, a Catholic city controlled by Spain and governed by an archduke. The representative of the English government at Brussels was a harassed and conscientious *chargé d'affaires* named William Trumbull, and Jonson brought a letter of introduction from an old friend of Trumbull's in Paris. The letter explained that Mr. Ben Jonson, who "cannot but be well known unto you by his reputation, having spent some twelve months' travel in this country in Mr. Raleigh's company, who was committed to his charge by Sir Walter his father, hath now taken a resolution to pass by Sedan into your parts." It continued with warm praise of Jonson, who possessed "extraordinary and rare parts of knowledge and understanding" and whose conversation was "honored and beloved in all companies." On a separate slip of paper, however, a more cautious and less flattering note was struck. "At Mr. Johnson's entreaty, I did accompany him with a letter of recommendation to you. . . . What is good in him I was content to relate, and indeed he hath many worthy parts; for the rest you shall soon make a discovery thereof."

There was little left for William Trumbull to discover about the habits of visiting Englishmen, for Brussels was on the direct route to the Spa and Trumbull was burdened with greater numbers of his fellow countrymen than even that patient man could have wished. When the old Countess of Pembroke arrived on her way to take the medicinal waters, she appeared with a coach and four horses and expected Trumbull to pay the duty on her tapestries. Lord Darcy reported that his sister had lost her umbrella on her way to the same destination, and would Trumbull please get her a new one. He was expected to watch over Lord Salisbury's son when he arrived in Brussels and to keep a relative of Sir Dudley Carleton's away from evil companions. He offered his house to the Countess of Worcester, gave storage room to Sir Thomas Somerset's trunk, and in his spare time shopped for miscellaneous articles desired by his friends, ranging from tooth cleaners and leather desk tops to a copy of *Don Quixote*.

Trumbull would already have known Ben Jonson by reputation, since a series of correspondents kept him informed of what was going on in every capital city in Europe. When Jonson's masque of *Oberon* was produced at Westminster, a friend of Trumbull's at The Hague sent him so complete and vivid an account of the whole thing that Trumbull's fervent "desire to come home to sweet England" was almost realized for a moment by proxy.

When Jonson returned to England in 1613, he found a great many changes. The most tragic was the death of Henry, Prince of Wales, which had taken place the previous November. In the last days of his illness Sir Walter Raleigh, who loved him, had sent a special remedy from the Tower that seemed for a moment to be effective and the dying man opened his eyes. But even that failed, and the most hopeful young prince in Christendom died at eight o'clock on a Friday evening, leaving behind a brokenhearted sister and all the plans he had been making for England. The Prince had intended to do great things, from rebuilding the English navy to financing Chapman's Homer, and "his papers showed him to have many strange and vast . . . projects" which now would come to nothing.

His sister's marriage was being celebrated when he died and it went forward on schedule in a glitter of dinners and plays and masques. Jonson was not there to supply any of the masques, but his *Alchemist* was one of the plays that the King's Men presented at Court during the festivities. In May the Princess Elizabeth and her round-faced young husband left England, and only three members of the royal family remained—the King, the Queen, and their lonely adolescent son, Prince Charles.

Six months before Prince Henry's death, the Secretary of State had died also. Towards the end he felt the wearying weight of his greatness as his father had before him, and left the Court in a vain attempt "to be more private at home." Then he journeyed to Bath, thinking "it was the best place to be at peace," and died on the way home on a Sunday in May. He was buried unmourned, for many men hated him, but he left a gaping hole that was not filled again in James' reign. "Our great, strange little lord is gone," and there was no one to replace him.

After Salisbury died, King James developed the addled theory that he did not need a principal Secretary of State. Since he had always greatly assisted Salisbury by meddling with the government, he decided that he could do all the important work himself, with an assistant secretary to handle the routine matters.

James found the task too much for him, and he should have chosen Salisbury's successor from one of the able career men in England. Instead he gave the seal of England to a blond young Scot named Robert Carr who had even fewer qualifications for the task than James. Carr had been the King's page in Scotland and had recently brought himself to the royal attention again by falling off a horse and breaking a leg. James had formed the habit of visiting him while the leg mended, and when he found that the young man's mind was a complete and affable blank he yielded to the fatal schoolmaster impulse that so often visited him at the wrong moment and took Carr as his protégé. The year before Jonson went to France, James was spending his mornings teaching Carr Latin, although, as one of the courtiers remarked bitterly, the young Scot did not even know how to speak English correctly. Still, he was handsome and grateful and teachable, and James convinced himself he was going to achieve a masterpiece and be the "creator, under God" of a perfect young man.

Carr was a well-meaning youngster, and Sir Robert Cotton vouched both for his honesty and his refusal to trade on the King's favor. One of Trumbull's London correspondents reported that the King's new favorite was "a very discreet and noble gentleman" and Carr made a reasonably conscientious effort to transact the mass of official business that had fallen from Salisbury's dead hands. He might have gone down in history as one of the most inoffensive of royal favorites if he had not been visited by a great misfortune: Frances Howard fell in love with him.

It was nearly seven years since the marriage of Frances Howard and the Earl of Essex had been celebrated in Jonson's *Hymenaei*, but a legal contract of that kind meant nothing to the Earl of Suffolk's daughter. She asked for an annulment of the marriage, on the ground that her husband was impotent.

The judicial proceedings were a farce, but in spite of her husband's indignant protests she got her divorce in September of 1613.

That Christmas Frances Howard married Robert Carr, now the Earl of Somerset. The wedding of course was a splendid affair and everyone showered the happy young couple with gifts. There were the duplications that are inevitable at weddings, and Sir Robert Cary and Sir Robert Mansfield both sent complete equipment for the fireplace in silver. There were also the usual murmurings, and the mayor of London made an unsuccessful attempt to avoid the expensive honor of entertaining the bride and groom on the plea that his house was not big enough for the occasion. But in general all was rejoicing, and the poets of England united in contributing verses to glorify the new Earl of Somerset and his bride.

John Donne, who warmly approved of the match, wrote Carr's wedding song, and George Chapman composed a long and learned poem to express his delight over the marriage. Chapman had come close to disaster the year before, when Prince Henry died, since the "dismayfull loss" of his patron meant that he no longer could afford to finish his translation of Homer. Chapman wrote frantically to every influential man he knew but no one would honor Henry's verbal promise, and he was like a man coming into haven after many storms when he found a new and generous patron in Robert Carr. When the first twelve books of *The Odyssey* were published in 1614, it was to Carr that Chapman dedicated them.

Chapman realized that many people disapproved of his patron's marriage to a divorced woman, and he tried to vindicate it in a long poem in which he compared her to Andromeda being rescued from the monster. The friends of the Earl of Essex naturally inquired if her first husband was supposed to represent the monster, and Chapman published an anxious explanation of his "poor mite in honor of the late nuptials." Chapman had intended the monster to symbolize the "base, ignoble, barbarous, giddy multitude"—the multitude that had sometimes dared to criticize his poetry and that now tried to criticize the marriage of his patron.

Jonson also contributed his share to the festivities. The commission for the actual wedding masque went to Thomas Campion, but Jonson wrote an Irish Masque which was shown at Court three days after the wedding. It was such a success that it was presented again the third of January. No doubt the show played better than it reads, for Jonson's stage Irish probably sounded well enough when it was delivered by trained actors and the Court enjoyed an impudence that could address the bride's father as "ty good man, Toumaish, o' Shuffolke."

Jonson wrote some verses to Carr in which he expressed the hope he would never know "discontent or sorrow." He also wrote a pretty little Challenge, delivered at Court by two boys dressed as cupids the day after the wedding, as well as the lines for the actual Tilt on the first of January. The Tilt ends when Hymen, god of marriage, celebrates the true love and happy concord of so notable a marriage.

If the poets could have made it so, Robert Carr would have led a happy life. He was a likable young man, and writers like Chapman, Jonson and Donne really hoped that his marriage would be successful. They did not know, any more than Carr himself knew, that his wife had recently committed a murder.

The victim was Sir Thomas Overbury, a writer and a former friend of Jonson's who had gained an ascendancy over Carr and had attempted to block the marriage. At the time of the wedding it was believed that Overbury had died in the Tower of natural causes; but too many agents were involved for the matter to be hushed up indefinitely, and less than three years after she had received Jonson's good wishes the Countess went on trial for murder.

Jonson was preparing his published works when the news came out, and all he could do was to suppress the identity of the prominent people involved in *Hymenaei, The Irish Masque* and the *Challenge at Tilt*. The situation was no fault of his and he extricated himself as tactfully as he could, but the whole episode illustrates the disadvantage of being a Court poet when the Court was that of King James.

# Chapter 19

ON THE 29TH OF JUNE, 1613, there was a fire in the Globe theatre, caused by two cannons that were being used in the opening performance of Shakespeare's new play, *Henry VIII.* The wooden theatre was burned to the ground, but the audience was so orderly that there was no loss of life. Ben Jonson must have returned from the Continent by then, since he says that he saw the blaze.

> The Globe, the glory of the Bank . . .
> I saw with two poor chambers taken in
> And razed, ere thought could urge, This might have been!

When the Fortune theatre also burned to the ground, eight years later on a winter night, all the "apparel and playbooks" of the company were destroyed. By great good luck, this did not happen in the case of the King's Men. Half of Shakespeare's scripts were not yet in print and existed only as playbooks, and if the Globe fire had been as complete as the one at the Fortune, plays like *Macbeth* and *Antony and Cleopatra* would have vanished forever. As it was, the Globe theatre was rebuilt the following year as "the finest that ever was in England" and no great harm had been done.

For a short time, however, the Globe was a smoking ruin, burned down to the piles that supported it in the swampy ground of the Bankside; and it apparently occurred to that vet-

eran builder of playhouses, Philip Henslowe, that this would be
a good moment to enter into competition with the King's Men
on the south side of the river. Henslowe did not own any theatre on the Bankside, since his lease on the Rose, had expired
many years earlier, but he was still interested both in actors and
in bear-baiting. He succeeded in combining the two by putting
up a theatre called the Hope and giving it a removable stage,
building it on the site of the rickety old Bear Garden.

Henslowe needed a reliable troupe of actors for his new
theatre and signed an agreement with Nathan Field. Field was
currently the head of a group of actors who had once been
under the patronage of the now-married Princess Elizabeth.
They had combined with his own group at the Whitefriars but
were still known as the Lady Elizabeth's Men. It was a short-
lived company and what prestige it had was chiefly owing to
Field.

Nathan Field was twenty-six when his company moved into
the Hope, a handsome, dark-eyed man and a veteran of the
theatre. He had himself turned playwright, and George Chapman composed some proud verses on the maiden script of his
"loved son." Field himself maintained a relaxed point of view
towards his literary effort, and when he was asked to supply
the conventional address to the reader he supplied instead an
unconventional one. "Reader, the salesman swears you'll take it
very ill if I say not somewhat to you. . . . Why should I write
to you? You never writ to me . . . I have been vexed with vile
plays myself a great while, hearing many; now I thought to
be even with some and they should hear mine too."

Ben Jonson, like Chapman, looked upon Field as a "loved
son," and it was undoubtedly because Field was head of the
company that he let the Lady Elizabeth's Men have his new
play. Jonson had named it *Bartholomew Fair* and it was produced at the Hope on the last day of October, 1614.

Jonson wrote his new comedy in the cheerful mood he had
showed in some of his recent masques, and in fact he opened
with the same device he had used in *Love Restored*. Again a

member of the cast comes out to report trouble backstage, but in *Bartholomew Fair* the confiding employee is the stagekeeper, who explains there will be a delay because one of the actors has a run in his black silk stocking. The stagekeeper further informs the audience that the play is a scurvy one and not the sort he himself would have written. "But these master-poets, they will ha' their own absurd courses; they will be informed of nothing." In fact, it is the stagekeeper's contention that the author kicked him "three or four times about the tiring house" merely for making one suggestion, involving a pump and a whore, that would have been the making of the play.

After this informal opening, the prompter comes onstage to make an agreement with the audience. The spectators are to agree "to remain in the places their money or friends have put them in, with patience, for the space of two hours and a half, and somewhat more. In which time, the author promiseth to present them . . . with a new, sufficient play called Bartholomew Fair, merry, and as full of noise as sport; made to delight all and to offend none." In return, the audience will kindly refrain from looking for dark political meanings in the script and feeling they can tell what great lady is signified "by the pig woman, what concealed statesman by the seller of mouse-traps" and so on. The play has no hidden meaning. It is merely designed "to delight all and to offend none."

Yet *Bartholomew Fair* was not without its definite purpose. As a classicist, Jonson was convinced of the importance of realism on the stage, and he saw his play as a kind of answer to the unrealistic and masquelike comedies that were so successful at the Globe. He was thinking in particular of Shakespeare's play, *The Tempest*, with its dances, its pageantry and its supernatural beings. Jonson objected to Caliban—that "servant monster" as he is called in Shakespeare's play. He objected equally to the stage device that brings in a magic banquet— a "living drollery" as it is called by one of Shakespeare's characters. Jonson would as soon have put a unicorn on stage as write an extravaganza like *The Tempest*, and he said so by quoting Shakespeare's own

phrases against him. Ben Jonson guaranteed the audience at the
Hope that the author would have no "servant-monster i' the
Fair . . . He is loath to make Nature afraid in his plays, like
those that beget Tales, Tempests and such like drolleries, to
mix his head with other men's heels." It is curious how Jonson
was haunted by Shakespeare. He even brings in a scathing mention of *Titus Andronicus*, which Shakespeare had written at the
beginning of his career and which Jonson ranked with another
*bête noire* of his, *The Spanish Tragedy*.

Jonson intended his own play to be taken seriously, as a
classical comedy, and he wrote a critical defense of it which
was designed as a preface to his translation of Horace's *Art of
Poetry*. The manuscript was lost, but it is easy enough to see
what Jonson's defense would have been. *Bartholomew Fair*
maintains the classic unity of time, since all the action takes
place in a single day, and it keeps to the classic principle of
decorum, since each of the characters behaves in a thoroughly
consistent manner throughout. In addition, the play has the
naturalistic tone of old Roman comedy. The horse courser talks
so exactly like a horse courser, down to the minutest jargon
of his trade, that Jonson might have successfully passed an examination in horse coursing himself.

Fortunately, Jonson was currently in a state of such lively
energy as a writer that there was no danger of the playwright
being overwhelmed by the critic. Moreover he had obviously
gone to the real Bartholomew Fair a great many times and had
taken a vast and uncritical delight in its goings-on. He enjoyed
its dirt, its noise, its vulgarity and its bounce, and whatever
Horace might have thought of the institution Jonson was
enough of a true Londoner to glory in it.

Bartholomew Fair was the annual cloth fair that was held
in the suburbs west of London in August. It was so huge it had
spilled over into four parishes, and so popular that by now the
clothiers were only a submerged pretext for the flood of activity
in what would now be called the Midway or the Fun Fair.
Most of the Fair consisted of a noisy and colorful mass of

booths for the roast pig and toy sellers, the gingerbread women
and ballad singers, the quack doctors, freaks and showmen—all
with the single ambition of getting as much money as possible
out of the customers' pockets before the Fair closed down for
another year. The dirt and the color and the noise must have
been notable even for a city as experienced as London, and
the occasion apparently became livelier each year. In 1614,
the year of Jonson's play, the city had made one much-needed
improvement and paved the whole Smithfield area, assessing the
citizens sixteen hundred pounds to cover the costs. This "reduced the rude vast place of Smithfield into a fair and comely
order," gave the booths a steadier underpinning and assured the
August visitors of not having to wade through mud if it rained,
but it is doubtful if it made the show itself any more decorous.

Jonson had a fine time peopling his own version of the Fair.
He was especially delighted with Ursula the pig woman, a fat
old harridan who sold hot roast pork in the dog days and
sweated like Falstaff. "I do water the ground in knots as I go,
like a great garden-pot." Ursula overflowed her chair, which
needed to be "let out o' the sides for me, that my hips might
play," smoked like a chimney, swore outrageously and was im-
mensely proud of her booth, which was festooned with green
boughs to keep the sun off her customers. Like the Wife of
Bath she had a high opinion of herself and describes herself
modestly as a "plain, plump, soft wench o' the suburbs . . .
juicy and wholesome." Early in the play she chases two of her
customers with a scalding pan and gets the worst of it, so that
she is put out of the action. But her greasy moon face presides
over the events of *Bartholomew Fair* like some disreputable
minor deity.

Jonson's showpeople have two things in common; they all
want to make money as quickly as possible out of those doomed
individuals, the customers, and they are all proud of their commodities. Joan Trash, the gingerbread seller, is very proud of
her little cookie figures, and even the mousetrap man takes an
interest in his wares. The corn cutter wanders about looking

for toes to trim; the pickpocket, equally alert, looks for purses. The whole stage of the Hope was crowded with an industrious group of moneymakers who are quite as disreputable in their way as the trio in *The Alchemist.*

One of Jonson's most endearing characters is a young man up from the country, one Bartholomew Cokes, who has fallen helplessly in love with the place. He calls it "my fair" because of his first name, and he is the perfect visitor. Cokes cannot buy just one ballad. He has to buy the "whole bundle" because he used to collect the pictures on them and paste them over the nursery chimney at home. He already owns a drum but he buys another from the hobbyhorse man and follows it with three jew's-trumps and a set of violins. Being interrupted by the gingerbread woman, who recognizes the customer of her dreams, he promptly buys the whole of her basket. By the end of the play Cokes has mislaid his friends, his purchases and even his hat; but he has had a fine time nevertheless and if Jonson feels any contempt for him it is a very affectionate contempt.

The one character in the play whom Jonson wholeheartedly dislikes is the Puritan, Zeal-of-the-Land Busy. The Puritans hated the Smithfield fair, as they hated the London theatres and the Mermaid tavern and many other places that Jonson enjoyed, and in return Jonson cordially hated the Puritans. Zeal-of-the-Land Busy has come to the Fair because he longs for roast pork but he has to supply himself with a noble reason for it. "I will eat exceedingly and prophesy; there may be a good use made of it too, now I think on't: by the public eating of swine's flesh, to profess our hate and loathing of Judaism." He eats two and a half servings of Ursula's pork, washes it down with a pailful of ale, and then gives his opinion of the Fair. "Thou art the seat of the Beast, O Smithfield . . . Idolatry peepeth out on every side of thee." He informs the trinket seller that his hobbyhorse is a "fierce and rank idol," he knocks over the little cookie figures of the gingerbread woman because they are an "idolatrous grove of images" and he finally ends his career of disapproval in the stocks.

This is not a realistic portrait of a Puritan, but it might be called a realistic portrait of what the average royalist believed a Puritan to be. It was undeniably true that many members of the sect had a gift for being pious on Sunday and making money on Monday, but on the whole they were not hypocrites. Theirs was rather the contrary fault of the self-righteous, that of being too fiercely and narrowly in earnest. Jonson's Puritan is a stage Puritan, just as the Irishman in *Bartholomew Fair* is a stage Irishman. But it is a good comic portrait and the audience at the Hope must have enjoyed it thoroughly.

Jonson's comedy is written in prose but it is not quite free from what one of the characters calls that "terrible taint, poetry." Jonson was at the height of his strength as a writer during these years, and his lines have a packed and nervous force that sets the play only a little below *Volpone* and *The Alchemist*. When young Cokes' tutor is describing the empty-headed innocence of his charge, the lines are those of a poet: "He that had the means to travel your head, now, should meet finer sights than any are i' the Fair, and make a finer voyage on't, to see it all hung with cockleshells, pebbles, fine wheat-straws, and here and there a chicken's feather and a cobweb."

The play is nevertheless a realistic one, and many of the touches that a modern reader might put down to Jonson's imagination are based on literal fact. For instance, Jonson gives his characters names like John Littlewit, Humphrey Wasp and Adam Overdo, but these are pale and almost conventional beside some of the names on the relief records in the Westminster parishes—Honey Killboy, Jeremy Tailcoat, Fridaysweed Savory, Tapertoe, Drinkall, Wildblood and the Widow Killbreath. Jonson's Justice of the Peace works out a ridiculous project for disguising himself and ferreting out the sins of the Fair, thus saving himself "spy money." But in this same year of 1614 the new mayor of London sent a proud report to the government in which he announced that he had not only ferreted out many brothels through his spy service but "had gone himself disguised to divers of them," thus striking a note of unconscious humor that the most satirical playwright could hardly have bettered.

The day after *Bartholomew Fair* opened at the Hope it was presented at Court before King James. Jonson wrote a special Prologue and Epilogue for the Whitehall production,

Your Majesty is welcome to a fair . . .

and the expense account of the Office of the Revels, which staged the Court version, lists "canvas for the booths and other necessaries." Nathan Field was familiar with royalty. At the beginning of his career he had acted before Queen Elizabeth and he had done many plays at Court since. But the present occasion must have been especially gratifying to him, for Jonson had given him a direct compliment in the text of *Bartholomew Fair*, linking him with Richard Burbage as the two best actors in London.

Field and his fellow actors were paid ten pounds for the performance, by warrant of the Lord Chamberlain who had general supervision of all the Court shows. For many years the Chamberlain had been the old Earl of Suffolk, and most of Jonson's plays and masques had been presented at Whitehall under him. But Suffolk had been advanced to the post of Lord Treasurer, in spite of his obvious unfitness, and the post of Lord Chamberlain had gone to his new son-in-law, Robert Carr.

No one at Whitehall approved of the rise of Robert Carr, except the Howard family who had helped him; and very few people approved of the Howards. By the time *Bartholomew Fair* was being produced, there was a concerted drive by the anti-Howard faction to produce a new favorite who might supplant Carr in the King's affections. On his way north the previous summer James had met a charming young man of twenty-two named George Villiers, and Villiers was now at Court being groomed by the anti-Howard party to unseat Carr.

Everything that Robert Carr might be, George Villiers was

a little more so. He was a little more handsome, a little more charming, and a little more eager to please. He was, in fact, almost pathetically eager to please, for he had been brought up by a widowed mother who was fiercely determined that her favorite son should make a great name for himself in the world. She had trained him in all the arts that might please a king, sent him to France for a final polish and then brought him home to train him again. When James was introduced to him in August, George Villiers was already a very promising courtier.

As soon as he arrived at Court, the anti-Carr faction took him in hand and continued his training. Young Villiers had the merit of being English rather than Scotch and he seemed to be an affectionate young man who would not soon forget his benefactors. Queen Anne smiled upon him, Sir Francis Bacon gave him excellent advice, and the Archbishop of Canterbury wrote him letters that were signed "your very loving father."

Then King James took a hand in the young man's education, resolved to create a masterpiece and shape him "platonically to his own idea." He had malleable material in George Villiers, who smiled politely at everyone with his "sweet and attractive manner" but had no very clear idea of what was happening to him. A shrewd Court observer remarked that "the King's eagerness to advance him so surprised his youth, that he seemed only to submit . . . without resistance . . . and rather to be held up by the violent inclination of the King than to climb up by any art or industry of his own."

Ben Jonson wrote a masque that Christmas, "the principal motive whereof is thought to be the gracing of young Villiers and to bring him on the stage." His mother had seen to it that the young man was a brilliant dancer, Jonson gave him a suitable background for his talents and the King authorized an expenditure of fifteen hundred pounds for the occasion.

Meanwhile Robert Carr had been behaving very unwisely. He insulted Villiers and tried to bully James, and more and more the King turned his affections towards the new favorite. Less than a year after the King had met him, George Villiers was made a knight and a Gentleman of the Bedchamber. The following New Year he was made Master of the Horse, in August he became a viscount, and the next January he entered the Privy Council as the Earl of Buckingham.

Meanwhile Robert Carr had gone downhill as suddenly as Buckingham had gone up. The murder of Sir Thomas Overbury had been discovered and it exploded into one of the most sensational murder trials of the century. The Countess pleaded guilty, since she could hardly do otherwise, but the sentence against her was ultimately commuted since her father was the Earl of Suffolk and since both Queen Anne and the amiable Buckingham were willing to intercede on her behalf. Carr pleaded innocent, and the fascinated Londoners had to arrive at six in the morning to get seats for his arraignment. In the end Carr also escaped with his life but he retired from the Court. His post as Lord Chamberlain was given to Jonson's good friend, the Earl of Pembroke, who had helped Buckingham to rise.

The Court of King James was a kind of stock exchange in which fortunes rose and fell as endlessly as the turning of a wheel. When Carr's wife was committed to the Tower she was assigned to the quarters of Sir Walter Raleigh, who had just been released and given a conditional pardon so that he could look for gold in Guiana. In a short time the wheel turned again, so that Raleigh ended his life on a headsman's block, and it is no wonder that one Englishman called the Court *terra infirma*.

Very few people succeeded in building a permanent career on so slippery a surface, but one of the few who did was Ben Jonson. That independent and unyielding poet not only was able to thrive in the insulated, hothouse atmosphere of Whitehall but he built a successful career for himself on its shifting foundations. In February of 1616 the achievement was made official. For Jonson was given a Court pension of a hundred marks a year, which would be a little over sixty-six pounds, and became what might be called the first poet laureate of England.

Jonson had many uses for the hundred marks, but it was the idea of being crowned for his work as a poet that especially pleased him. In one of his masques he had presented the spirits of ancient poets "in a priest-like habit of crimson and purple, with laurel garlands." Jonson could not very well roam about in crimson and purple, but he could feel on his head the laurel garland. For he was now the poet laureate, the King's poet.

Two years earlier Jonson's learned friend, John Selden, had published a little book called *Titles of Honor.* Selden had omitted any mention of the post of poet laureate in his list of titles and Jonson suggested that he might like to remedy the omission. In the next edition Selden included a discussion of the poet laureateship, both in England and abroad. "Thus have I . . . performed a promise to you, my beloved Ben Jonson . . . And so you both fully know what concerns it, and your singular excellency in the art most eminently deserves it."

Selden's account is actually a little misleadiing. There had never been an official poet laureate in England and when John Skelton claimed the honor he was referring to an academic distinction given him at Oxford. But if the post did not officially exist, Ben Jonson was quite ready to create it. He was convinced he "deserved the bays" and he succeeded in establishing his position so firmly in the popular mind that when the Court pension went to another poet after his death the post of laureate went to him also.

Perhaps it was this single-mindedness of Jonson's that made it possible for him to succeed in a Court where so many failed. Unlike Sir Thomas Overbury he did not want power, and unlike most of his fellow courtiers he did not want money. The one thing he wanted was the honor due him as a poet, and for this there was much less competition.

Moreover, it was a desire in which there was no possibility of degradation. Intent on a different goal, Jonson did not bow to the two gods of Whitehall, money and power, and he was never contaminated by the hot, greedy winds that blew through the Court and destroyed so many people.

# Chapter 20

SIR WALTER RALEIGH was released from the Tower in March of 1616, having been in prison for more than a dozen years, and one of the first things he did was to go around London to see the "sights and places built or bettered since his imprisonment." He saw many changes, for the city had flourished like a great tree in the quiet and prosperity of the new reign. A London chronicler mentions, with legitimate civic pride, that London was "so much increased with people and building, as no known city of the universe may compare with it." Nowhere else in England was there a similar growth of population and King James, who disliked the place, remarked bitterly, "Soon London will be all England."

As London turned itself into a modern city, the old ways broke down one by one; and the increasing dilapidation of St. Paul's, which everyone talked about repairing and no one did, might have served as a symbol of the slow dissolution of the medieval point of view. The building trade, which had been under such strict, medieval supervision when Jonson was a young man, found that it could not keep pace with the hundreds of new houses that were put up annually if it held to the old apprentice system, and a flood of cheap, unskilled labor was dissolving the careful limits that had been set up by the building guilds.

Guild supervision was not the only legacy from the past that was breaking down. The old medieval standards of power, based on land and position, were collapsing under a single new force: money. London was the money-getting and money-spending center of the kingdom, and the orgy of speculation in which the city indulged was only matched by its orgy of spending. Everyone who had money or who wanted it came to London, and country gentlemen were beginning to establish town houses for the winter season at "the instigation of their wives," who longed to buy new clothes and do all the fashionable urban things. Occasionally these people ruined themselves in the process, and when Lady Webbe died of the smallpox her friends could not altogether regret her passing. For she "loved this town too well, which in short time would have drawn her and her husband dry as well in purse as in reputation."

The evil glitter of gold that Jonson had attacked in *Volpone* and *The Alchemist* grew brighter year by year as the prosperity of the city increased, and the money that came so easily departed easily too. At a gambling party at the Three Tuns in Newgate Market, one young man won fifteen hundred pounds. He lost most of it the next day and killed himself by taking poison.

A Londoner writing in 1615 noted that Sir George Hayward had recently gone mad and added that he had never heard of so many people going insane "in all my time . . . as I have within these two or three years." It was not surprising, for there was little in the London atmosphere to contribute to stability and good sense; and even the most sober of citizens could be caught up unwillingly in the hysteria of the period. Jonson's good friend, Richard Martin, that gay and delightful man, applied in 1618 for the post of Recorder and was "told it should be done for him but that he must be thankful." Martin was quite prepared to be thankful and after his election he duly distributed two or three hundred pounds in gifts. He was then informed that he still owed fifteen hundred pounds, since the post had been obtained for him after a series of bribes and private arrangements of which the new Recorder knew nothing. "It lay so heavy at Mr. Martin's heart after he knew of it that he fell ill . . . and took his chamber and never came forth until he was carried to burial."

The man who finally got the job was Robert Heath, "a great agent in new suits and projects for greedy courtiers." He was an unworthy successor to a good lawyer and an honest man, but agents like Heath flourished for an obvious reason. The Whitehall courtiers could not be expected to stand idly by while a great golden stream of ready money flowed through the London shops and industries. It was true that the courtiers had no goods to sell and could not compete with the London businessmen who sold jewelry and silks and furniture and flowers made of pearl for ladies' hairdresses. But the single commodity that the courtiers possessed, although intangible, was a reliable one and capable of earning a great deal of money for them. They sold influence.

If a group of London businessmen wanted to form a joint-stock company or get a monopoly for some kind of manufacture or trade, they were obliged to get a royal charter. It was the function of men like Heath, who were called "projectors," to float various schemes that could be protected by monopolies, and part of their job was to bribe the various courtiers whose protection had to be gained before the deal could be pushed through. The courtiers did not look upon this as bribery. They considered it a reasonable payment for services rendered. Lady Bedford, for instance, was a woman of unimpeachable virtue and respectability, and yet when two projectors were trying to push through a patent for the exclusive manufacture of gold and silver thread they gave her "five hundred pounds apiece to be interested in that patent." King James once remarked cheerily to the Venetian ambassador that if he had tried to set in force the Venetian system of punishing bribery he would "soon not have a single subject left."

The system of granting monopolies was a kind of extension of the old guild theory of "protection." The idea of unrestricted competition had not yet entered the public mind and it was felt that if a businessman invested time, thought and money in a new way of making starch or packaging playing cards he was entitled to freedom from competition. But the guild system of preventing competition was old and respectable, while the new system of monopolies was not only a mushroom growth but singularly open to abuse. Apart from anything else it usually involved a rise in prices, since the holder of the patent could charge what he pleased and was saddled with a large initial investment in bribes which he had to recoup. A furious Elizabethan Parliament submitted a whole list of commodities that had doubled and tripled in price under the new system.

Monopolies had been bad enough under Elizabeth but they became far worse under James, whose need of money was so desperate that he was willing to agree to almost any scheme that would bring him some ready cash. Since the King did not have the power of direct taxation he could not touch the money that flowed through London in a golden stream, and like his own eager courtiers he entered into the money-making schemes that were hatched in the fertile brains of the Jacobean projectors. He was promised, for instance, a profit of ten thousand pounds a year on the patent for gold and silver thread, and he was not inclined to investigate too closely a project which was later discovered to be a vicious and almost criminal racket.

When the Earl of Salisbury was alive, he did not let James make a fool of himself by embracing every money-making scheme that came his way. If the Secretary of State introduced the King to a business investment it was a legitimate one, like the New River company in which James held shares and which succeeded in bringing a new supply of much-needed drinking water to London in spite of the bitter opposition of local landowners.

After Salisbury's death the King promptly became involved in a deplorable scheme to make money out of the textile industry. The plan was brought to him by Alderman Cockaigne of London, and in fairness to James it must be said that Cockaigne's plan looked well on the surface. There was a great deal of unemployment in the textile industry, and the alderman pointed out that it was foolish to send English cloth abroad to be dyed when he could take up the slack by having it done at home. Six hundred thousand pounds might be earned under the new system, and the King could have half of it.

Cockaigne spent a great deal of money about the Court, bribing important people like Lady Bedford to use their influence with the King, and he got a royal charter without too much difficulty. A proclamation of 1614 rejoiced in "this great and happy alteration for the better" and the only group which could not be expected to rejoice was the great London company of the Merchant Adventurers. Their charter, which permitted them to handle most of the export trade in cloth, was taken away from them and given to Cockaigne's group, which called itself the New Merchant Adventurers.

By 1616 the project was already in serious difficulties. The inexperienced English dyers were spoiling the material, and the Dutch had retaliated after the blow to their own dyeing industry by prohibiting entry to the finished English cloth. The glittering profits that Cockaigne had promised were so far nonexistent. Still, Cockaigne felt that if he could keep the King's favor all might yet be well, and with the profound Jacobean conviction that everything could be solved by lavish entertainment he put on a huge banquet.

Ben Jonson wrote the script for Alderman Cockaigne's banquet, and dyers and cloth dressers with their shuttles "were presented to the King and spake such language as Benjamin Johnson put in their mouths." An earlier royal banquet in which Jonson had assisted had been lavish enough, but the New Merchant Adventurers spent three times as much money as the Merchant Tailors had done, and where the Merchant Tailors had presented James with a hundred pounds of gold the New Merchant Adventurers presented him with a thousand.

Cockaigne was knighted at the banquet but he could not save his company, since both the cloth and the profits had failed to materialize. Moreover, the original company of Merchant Adventurers had been quietly bribing its way back into favor, and after a judicious spending of seventy thousand pounds it regained its old charter. This expense was passed on through the clothier to the consumer but the old prosperity could not be so easily regained. In their greed for money the King and Court had gambled with England's most important single export and had dislocated its delicate economy so completely that the depression of 1620 was the direct result of their tampering.

Ben Jonson was no economist and he was not acquainted with the ramifications of Cockaigne's business project. But he did know that the craze for easy money which had hit the Jacobean Court was an evil thing, and that the gullibility on which the projectors were feeding was the same hope of getting something for nothing that he had pilloried in *The Alchemist.*

Jonson wrote a new play on the subject and called it *The Devil is an Ass.* The title comes from a small devil named Pug who hopes to distinguish himself in London and finds that the city is too much for him.

> Why, Hell is
> A grammar-school to this!

All Pug desires as the play progresses is to escape to a calmer and cooler atmosphere. "O Chief, call me to Hell again and free me!" He finally succeeds in leaving London, beaten and discredited, having found he was quite unable to cope with the superior deviltries he found on earth.

The focus of the plot is a greedy squire who has come up from Norfolk to make money in the city, but the most interesting characters are a projector named Meercraft and his colleague at Court, Lady Tailbush. Meercraft thinks up the various projects and arranges for their financing, while Lady Tailbush does contact work at Court. The pair are currently working on a new kind of cosmetic which she is enthusiastically advertising among the proper people. She had every reason to expect success, since supplying the Court with cosmetics had become a

large and flourishing industry. (When Lady Bedford left off
artificial aids to beauty after a serious illness, it was observed
how very "strangely" she looked among so many painted
faces.)

Lady Tailbush has a single project but Meercraft has a dozen.
He is "the Wit, the Brain, the great Projector" and he can
think of ideas as fast as he can find anyone to invest in them.
In Meercraft's opinion, any intelligent man can make money
work for him.

> Sir, money's a whore, a bawd, a drudge,
> Fit to run out on errands . . .
>    Coin her out of cobwebs,
> Dust, but I'll have her. Raise wool upon egg-shells,
> Sir, and make grass grow out of marrow-bones
> To make her come.

Meercraft has worked out a new way of dressing dogskins
that is guaranteed to bring in twelve thousand pounds, and he
can cut the cost of wine in half by making it out of raisins. As
a good promotor should, he allows for every contingency. He
has a project to introduce into England the Italian custom of
using forks and has made a private arrangement with the linen
drapers not to put any difficulties in his way; for one of the
main points that he has stressed in the advertising copy of this
particular prospectus is that forks will be "a mighty saver of
linen."

But Meercraft rises to his noblest height of invention in the
matter of toothpicks. He hopes to get a monopoly on "serving
the whole state with toothpicks" and has worked out elaborate
plans to break down any resistance on the part of the customers.
His advertising shows how dangerous it is to the health to use
inferior toothpicks,

>      what diseases
> And putrefactions in the gums are bred
> By those are made of adulterate and false wood.

He furthermore intends to start his campaign with the very young, and plans

> to have a book
> Printed to teach their use, which every child
> Shall have throughout the kingdom that can read
> And learn to pick his teeth by.

Moreover, toothpicks are socially desirable as well as healthful, since they "preserve the breath pure and . . . free from taint." Meercraft has thought of everything, with as much ingenuity as the whole staff of a modern advertising agency, and no doubt men like him deserved the success they achieved in the Jacobean world of business.

Aside from the satire, which is magnificent, the play is not one of Jonson's best. The plot is complicated and loosely constructed, and it lacks the unity of tone that is found in his greater plays. A subplot tells the story of a London gallant in love with the squire's wife and is obviously intended as part of the satire; and yet a lyric note creeps into it which Jonson, for all his realism, was not able to destroy in himself. It appears when the lover describes the wife's nights:

> The cold
> Sheets that you lie in, with the watching candle . . .

It appears also in the lover's plea for her favor, the ancient appeal echoed and re-echoed by so many poets.

> Ere your spring be gone, enjoy it. Flowers,
> Though fair, are oft but of one morning. Think,
> All beauty doth not last until the autumn.
> You grow old while I tell you this. And such
> As cannot use the present are not wise.

This is an adaptation of Horace's "*Carpe diem*" and is almost Greek in its steady, luminous simplicity.

It is in this same play that Jonson inserted one of his loveliest songs:

> Have you seen but a bright lily grow,
>     Before rude hands have touched it?
> Have you marked but the fall of the snow,
>     Before the soil hath smutched it?
> Have you felt the wool of the beaver,
>     Or swansdown ever?
> Or have smelt o' the bud o' the briar,
>     Or the nard i' the fire?
> Or have tasted the bag o' the bee?
>     O, so white! O, so soft! O, so sweet is she!

*The Devil is an Ass* was presented at the Blackfriars by the
King's Men in the autumn of 1616. Jonson did not record the
casts of his later comedies, but it is probable that Richard Robinson played the part of the squire's wife. Robinson was one of
the many young actors that Jonson liked and encouraged, and
in the same way that Jonson put a direct compliment to Nathan
Field in *Bartholomew Fair* he put a direct compliment to Robinson in *The Devil is an Ass*. Jonson was generous in his praise,
and on the whole the actors at the Blackfriars could not have
found him a difficult man to work with.

Whenever a playwright used a topical subject there was always a risk of repercussions, especially in the case of a writer
as vigorous as Jonson. Someone at Court protested to the King
because he felt he recognized himself in Meercraft's project to
raise "eighteen millions" by draining land, and the King told
Jonson to "conceal" the resemblance. Jonson obliged and the
play as it stands now does not have any episode that is traceable
to a single individual. Nevertheless it reflects one aspect of
Court life so accurately that many people could have recognized themselves in Jonson's mirror if they had cared to look.

King James himself had special reason to be interested in the
last scene of the play, in which the squire pretends to be possessed by a devil. One of the most unpleasant aspects of the be-

ief in witchcraft was the fact that many people, particularly
mall boys, had learned how to counterfeit demonic possession.
They could assume all the symptoms—foaming at the mouth,
welling, vomiting pins and so forth—and then they accused innocent people of being witches who were tormenting them.
When King James was on his summer progress in 1616, just
before Jonson's play opened, he found six witches in prison in
Leicester, awaiting trial for having tormented a thirteen-year-
old boy who was the nephew of a prominent preacher. Nine
other witches whom the boy had also accused had been hanged
before James arrived. The King had already succeeded in un-
masking two impostures of a similar kind, and as soon as he examined the boy he knew he was an hysteric. But even at that he
was able to save the lives of only five of his subjects for the
sixth had died in jail. Jonson speaks in his play of "a boy o'
thirteen year old" counterfeiting the devil "but t'other day"
and it was almost certainly the Leicester tragedy he had in mind.

James wanted to see justice done in his kingdom and occasionally he managed to achieve it. He also wished to have a
quiet, orderly and moral Court. He thoroughly disliked smoking and cosmetics and the clutter of overdressed, extravagant
women who overran Whitehall, just as he disliked the way
everyone, including himself, had to worry about money. Yet,
on the whole, King James sincerely believed that he was running his kingdom efficiently and well. He had a fundamentally
placid temperament in spite of his occasional rages and was able
to amble his way through his dissolute Court with the contented conviction he was doing all that any reasonable man
could expect of him. Ben Jonson thought the same, since he
apparently had a real liking for the man he called "best of
kings" and his frequent criticism of James' Court was never at
any time a criticism of King James.

# Chapter 21

THE YEAR THAT BEN JONSON wrote *The Devil is an Ass* was the same year in which he was given his Court pension. It was also the year of a much greater triumph, for it was in 1616 that Jonson published his collected works. All his best plays, all his masques, his entertainments and his verses were gathered together in a magnificent folio volume of more than a thousand pages and offered to the public.

It was the first time in English literary history that a poet had presented himself to posterity in so formal a manner, enshrining his plays in the dignity of a folio instead of in small cheap quartos, and it was inevitable that Jonson should be the one to do it. Long ago he had decided that he was a dedicated man—a priest of Apollo—but now he was in a position to make the whole country acknowledge it instead of merely murmuring it intensely to himself.

The book was published by William Stansby, a prominent London printer who turned out so handsome a volume that even Jonson should have been satisfied. The title page is as crowded with symbolic figures as the one in Raleigh's *History*, but it is much more handsomely and massively designed and looks not unlike the triumphal arches that Jonson did for King James. The figure of Tragedy, crowned and sceptered, stands on one side of the pillars, with Comedy on the other, and in the opening between is printed the proud title: THE WORKS OF BENJAMIN JONSON.

No previous writer had seen fit to raise a group of play scripts to the dignity of "Works" and several of Jonson's contemporaries were inclined to jeer at him for it. But Jonson had always looked upon his plays as poems, and in the first section of the folio he printed the nine that he felt were worthy of immortality. He opened with *Every Man in his Humour*, dedicated to William Camden, and closed with *Catiline*, dedicated to the Earl of Pembroke.

Jonson's theories on comedy had matured considerably in the eighteen years since he had written *Every Man in his Humour*. He had become more deeply convinced of the truth of Cicero's definition of comedy—"a copy of life, a mirror of custom, a representation of truth"—and he could see many ways in which his first Humour comedy fell short.

A lesser man than Jonson might have been content to give the play a superficial realism by crossing out the Italian allusions and putting in English ones, so that Sister Hesperida became Dame Bridget and the Italian academies became English universities. But Jonson, with his usual thoroughness, went deeper and rewrote the whole play. He made the people livelier and more recognizable, the dialogue more relaxed and realistic and planted the whole thing firmly in a London climate. In the original version of the play, Lorenzo senior denounces his son's behavior in a string of commonplace platitudes, but when he is changed to old Mr. Kno'well he gives a brisk and realistic discussion on the current slackness in dealing with children.

> Can it call, whore? cry, bastard? O, then kiss it.
> A witty child! Can 't swear? The father's dearling!
> Give it two plums.

Old Mr. Kno'well disapproves not only of the current notions of sophistication that encouraged this sort of precosity in children, but even more of the standards the parents themselves were offering,

> repeating still
> The rule, "Get money;" still, "Get money, boy,
> No matter by what means."

Jonson was the same satirist he had been eighteen years earlier
when he offered the play to Shakespeare's company; but in the
years since then he had collected a great many more things to
be satiric about, and he knew much better how to achieve the
kind of naturalistic comedy he had been trying to write in 1598.

Jonson cut out of the revised version what had once been the
pride of his heart, the long speech at the end of the play in
which the dignity of poets is defended. Jonson still believed
that poetry was fit to be seen only by "grave and consecrated
eyes." But he also knew that the speech was out of context and
would only mar the realistic tone he was trying to give the play.

Nevertheless, Jonson had no intention of abandoning the
point he had made and so he rewrote the idea and presented it
as a Prologue, including in it the most detailed and vigorous attack he ever made on the practices of his fellow playwrights.
He had been attacking the contemporary theatre for years because it was not neat, orderly and realistic, and he packed into the
Prologue's thirty lines a final broadside against the "ill customs"
of the current stage. They are the same ones that Sir Philip Sidney had objected to, and Jonson sometimes uses an echo of Sidney's words.

> To make a child, now swaddled, to proceed
> Man, and then shoot up, in one beard and weed,
> Past threescore years; or, with three rusty swords
> And help of some few foot-and-half-foot words,
> Fight over York and Lancaster's long jars.

Jonson declares that he himself is offering the audience a naturalistic play,

> as other plays should be.
> Where neither Chorus wafts you o'er the seas;
> Nor creaking throne comes down, the boys to please;

Nor nimble squib is seen, to make afeard
The gentlewomen; nor roll'd bullet heard
To say it thunders; nor tempestuous drum
Rumbles to tell you when the storm doth come.
But deeds and language such as men do use,
And persons such as Comedy would choose
When she would show an image of the times
And sport with human follies, not with crimes.

It is conceivable that Jonson did not have Shakespeare in mind when he was writing this, but it is nevertheless true that the whole list of the offenses, with the exception of the child who shot up to threescore years on stage, can be matched somewhere in Shakespeare's plays. There is the apparatus that came "creaking" down from the stage heavens carrying Jove enthroned on his eagle in *Cymbeline*, the stage storm in *King Lear*, the Chorus that wafted the audience overseas to France in *Henry V*, and the series of history plays that do nothing but recount the "long jars" between the houses of Lancaster and York.

Shakespeare himself once remarked mildly that it was difficult to show a battlefield on stage, equipped only with what Jonson calls three rusty swords and what Shakespeare himself spoke of as "four or five . . . ragged foils." Even the versatile stage of the Globe had its obvious limitations.

> Can this cockpit hold
> The vasty fields of France? or may we cram
> Within this wooden O the very casques
> That did affright the air at Agincourt?

Shakespeare answered himself by saying it could be done as long as the audience was willing to help out with its imagination. But Ben Jonson did not wish to appeal to the imagination of the audience; he preferred to attack through the intellect. He could not forgive the contemporary theatre for its lack of realism, its lack of decorum, and its complete lack of interest in classical theory, and it was characteristic of him to open his collected works by saying so.

Jonson himself was so firmly in the grip of classical theory that he had the printer set up the text of his plays by the same method that had been used in the first European editions of Plautus and Terence. The system is still used in printing Roman comedy, but it was never easy to read or especially practical. Jonson also tried to be classical in his spelling, so that *Comedy* always appeared as *Comoedie.* Somewhat carried away, he even went so far as to have *porpoise* appear as *porcpisce*, and the printer wisely put some of these classical gestures back into normal English spelling, just as a subsequent printer had to do in the case of that other determined classicist, John Milton.

This sort of thing represents the useless fringe of Renaissance learning, and in general Jonson resisted any temptation to show off his erudition in the folio. But he wanted his plays to be printed as accurately as possible and he must have visited the printer frequently and surrounded himself with a whole series of page proofs as he went through the text of each play with microscopic attention. He systematized and modernized the punctuation, and whenever he caught a past error of his own he corrected it instantly. In the original text of *Sejanus*, for instance, he had a Roman courtier swear by Castor. Then he discovered later, through his reading of Aulus Gellius, that this oath was used only by women and carefully rewrote the line.

Unlike the plays, the masques in the folio are printed very carelessly. Jonson cannot have read proofs on this section, or he would certainly have stopped the printer from turning Martial's Epigrams into Epistles. The trouble here was evidently lack of time; the masques were printed so late that it had been possible to make use of the disclosures of the Overbury murder trial, which occurred the same year, and to suppress the fact that some of Jonson's work had been written for the defendants. The Challenge at Tilt that he had recently done for Carr's marriage was now discreetly listed as having been done merely "at a marriage."

The masques, having been printed last, were at the end of Jonson's folio. The plays were at the beginning, and in between were two collections of Jonson's poetry.

The first and longer of these, the Epigrams, had apparently been issued as a separate book four years earlier. "A book called Ben Jonson his Epigrams" was entered in the Stationers' Register in May of 1612, and a Scotch poet listed it among the books he had read that year. No record otherwise remains of the edition and possibly it did not sell very well. Jonson has a haughty epigram, "To my Bookseller," in which he accuses him of considering a book "good or bad" according to how well it sold. He announces that he does not wish to have his book advertised on walls and posts to attract a stupid public, and the whole epigram is of the kind that authors frequently write when their work has not done well financially.

Jonson took his Epigrams very seriously and went so far to refer to them as "the ripest of my studies." In Jonson's opinion most of the poets who wrote epigrams did them improperly and he himself was practically the only one to follow "the old way and the true." He felt a special contempt for his nearest rival, John Owen, whose Latin epigrams were read not only in England but all over Europe. Owen was headmaster at Warwick School, and Jonson said that he was nothing but "a pure pedantic schoolmaster, sweeping his living from the posteriors of little children and hath no thing good in him." Owen's epigrams, according to Jonson, were "bare narrations," while his own were in the true classic tradition.

Jonson's short poems are not epigrams in the usual meaning of the word. They are an attempt to reach back through Martial to the wide range of the *Greek Anthology* and to give the form the dignity and variety it once possessed. Jonson's epigrams include grave and dignified lines to men like Salisbury and Egerton, and loving verses to close friends like the three members of the Roe family. There are tender verses of mourning for his dead children, of admiration for musicians and fellow poets, and there is an especially charming letter in verse he sent to the Countess of Bedford with a copy of Donne's satires.

There are also satires of Jonson's own among the epigrams, spirited attacks on people and habits he disliked and especially on the effeminate young witlings he had encountered at Court. Jonson attacked, without naming her, a woman who took drugs to avoid becoming pregnant since she did not want to miss any of the festivities at Court. He attacked the throng of fledgling statesmen who had spent a few weeks at Whitehall and considered themselves experts on every problem that was facing Europe. He attacked greed and dishonesty and pretense; and at one point he even attacked himself, because he had praised a "worthless lord."

Jonson dedicated his Epigrams to the Earl of Pembroke, as he had also dedicated his martyred and beloved *Catiline*. He felt that Pembroke was one of the finest men at Court, and in a way he was probably right. Pembroke was not a man of remarkable intelligence, but he showed a kind of steadiness in that wavering atmosphere that made him, in the phrase of a younger contemporary, "the most universally loved and esteemed of any man of that age." The only fault that could be found with him was the fact that, because of an unhappy marriage, "he was immoderately given up to women." But he chose his women more for their wit than their beauty, and he had always shown himself a good friend to any writer of intelligence. Jonson had known him for at least eleven years and honored him both as a good friend and a generous patron.

Although Jonson's dedication shows profound respect, he could not help feeling that he was presenting Pembroke with something of great value. He asked the Earl for the protection of his patronage, "in thanks whereof, I return you the honor of leading forth so many good and great names as my verses mention." He then made the typically Jonsonian addition—"amongst whom, if I have praised, unfortunately, anyone that doth not deserve . . . I hope it will be forgiven me." It was not the custom to indicate in public that great men were not always worthy of the praise that was lavished on them, but Jonson was not interested in following customs. He then turned in admiration to his own work: "They are no ill pieces, though they be not like the persons." Jonson might be a Court poet, but no one could accuse him of undue self-abasement.

In addition to the Epigrams, Jonson included a shorter group of fifteen pieces. He named these "The Forest" because "the ancients called that kind of body *Silva* . . . in which there were works of divers nature." This section includes a religious poem, an ode, some epistles to great ladies, and the most famous poem that Jonson ever wrote—the song "To Celia" that is usually called by its first line.

"Drink to me only with thine eyes" is an almost perfect example of a classical poem, achieving the balanced Greek harmony and the lucid singing line in which each word fulfills its purpose and there is not one too many. The poem was born of Jonson's learning, for he built it up out of five separate prose passages from the *Epistles* of Philostratus. He was used to turning prose into poetry, since that was the way Camden had taught him, and frequently his poetry sounds like rhymed prose. Often enough he failed, but here he succeeded. Nor can the success of so lovely a lyric be laid to some kind of a happy accident, for an earlier draft begins:

> Drink to me, Celia, with thine eyes,
> And I'll pledge thee with mine . . .

This was satisfactory enough, and faithful to the Greek original. But Jonson was not content, and he kept on working on the poem until he had exactly what he wanted

> Drink to me only with thine eyes,
> And I will pledge with mine;
> Or leave a kiss but in the cup,
> And I'll not look for wine.

The thirst that from the soul doth rise
Doth ask a drink divine;
But might I of Jove's nectar sup,
I would not change for thine . . .

Jonson opens "The Forest" with a song entitled "Why I write not of love"—a resolve of which he was fortunately incapable. Jonson's love songs, both here and in his later collections, show none of the passion and torment of the Elizabethans, and to judge by his verses Jonson never set any lady's foot upon his neck and then lamented under its weight. He took a civilized delight, not unlike Horace's, in both love and ladies, and the melodious laments of the Elizabethan sonneteers were as alien to his pen as they were to his temperament.

"The Forest" shows Jonson the lover, and it also shows Jonson the moralist. Like many city dwellers he was convinced that a simpler, steadier way of life could be found in the country, and a long poem to Sir Robert Wroth hymns the moral advantages that Sir Robert had been able to find by avoiding Court masques and living quietly among his own partridges.

An even more charming ode to the simple life is Jonson's poem on Penshurst. This was the country seat of Sir Robert Sidney, Philip's younger brother, and Jonson wrote as a delighted guest who approved of everything about his democratic and open-handed host. At Penshurst he never had to put in a special request for a fire in his bedroom and no one cared how much he drank. His host treated all the guests alike, whatever their social rank, and Jonson valued that in him. He also valued the people whose manners did not change with their alteration in rank, and another of the poems in "The Forest" praises Katherine, Lady Aubigny. Her husband had been Jonson's generous patron, and Jonson praises the "even and unaltered gait" she has been able to maintain in spite of being a great man's wife.

What Jonson chiefly disliked about Court life was its lack of moral independence, and the men and women he praises in his verses are chiefly the ones who had enough strength to live their lives in their own fashion. Jonson himself had been able, to a remarkable degree, to "live exempt from all the nets" that Court life spread, and he liked best the people who had done the same. He was a classicist in this as in much else, for he hated a lack of self-control.

"The Forest" was followed by Jonson's Court assignments— the entertainments, the masques and the barriers—with all the lofty idealism and devoted learning that he had lavished on what he called "the short bravery of the night." Whatever Jonson did he did well, and his collected works are a fitting memorial to a lifetime's devotion to poetry. King James could hardly have chosen a better poet laureate, or Jonson a more fitting time to bring out his volume.

In this same year of 1616 King James brought out a folio edition of his own collected prose, *The Works of the Most High and Mighty Prince James*. The bishop who supervised the publication stated somewhat defensively that it was "neither unlawful nor inconvenient for a King to write," especially since James came from a literary family. His father had translated Valerius Maximus into English, and his mother had done a book of French verses with a needlework cover she had made herself. At the moment most of James' prose was being written in defense of the Protestant position against men like Cardinal DuPerron, a fact which no doubt explains his choice of a patron for one of his pieces. It was dedicated to Jesus Christ from "His most humble and most obliged servant James." The title page of James' folio was as ornamental as Jonson's with Peace and Religion propping up a variety of ornamental devices; and no doubt James felt the same quiet satisfaction over his collected works that Jonson did, if with somewhat less reason.

In this same year of 1616, two poets who had been friends of Jonson's died. One of them was Francis Beaumont, still in his early thirties, who had recently married and retired to the country. His friendship with Jonson dated back at least to 1607, when Beaumont wrote some verses commending the work of his "dear friend," and Jonson must have valued Beaumont's approval since three sets of complimentary verses from him are printed in the front of the folio. Beaumont's career had been as brief as it was brilliant, culminating in the successful masque, "fraught with art, state and delights," that he wrote for the Princess Elizabeth's wedding. After his death in March he was buried in Westminster Abbey, in the corner near Geoffrey Chaucer and Edmund Spenser that was already beginning to be reserved for poets.

The following month William Shakespeare died in his native Warwickshire. Like Beaumont, he had been in retirement; but since he had been an actor all his adult life and in close association with the business end of the theatre there was little talk of burying him in Westminster Abbey. Although a few men like William Camden had expressed their admiration for Shakespeare he had made no real stir in literary circles, and except for the grief of his friends his death would not have been much noticed in London.

Jonson's friendship with Shakespeare dated back at least eighteen years, and although the older man had been living in Stratford he had frequent business in London and Jonson had probably seen him fairly often. Both Jonson and Shakespeare had contributed to a tilt show put on three years earlier, with Shakespeare composing the *impresa* carried by the Earl of Rutland and Jonson writing the only speech delivered that day, that of the two Rich brothers.

Towards the end of the seventeenth century a story was current that Jonson had gone down to Warwickshire just before Shakespeare died and that the two men had a "merry meeting." Tht story itself is apocryphal, but it would be pleasant to feel that Jonson saw Shakespeare once more before he died. For Ben Jonson loved Shakespeare as a friend, however much he may have disapproved of some of his ways of writing; and when Shakespeare's own complete works were published in folio, seven years later, the lines that Jonson wrote for it were headed,

To the memory of my beloved.

# Chapter 22

J ONSON CONTINUED WRITING COURT shows, and one of the most charming was an entertainment he wrote in 1616 called *Christmas, his Masque.* This rather Dickensian little piece shows old Captain Christmas as a Londoner with a large family who arrives at Whitehall to present a show.

I bring you a masque
From little, little, little, little London.

The old gentleman herds in his ten sons and daughters—Mince Pie with her spoons, Wassail with ribbons and rosemary, Carol with a red cap and a flute—and introduces each of them in cheerful doggerel.

The Captain's troupe means well, but they do not have an easy time of it. There is trouble over the properties, since someone has forgotten the clove for the orange, Mumming has mislaid his vizard and Misrule feels his suit is too small for him. Moreover, the little boy they have hired to play Cupid is so overcome by the splendor of the audience that he cannot give his lines. In this he is unlike his mother, who came along to supervise him and who talks steadily. "Speak out, Robin," she implores him, but Robin cannot. This is all the more unfortunate since his mother, a superb example of a stage-struck parent, has been boasting about the offers her actor son has been receiving. "I could ha' had money enough for him, an I would ha' been tempted and ha' let him out by the week to the King's Players; Master Burbage has been about and about with me, and so has old Mr. Heminges too."

A month or so later Jonson was commissioned to do a masque for Lord Hay, who was planning a magnificent entertainment for the French ambassador and had asked Lady Bedford to be his hostess. Jonson collaborated with Nicholas Lanier, a distinguished musician who came of a French family, and between them they produced what might almost be called the first English opera. "The whole masque was sung after the Italian manner, *stylo recitativo*." Jonson wrote flowing, simple lyrics, full of vowels and smooth rhymes, to accompany the music and to tell a little fable of some lovers who believed themselves to be ghosts. The text of *Lovers Made Men* was printed and distributed as souvenirs among the guests of the evening, to be remembered long after the banquet supplied by Lord Hay's thirty master cooks had been forgotten.

During this same season, on Twelfth Night, 1617, another of Jonson's shows was presented at Court. Young George Villiers had just become the Earl of Buckingham, and the usual Court masque became that year a showcase for his talents as a dancer. It also shows the range of Jonson's talent, for *The Vision of Delight* is as light and graceful as the season it celebrates. Buckingham and his fellow dancers were dressed as "the glories of the spring"; and although Jonson's spring is that of a city man who regards frisking lambs and early nightingales from a respectful distance, the result is charming. Especially lighthearted is a discussion of dreams that would have delighted Edward Lear.

> If a dream should come in now, to make you afeard,
> With a windmill on his head and bells at his beard,
> Would you straight wear your spectacles here at your toes,
> And your boots o' your brows, and your spurs o' your nose?

Jonson introduces a lovely jumble of whales, mousetraps, ostriches, fleas and puddings and offers every kind of dream that is available,

dreams that have wings,
And dreams that have honey, and dreams that have stings.

Jonson liked nonsense for its own sake and so, apparently, did the Court that employed him.

One of the guests of honor at this particular masque was the Princess Pocahontas, who was on a visit to England. As the daughter of a foreign monarch she was given a seat worthy of her station, although she no longer looked like the Indian princess she was. She had become a Christian since her marriage to an Englishman and went by the new name of Rebecca, and she appeared at Court like any other English lady in a ruff and a farthingale.

The following year Jonson was assigned an extremely important masque, the first to be given by Prince Charles, who was now the Prince of Wales. King James was experiencing his usual difficulty with finances, but he set aside four thousand pounds for his son's debut in Jonson's *Pleasure Reconciled to Virtue*.

Charles had not danced in a masque since he appeared eight years earlier as the west wind, a sober little ten-year-old in a green tunic and silver wings. Unlike his handsome and athletic elder brother, Prince Charles had a sickly childhood. He could hardly "stand alone, he was so weak in his joints and especially his ankles" and although he was now fully recovered he could not be expected to compete on equal terms with that beautiful young animal, the Earl of Buckingham, who was to be his fellow dancer. Charles' suit was white and crimson, with silver roses on his shoes and a great plume of egret feathers on his head; but he might well be forgiven if he looked forward to his public debut as a dancer with a little trepidation.

Ben Jonson also had his emotional moments as the work on the masque progressed. He was once more collaborating with Inigo Jones after a hiatus of seven years, and it may have been on this occasion that Jonson "said to Prince Charles of Inigo Jones, that when he wanted words to express the greatest villain in the world he would call him an Inigo." Jones had been in Italy while Jonson was in France. He had traveled in the train of that splendid and Italianate nobleman, the Earl of Arundel, and had devoted himself in the hot summer days to pacing distances and measuring architectural details. He arrived back in England even more firmly dedicated to the doctrine of Italian supremacy in architecture, and as soon as he started work with Jonson the old war between the poet and the stage designer began again.

It was Jones who won the battle this time, for the stage settings for the new masque were exceedingly elaborate. The curtain opened to disclose a complicated structure intended to represent Mount Atlas, the "top ending in the figure of an old man, his head and beard all hoary and frost as if his shoulders were covered with snow; the rest wood and rock." Not content with this, Jones had rigged up a contrivance whereby "the enormous head . . . rolled up its eyes and moved itself very cleverly." Out of the mountain came Comus, the god of good cheer, carried in a kind of bath chair that Jones had designed for him, and the antimasque was performed by some little boys dressed as bottles in "huge wicker flasks" that Jones had contrived. Behind the mountain Prince Charles and his eleven fellow masquers were waiting to enter, and Jones had arranged some special effects for that also. "Mount Atlas then opened, by means of two doors which were made to turn, and from behind the hills of a distant landscape the day was seen to dawn."

After all the hard work and the high expectations, it is sad to report that the masque was not a complete success. "It came far short of the expectation, and Mr. Inigo Jones has lost in his reputation . . . Some extraordinary device was looked for (it being the Prince his first masque) and a poorer was never seen." Even the distinguished masquers did not come off well; when they paired off with the ladies, in the dance that always followed the formal one in the masque, they "began to lag. Whereupon the King . . . got impatient and shouted aloud: 'Why don't they dance? What did they make me come here for? Devil take you all, dance!' " The day was saved by Buckingham, who leaped forward and put on an intricate and brilliant display that evidently satisfied his fretful monarch. As for the young Prince of Wales, one of the spectators reported that he was very good at bowing, "being very formal in making his obeisance."

Ben Jonson did not escape censure for his part in the masque. "The poet is grown so dull that . . . divers think fit he should return to his old trade of bricklaying." Whatever others might think about the comparative failure of the great masque, the former bricklayer remained quite unmoved. In fact, he announced that it had "pleased the King so well" that he wished to see it again.

It is true that the masque was shown a second time and that Jonson showed some ingenuity in writing a new antimasque for it. He called it "For the Honour of Wales" and introduced two comic Welshmen who disapprove of the original masque and wish to see it revised. Jonson had made himself familiar with Welsh geography and he knew enough about the language to be able to use *tawson* for *shut up* and other useful phrases. Nevertheless his characters are stage Welshmen and there is no effort to be realistic.

Whatever the Court may have thought of the first masque, there was much praise for the "pleasant, merry speeches" of Jonson's addition. Moreover, the poet had the wit to turn the criticism back on the critics by having his comic Welshmen agree with them. They feel it is outrageous to have "our young master Sarles . . . the first time he ever play dance, to be pit up in a mountain (got knows where) by a palterly poet." The jokes are good-humored and in spite of the disapproving report from one member of the audience there is nothing in the text to make a "Welshman choleric." In any case, Jonson had the tact to end with a sober little tribute to Wales given in good English.

In the course of the show, the two Welshmen give King James a cordial invitation to visit Wales, assuring him that he will be "as welcomely there" as he was in Scotland the previous summer. The King had been intending for years to go back to Scotland, but it was difficult to raise enough money to make the visit. When he had finally succeeded, the previous summer, Inigo Jones supervised such items as the portable royal chapel and Buckingham went along because James was unwilling to be parted from him.

The King said that he went to Scotland out of a "salmon-like instinct" to see his native soil, and Jonson had begun to feel stirrings of the same instinct. He had never visited the home of his ancestors, so far as is known, but now that he was a Court poet and a man of consequence he might have had a special reason for wanting to make the trip. Moreover, he had met and liked a great many Scots at Whitehall and he could be sure of warm hospitality if he made the trip north.

Like King James, Jonson never had much money on hand; but, unlike King James, he planned his trip economically. Jonson went to Scotland on foot, which was something of an achievement for a man in his middle forties who had, as he cheerfully admitted, a "mountain belly." The chief strain seems to have been on his shoes. He had to buy a new pair at Durham, and was firmly resolved they should last him through Scotland and back to Durham again.

Ben Jonson arrived in Scotland in the summer of 1618, and when he reached Edinburgh he found it comparatively deserted, just as London would have been in the summer. Edinburgh was a small-scale combination of London, Oxford and Westminster, since it was the principal city in Scotland and sheltered the law courts, the university and the parliament. Scotland was not a rich country and the capital city consisted chiefly of one beautiful street surrounded by slums. The merchants had built comfortable balconies on their homes, but a pleasanter place to stay in the summer was the little town of Leith, a mile away, which served Edinburgh as a seaport. Jonson went there as the guest of a prominent shipowner named John Stuart and he apparently spent much of the summer with him.

Shortly after Jonson left London, a versifier named John Taylor set out on a walking trip of his own to Scotland. Taylor had left the navy to turn waterman, as so many old sailors did, and then he drifted into writing. He wrote easy, journalistic verses on various topics of the day and had recently found there was a good market for travel reports. As a practical man, Taylor made sure of his readers before he embarked on his trips, and before he left for Scotland he had collected sixteen hundred people who were willing to subscribe to a versified account of his travels. Jonson told a Scotch acquaintance furiously that "Taylor was sent along here to scorn him," but Taylor assured his sixteen hundred subscribers that anyone who said he took up the "project either in malice or mockage of Master Benjamin Johnson" had a wide imagination and a shallow brain. While Taylor was in Edinburgh he went out to Stuart's house in Leith to pay his respects to the poet whose "rare capacity" he had hymned six years earlier and Jonson forgivingly gave him twenty-two shillings.

If Jonson had been somewhat ruffled in his feelings by having Taylor imitate his walking tour, he could find comfort in the respectful way he was being treated in Scotland. As Taylor reported to his fellow countrymen: "He is amongst noblemen and gentlemen that know his true worth." The city of Edinburgh was so delighted to have Jonson in its midst that during the autumn the Town Council made him an honorary burgess and guild brother, with a special banquet in his honor. The task of inscribing Jonson's burgess ticket was entrusted to one Alexander Patterson, who was paid over thirteen pounds for the writing and gilding, and the banquet itself was a splendid affair that cost over two hundred pounds.

A frequent visitor in Edinburgh was William Drummond, who owned the beautiful estate of Hawthornden seven miles away in the river valley. Drummond was a poet and might almost be said to be the only poet Scotland possessed, since most of the Scottish men of letters had traveled to richer fields and were living in England. Drummond had once been a traveler himself, but since his father's death he had been living quietly in seclusion, surrounded by his books and his manuscripts. He wrote a few verses on public matters, for when Prince Henry died he did an elegy that was printed in black borders and went into three editions, and when James came up to Scotland a schoolmaster encased in a plaster lion recited some verses that Drummond had written in the King's honor.

Drummond deprecatingly called his verses "the warblings of the wild birds in the solitary forests" but in actual fact they were civilized and graceful echoes of the French and Italian schools. Drummond was a learned man who had been educated abroad, and his library contained eight times as many books in foreign languages as in English. Since Ben Jonson was also a learned man and a distinguished poet, it was natural that Drummond should extend the hospitality of Hawthornden to him; and Jonson went there for a visit of several weeks in the Christmas season.

The two men were wholly unlike, and it must frequently have occurred to Drummond that his idea had been a very great mistake. Jonson entered that placid, secluded household like a high wind, prepared to regale his host with his own views on art and life and to do a great deal of drinking. The gentle, sentimental Drummond was wholly unprepared for Jonson's impact, which stronger men than he had found rather overwhelming.

Jonson's effect on Drummond was fortunately preserved for posterity, since the unhappy laird of Hawthornden jotted down everything he could remember that Jonson said, ending with an embittered character sketch of his hard-drinking guest. Drummond missed the point of some of Jonson's jokes and was apparently incapable of recognizing where Jonson was serious and where he was not, but if his earnest jottings do not give a complete picture of Jonson himself they give an excellent picture of Jonson's effect on Drummond.

It is true that Jonson made no effort to be tactful. He happened to dislike, for instance, the Italianate love songs on which the Elizabethans of his boyhood had lavished so much art and of which Drummond was a devoted and skillful follower. He kindly informed Drummond that his verses, though good, were "not after the fancy of the time" and he even went so far as to attack that demigod of the sonneteers, Petrarch. He "cursed Petrarch for redacting verses to sonnets," and the unhappy Drummond was not accustomed to guests who went about cursing Petrarch.

Jonson's remarks on women were equally distressing to Drummond. Drummond had been engaged to a Miss Mary Cunningham, who died, and since then he had faithfully been mourning his lost love like some melodious dove. Two years earlier he had published a volume of verses that were chiefly a memorial to his beloved; and he was not in a state of mind to appreciate Jonson's reminiscences on his own love affairs, which had been neither romantic nor constant. "He thought the use of a maid nothing in comparison to the wantonness of a wife and would never have ane other mistress." In one of Jonson's comedies a woman made a remark that echoed the attitude of a great many women at Court:

> I do think
> If nobody should love me but my poor husband
> I should e'en hang myself.

Jonson had apparently saved many ladies from this fate, and it was an atmosphere to which Drummond, with his sentimental idealism and his lovely, gentle lyrics, was wholly unaccustomed.

With great precision, Jonson managed to dance on all his host's finer feelings. During the past year, for instance, Drummond had struck up a fervent long-distance friendship with Michael Drayton and had been writing him reverent letters about his works. "Long since, your amorous and truly heroical *Epistles* did ravish me, and lately your most happy *Albion* put me into a new trance." Since Jonson had known Michael Drayton for twenty years and since Drummond had no hope of meeting his new-found and "beloved" friend in person, he was naturally eager to hear anything Jonson might tell him.

In return, Jonson could hardly have been more tactless. He said that Drayton was afraid of him and that he, for his part, had no esteem for Drayton. He said that the long poem which Drummond had termed "most happy *Albion*" would have been satisfactory enough if Drayton had done what he set out to do, but that Drayton's "long verses pleased him not." He then dredged out of his capacious memory a case twenty years earlier in which Drayton had not used the possessive correctly in the title of a poem. He then quoted an epigram in which Sir John Davies had jeered at one of Drayton's sonnets, and this concluded everything that Jonson wished to say about Drayton.

Jonson's reports on other literary figures were equally unsatisfactory. He said that Spenser's stanzas did not please him, that Daniel was no poet, that Beaumont was too fond of himself, that Middleton was a base fellow, that John Day was a rogue and Abraham Fraunce a fool, and that apart from himself almost no one knew how to write a masque. Some of this may have been Jonson's considered opinion, but most of it sounds like a man talking at random after one drink too many and with no idea that his host was taking it all down.

If Drummond had been a little more alert and a little more sympathetic mentally he would have noticed how often Jonson contradicted himself. First Jonson said firmly that "Spenser's stanzas pleased him not, nor his matter" and then he admitted that he had "by heart some verses of Spenser's *Calendar*." He could state that John Donne "deserved hanging" for his irregular scansion and then call him "the first poet in the world in some things." In the face of some of his own best verses he could announce that he approved only of couplets and detested "all other rimes." And after a lifetime of selfless devotion to poetry he could advise Drummond to abandon it because it had "beggared him, when he might have been a rich lawyer, physician or merchant." Jonson himself said elsewhere, "There is no statute law . . . bids you be a poet against your will" and he had not suddenly reversed, in his talks with Drummond, the principle on which he had based his whole life. He was merely saying, with his usual vigor, anything that happened to come into his head, and if Drummond had known him better he would not have taken him so seriously.

At one point in the discussion the name of Shakespeare came up, and again, as in the case of Drayton, Jonson went out of his way to disparage the kind of writing that Drummond admired. Drummond had read Shakespeare but was instinctively drawn to his earlier and more romantic work. It was not the great tragedies that could be found in Drummond's library, but *Venus and Adonis, The Rape of Lucrece, Romeo and Juliet* and *Love's Labour's Lost*. Writing of this kind was a beautiful echo of the mood of the Italian sonneteers which Drummond admired and Jonson did not. He told Drummond firmly that Shakespeare lacked "art." He then attacked Shakespeare's carelessness for putting a seacoast in Bohemia, "where there is no sea near by some hundred miles," and that was all that Jonson wished to say about Shakespeare.

If Drummond had been really capable of listening, Jonson might possibly have been willing to discuss English drama intelligently and explain his basic objection to the romantic school of playwrights. He had carried to Scotland with him the preface he had written for his translation of Horace's *Art of Poetry*, and this contained a discussion of Horace and Aristotle and a general survey of basic principles. Jonson had cast it in the form of a dialogue between himself and John Donne, whom he called "Criticus." The manuscript is now lost, but Jonson read it to Drummond; and Drummond had so little interest in its contents that he failed to report anything specific about it. Drummond had very little sympathy with the ideas that most interested Jonson, and that is why his notes finally evaporated into page after page of jokes and after-dinner anecdotes.

Drummond did achieve one thing, however, and that was to get Jonson to talk about himself. Jonson told his host about his schooling, his hatred of bricklaying, his duels in the Low Countries and elsewhere, the vision of his dead son, the banquet with his mother, his friends and his fights. He even told Drummond little things about himself. "He hath consumed a whole night in lying looking to his great toe, about which he hath seen Tartars and Turks, Romans and Carthaginians, fight in his imagination." A man who could get this sort of information from Jonson and then remember to put it down deserves the full gratitude of posterity.

For the rest, it must be remembered that Drummond was a sorely tried man, especially since he was unlucky enough to bring out the schoolmaster in Jonson. Jonson could see himself educating Drummond, whose sheltered life and delicate idealism must have seemed a little wispy to so unsheltered and vigorous a humanist, and he assigned his host a course of reading in the Latin classics. Jonson seemed to feel that a little less indulgence in French love poets and a little more time spent in the bracing atmosphere of the Romans would do his host a world of good, and he twice told Drummond to study Quintilian, "who (he said) would tell me the faults of my verses as if he had lived with me."

Drummond was not a schoolboy; he was a grown man and an honored poet and it is not likely that he enjoyed being lectured by Jonson. It is with unmistakable malice that he lists some of Jonson's comments on French and Italian authors and then adds as a kind of footnote: "All this was to no purpose, for he neither doth understand French nor Italian." As a matter of fact, Jonson must have known French fairly well after so many months spent in Paris, and he knew enough Italian to be able to repeat a madrigal by Parabosco, as Drummond himself admitted. But by this time Jonson's host was in no state of mind to be fair and weigh all the evidence.

Drummond's profound irritation found its release in the short sketch of Jonson that concludes the notes. Ever since the days of *Poetaster*, seventeen years before, Jonson had been accused of callousness in his friendships. "He will sooner lose his best friend than his least jest." The charge was untrue, as a multitude of Jonson's friends from Camden to Donne could testify, but Drummond in his present temper was quite ready to believe it. "He is a great lover and praiser of himself, a contemner and scorner of others. Given rather to lose a friend than a jest. Jealous of every word and action of those about him (especially after drink which is one of the elements in which he liveth). A dissembler of ill parts which reign in him, a bragger of some good that he wanteth. Thinketh nothing well but what either he himself, or some of his friends and countrymen, hath said or done."

At this point Drummond must have paused in his summing-up. Almost in spite of himself he had to acknowledge that this was not the whole truth about his energetic guest. Even a poet whose feelings had been hurt could not fail to be aware of the warmth and generosity that were so fundamental a part of Jonson's nature, and Drummond ended his survey with a final sentence that was both just and acute: "He is passionately kind and angry, careless either to gain or keep, vindictive, but if he be well answered, at himself." Drummond, pursuing his sober, gentle way in the valley could only dimly understand Jonson storming among the hills, but he was aware of the Englishman's force however little he liked him.

The two men parted on outward terms of great cordiality, and Drummond asked Jonson to write out some verses for him as a farewell gift. Jonson sent him the manuscript in the middle of January with the following inscription: "To the honoring respect born of the friendship contracted with the right virtuous and learned Mr. William Drummond . . . I, Benjamin Jonson, whom he hath honored with the leave to be called his, have with mine own hand, to satisfy his request, written this imperfect song." The "imperfect song" was the little love lyric, "The Hour Glass." Jonson also sent Drummond a lighthearted and civilized portrait of himself as a lover that he called "a picture of myself."

I now think Love is rather deaf than blind,
    For else it could not be,
        That she,
Whom I adore so much, should so slight me,
    And cast my love behind.
I'm sure my language to her was as sweet
      And every close did meet
     In sentence, as of subtle feet,
        As hath the youngest He
That sits in shadow of Apollo's tree.


O, but my conscious fears,
    That fly my thoughts between,
    Tell me that she hath seen
      My hundred of gray hairs,
      Told seven and forty years,
Read so much waste, as she cannot embrace
    My mountain belly and my rocky face,
And all these through her eyes have stopped her ears.


So unconventional a lover was not the right sort of man to spend Christmas in the earnestly idealistic company of William Drummond.

After Jonson went back to England the two men exchanged a few letters. Jonson was planning to write a book about Scotland, with his own "adventures" set against a background of local color, and, being Jonson, he wanted everything accurate. He was prepared to check on the borough laws of Edinburgh, the appearance of Loch Lomond, and anything else that Drummond could tell him.

Drummond was a man who took his own letters seriously. He made careful first drafts and kept copies of all his correspondence in a register that bore the solemn title: "Letters Amorous, Complimental, Consolatory, Military, Historical." The letters to Jonson really needed a new heading, Instructional, for Jonson wished to be informed on a huge variety of subjects, from the form of the oath taken by Scottish knights to the "students' method" at St. Andrews. Drummond even sent him a complete list of all the emblems that the late Mary Queen of Scots had embroidered in silk thread on a bed of state.

Jonson apologized charmingly for making so many requests. "I hope they shall neither burden nor weary such a friendship, whose commands to me I will ever interpret a pleasure." Nevertheless, for all the polite sentiments on both sides, the friendship came to nothing, and anyone who had stopped by during those winter weeks at Hawthornden would have had no difficulty in understanding the reason.

# Chapter 23

THE SUMMER AFTER JONSON'S meeting with Drummond he paid a visit to another poet. He went to Oxford as the guest of Richard Corbet of Christ Church College. Jonson had known the Corbet family for some time, and when Richard's father died earlier this same year Jonson had written a very loving epitaph for him. He felt he had lost a "friend and father" in the gentle old man, and he apparently felt towards Vincent Corbet's only son as he might have felt towards a lively younger brother.

Richard Corbet, like Jonson, had gone to Westminster School, and, like Jonson, he had failed to win a university scholarship. Nevertheless he succeeded in entering Christ Church College, where he became famous for his jokes, his exploits and his irrepressible sense of fun. He trained for the ministry and finally became what one Oxford historian called "a most quaint preacher" and a special favorite of King James. Even after he became a bishop, Corbet persisted in writing verses. For this, "he was reproved by the graver sort; but those who knew him well took no notice of it." Nor did Corbet take much notice of the graver sort, since even in his old age he "loved boys' play very well."

Corbet's verses were not in the least like Drummond's. Whereas Drummond wrote delicate translations from French and Italian and mused on Phoebus and the nightingales, Corbet wrote lively, civilized, almost eighteenth-century verses on any subject that happened to catch his fancy. His most famous poem is his "Proper New Ballad Entitled the Fairies' Farewell," in which he gravely surveyed the current state of the fairies in England, but he could also write engaging verses on the dirt of Paris and the pretentions of the Puritans or compose a poem candidly entitled "Nonsense."

Corbet was the right sort of man to have Ben Jonson as a guest. They both appreciated good living and "boys' play" and did not hold with trying to maintain too much dignity, and if Corbet had written out a report of Jonson's visit it would have been very unlike Drummond's. Moreover, Oxford was not the sort of university that carefully counted the number of drinks a man might take. As one graduate remarked, "The whole time of my life besides did never so much transport me with drinking as that short time I lived at Oxford, and that with some of the gravest bachelors of divinity there."

Quite apart from Corbet's private hospitality, Christ Church College as a whole was delighted to welcome any graduate of Westminster School. When a Westminster boy went to Oxford on a school scholarship he always went to Christ Church, and it was the custom for the new arrivals to be welcomed there with what was called the Westminster Supper. The Dean and Chapter of the College had tried to suppress this supper on the grounds that it had grown to an "intolerable excess," but the institution was still flourishing when Jonson came to Oxford. Perhaps the Dean's heart had not really been in the suppression, for he was a graduate of Westminster School himself. So was the Dean before him. And as for the Dean that followed—that was Richard Corbet himself, who took the post a year after Jonson's visit at the early age of thirty-seven.

A short time after Corbet was made Dean of Christ Church College, John Donne was made Dean of St. Paul's. A Londoner was moved to remark that if only Ben Jonson could be made Dean of Westminster, the land would then be "furnished with three very pleasant poetical deans." If Jonson had entered Oxford in his teens instead of being apprenticed to a bricklayer, he might very well have been trained in divinity and ended in some high ecclesiastical position; he admitted to Drummond that he had "a mind to be a churchman." In that case some of his poetry might have come into being but there would have been no *Volpone* and no *Alchemist*, so perhaps it is just as well that Jonson was forced to conduct his education in his own way.

When Ben Jonson came to Oxford in 1619 he was one of the most learned men in England, and Oxford gave him the formal honor that the onetime bricklayer so thoroughly deserved. On the 17th of July, 1619, a letter from the Chancellor of Oxford was read out, suggesting that Jonson be given the honorary degree of Master of Arts, and two days later, in full Convocation, the degree itself was bestowed upon him.

Honorary degrees of this kind were not uncommon. The Chancellor of Oxford (who was Jonson's good friend, the Earl of Pembroke) had been given a similar one in 1605, when King James paid a visit to Oxford and nearly every nobleman in his train was given an M.A. William Camden was offered the same honor in 1613 and refused it, apparently feeling he was too old for an honorary degree to be of much value to him; and it was two less important individuals, John Walter and Thomas Fleming, who were given honorary degrees by Oxford that year. Three years later one of the recipients was Sir Francis Stewart, a literary friend of Jonson's and, like Camden, a graduate of Christ Church. When Jonson issued his collected works that same year, *Epicoene* appeared with a dedication to Sir Francis Stewart, which was a greater honor than Oxford could give him.

Although Camden had refused the degree of Master of Arts for himself, it must have been a great satisfaction to have it given to Jonson, for it was Camden who had started the small schoolboy on the road that led to this final honor from his beloved Oxford. Camden could not help feeling that his own university, his "dear nurse and mother," was more important than Cambridge. In his *Britannia* he had striven to be equally fair to "these two most flourishing universities of ours" but he gave less space to Cambridge, and he was a little facetious with some colleagues of his who tried to assign a very early date to its founding.

Jonson tactfully spoke of Oxford and Cambridge as those "most equal sisters" when he dedicated *Volpone* to them, and in fact they seem to have treated him in much the same way. When Jonson was in Scotland he told Drummond he was "Master of Arts in both the universities," so that both institutions must have planned at about the same time to give him honorary degrees. The only other known relationship between Jonson and Cambridge is that the president of St. John's College asked him to write some verses for a reception that was given King James when he visited there in March of 1615.

As a Master of Arts, Jonson must have had a very pleasant time at Oxford. He now had the right, for instance, to use Sir Thomas Bodley's collection of books, which was currently being called the University Library. The books were nobly housed, with all the dignity and exclusiveness that Bodley himself would have wished. The founder had refused to permit any playbooks on his shelves, because of the "scandal" they would bring to "so noble a library," and so all the quartos of Shakespeare's plays were safely excluded. But in its way it was a magnificent collection and Jonson, who was building a notable library of his own, would have had a happy time there.

Jonson could not linger at Oxford indefinitely. He was a Court poet as well as a scholar, and well before Christmas he was back in London working on his latest masque. He had not supplied a masque the previous Christmas, which he had spent with Drummond, and the gratifying news went up to Scotland that his "absence was regretted."

On a January day while Jonson was still in Scotland, the Banqueting Hall had burned down. Some people said the fire began when a workman kindled a flame to heat his gluepot, but the place was so crowded with paper and oiled cloth and dry fir boards that the only surprising thing was that the disaster had not happened earlier. The Privy Council hurried *en masse* to the scene, with the Earl of Pembroke in particular distinguishing himself as a fire fighter, and plans were immediately made to rear a much more splendid building with Inigo Jones as the designer.

Two months after the hall of the masques burned to the ground, the great patroness of the masques died. Queen Anne had endured a long illness, and she clung to the comforting presence of her two Danish attendants as she lay dying in state at Hampton Court. The Queen had been fairly happy in England with her banquets and her masques, "content in her own house with such recreations as might not make time tedious to her." But she had never been especially popular, and the outburst of grief that March was not caused by her death. It was occasioned by the death of Richard Burbage, chief actor of the King's Men, who died eleven days later. Middleton, who accused the Londoners of treating Burbage like a "mortal god on earth," said they had no right to mourn him more than their own queen. One rather extravagant versifier declared that some of Shakespeare's greatest heroes had vanished along with the man who had interpreted them.

> King Lear, the grieved Moor, and more beside
> That lived in him, have now forever died.

Most of Ben Jonson's best plays had been produced with Burbage heading the cast, and Jonson must have missed him both professionally and as a friend.

Queen Anne's responsibilities towards the masque were taken over by her son Charles, and when a warrant went out to the theatre people—"to warn Mr. Ben Johnson, the poet, and the players at the Blackfriars to attend his Highness that night following at Court"—the messenger was sent by the Prince's gentleman usher. Jonson called his masque for Charles *News from the New World,* and like the successful Welsh piece he had written for him earlier it was mostly in prose and briskly topical. Jonson mentioned his recent trip to Scotland with an aplomb that a lesser man might well envy. "One of our greatest poets (I know not how good a one) went to Edinburgh o' foot . . ."

Jonson did another masque during the summer, a pretty thing in the pastoral tradition, full of buttercups and cowslips, that he called *Pan's Anniversary*. It was apparently written for the King's birthday in June, and the following January Jonson assisted in celebrating the birthday of another important individual, the Lord Chancellor of England.

The Lord Chancellor was Sir Francis Bacon, who had at last found the high road to political success after a lifetime of delays and disappointments. He celebrated his birthday in York House, the great mansion that had been given him when he became Chancellor three years earlier; and he was celebrating not only his sixtieth birthday but the fact that he had recently become Viscount St. Albans and assumed a coronet.

Bacon was one of the very few people whom Jonson wholeheartedly admired, and Bacon apparently liked Jonson. When the poet set out for Scotland, Bacon remarked lightly that "he loved not to see poesie go on other feet than poetical dactyls and spondees" and Jonson repeated the mild joke. When he wrote the birthday song for the celebration at York House, he rejoiced that so great a man as Bacon had at last assumed his rightful place in the world.

> Hail, happy genius of this ancient pile!
> How comes it all things so about thee smile?
> The fire, the wine, the men . . .

Three months later the crash came. Bacon was arraigned before the House of Lords on a charge of taking bribes and had to plead guilty. He spent the remaining years of his life in poverty and disgrace, hounded by creditors and deprived of York House, but Jonson's admiration for him did not waver. "He seemed to me ever, by his work, one of the greatest men, and most worthy of admiration, that had been in many ages. In his adversity I ever prayed that God would give him strength, for greatness he could not want." The words are another man's, but Jonson copied them out because they expressed so exactly his own convictions.

As for Bacon himself, he crawled where he had to crawl and sent begging letters to James and Charles and Buckingham. But in his heart he never doubted that he would be vindicated to posterity. He saw himself in the company of Demosthenes, Cicero and Seneca—"all three persons that held chief place of authority in their countries; all three ruined . . . as delinquents and criminals; all three famous writers; insomuch as the remembrance of their calamity is now, as to posterity, but as a little piece of nightwork remaining amongst the fair and excellent tables of their acts and works." Bacon was right about himself. His faults and weaknesses as a man are now only "a little piece of nightwork" against the splendor of his scientific curiosity and the greatness of his writing.

The Parliament that destroyed Bacon was the Reform Parliament of 1621, and whatever the rights of the matter in the case of the great Chancellor there is no doubt that most of the reforms were long overdue. Graft had flourished all over England, with Whitehall as its center, and a long parade of witnesses came to give testimony in the House of Commons on the sort of conditions that Jonson had attacked in *The Devil is an Ass*. Jonson's Meercraft was exemplified in real life by Sir Giles Mompesson, a talented and unscrupulous projector who had been developing monopolies for licensing inns, for freighting, for special uses of sea coal and especially for the notorious patent on gold and silver thread. His business associate was Buckingham's brother, who was too "great a man" to be attacked by the cowed workmen in the trade, and the company was run on a vicious system of threats and extortions. Mompesson even possessed a warrant, signed by Chancellor Bacon, permitting the imprisonment of anyone who tried to interfere.

It is possible that all this dishonesty might have gone on

flourishing unchecked if the nation had been still enjoying the carefree prosperity of the previous decade. But a depression began to creep over England, and by the time Parliament convened there had already begun to be riots among the unemployed.

The cloth trade was especially hard hit, and the Londoners were inclined to blame Alderman Cockaigne and his greedy tinkering with cloth exports for the whole of the depression. When a spectacular fire destroyed his packed warehouse, his fellow citizens hailed it as the judgment of God on an evil man who had tried to destroy England through misuse of a monopoly. London had reason to be bitter, for the shops in that thriving city were beginning to stand empty. Even the owners of the splendid buildings in Goldsmiths' Row, "the beauty and glory of Cheapside," found there was no market for the luxury trades and began to rent out space to haberdashers instead of jewelers.

King James was shocked by this latest development, which apparently offended his aesthetic sense. After a visit to the city he announced firmly that all the "petty trades" would have to leave Goldsmiths' Row so that the beautiful gilded structures could go back to their original splendor. Six weeks after this weirdly unrealistic remark, James permitted the monopoly for gold and silver thread to be set up again "under color of a new corporation," and Sir Giles Mompesson, who had been banished from England by the Reform Parliament, was back in Whitehall again. Less than two years after the men of the Parliament had returned to their homes, the work they had done was destroyed.

James meant well, and his speech when he opened Parliament had been one of some humility. "Deal with me as I deserve at your hands; I will leave nothing undone that becomes a just king." But before the House of Commons disbanded, James had recovered his self-confidence and was lecturing them on their temerity in attempting to improve his kingdom. "We wish you to remember that we are an old and experienced king, needing no such lessons." It would have taken a stronger and more intelligent monarch than James to check the corruption that was flourishing in England, and the well-intentioned old man had the special handicap of being happily convinced that he was doing everything that could be expected of him.

Meanwhile, James was engaged on his pet project. He was trying to train Buckingham to become a great statesman who would rule England wisely and well under his protector's fatherly hand. Of all James' ideas this was probably the worst and yet like all James' ideas it seemed reasonable enough on the surface. Its only fault was that James was incapable of teaching good sense in politics and Buckingham was even more incapable of learning any.

James loved Buckingham deeply, for he gave the King just the sort of half-teasing and affectionate deference that the lonely old man had never found in his own sons. By now, Buckingham was calling the King his "dear dad" and the King was calling him his "sweet and dear child." When Buckingham married in 1620, the King widened his heart to include "Kate" and wrote anxious letters to his "sweet daughter" on the state of her health. James could even include Buckingham's greedy brothers and his fiercely ambitious mother in his affections, for the sake of the warmth and joy that Buckingham had brought into his life. All his life James had wanted to be loved, with that fatal longing that destroyed so many of the Stuarts, and now he had found the ideal family group. It was uncritical, devoted, not too clever and entirely of his own making. He could relax into it with perfect contentment and forget for a time that such things as depressions and Parliaments existed.

Buckingham had been made a marquis and had then been given the position of Lord High Admiral, and in 1620 he acquired a country estate worthy of his honors. It was a property in Rutlandshire that had belonged to the Countess of Bedford, a mansion on a hill surrounded by beautiful woods and not far from the home of his father-in-law, the Earl of Rutland.

The following summer, James arrived at Buckingham's estate of Burley-on-the-Hill for a visit. He was there on the third of August, which happened to be the anniversary of the day, seven years earlier, on which Buckingham had first been presented to James, and it was clear that a special masque was needed for the occasion.

The tone of the masque had to be exactly right, respectful yet lively and with an undertone of teasing, and Buckingham commissioned Ben Jonson to write it for him. Jonson knew all the noble performers well and was not likely to be awed by the occasion into turning out something dull. Buckingham's faith in him was completely justified, for Jonson turned out that charming and impudent piece, *The Gipsies Metamorphosed*.

The gipsies consisted of Buckingham, his brother-in-law and various young friends of his, who put walnut juice on their faces and memorized Jonson's jingling verse before they presented themselves at the head of a roving band. Since they were gipsies they were naturally expected to tell everyone's fortune, beginning with a lively one for the King.

> You live chaste and single and have buried your wife
> And mean not to marry by the line of your life.
> Whence he that conjectures your qualities learns
> You're a good honest man and have care of your bairns.

King James' talents as a scholar and writer came in for a kindly pat:

> Some book craft you have and are pretty well spoken . . .

Lines like this could never have been delivered by a hired actor; but everyone knew that it was Buckingham behind the walnut juice, and the speech was just impertinent enough to be entertaining.

The fortunes of the great ladies present were also told by the gipsies, and here Jonson had to tread warily. It needed a man who knew the Court well to negotiate the narrow line between a joke and an insult, but Jonson managed it triumphantly. Buckingham's wife Katherine was gently teased for her worshiping devotion to her husband.

> Lady, either I am tipsy
> Or you are to fall in love with a gipsy.
> Blush not, Dame Kate,
> For early or late
> I do assure you it will be your fate.

Husbands were not mentioned in the case of the host's mother, that redoubtable lady who had become Countess of Buckingham while her nondescript third husband remained a mere knight. Instead the praise was concentrated where it would please her, on her children like "George and Sue." Her daughter-in-law, Lady Purbeck, was given a studiously vague fortune that concentrated on her beauty and did not mention domestic matters; for her husband was going insane, and later in this same year she left him to live with another man. As for Lady Purbeck's mother, who had bitterly opposed a marriage into Buckingham's family, she was complimented with equal caution. Jonson knew where to be impudent and where to be careful, and Buckingham could not have chosen a better man.

Jonson liked to be as realistic as possible and he delved deeply into the whole matter of gipsy lore and gipsy language. It was actually thieves' slang rather than gipsy slang that Jonson used, for his reference book was one that had been compiled by a Kentish magistrate who studied the roving underworld of beggars that came his way. Thomas Harman had started his investigations as a hobby, but he became so fascinated by the people he encountered that he compiled an accurate sociological survey that was much used by poets and pamphleteers. It was Harman who recorded such familiar definitions as *prat* for *buttock* or *duds* for *clothes*, and Jonson was one of many writers who used him as a kind of dictionary.

In parts of the masque, and especially in the antimasque of

the villagers, Jonson achieved a cheery vulgarity of his own
that quite matched that of any wanderer of the road, and the
most indecent verses were the ones that were most popular.
The doggerel account of Cock-lorell and the Devil was copied
and recopied and exists in more transcripts than any other verse
of Jonson's. On the other hand, the gipsy masque is graced with
one of the most delicate and charming lyrics that Jonson ever
wrote:

> The faery beam upon you,
> The stars to glisten on you,
>    A moon of light
>    In the noon of night
> Till the firedrake hath o'er gone you.
>
> The wheel of fortune guide you,
> The boy with the bow beside you
>    Run aye in the way
>    Till the bird of day
> And the luckier lot betide you.

*The Gipsies Metamorphosed* was such a success that it clearly
had to be repeated. Two days later James left Burley-on-the-
Hill to visit Buckingham's father-in-law, the Earl of Rutland,
and the masque accompanied him. It was presented at Belvoir
Castle on the fifth of August and Jonson wrote a few lines to
fit the new host, who was now

> the good man of Bever,
> Our Buckingham's father.

Next month James was at Windsor and the masque followed
him there. But the King was now surrounded by Privy Councilors
instead of Buckingham's female relatives, and Jonson had
to make extensive alterations. He wrote a lighthearted prologue, apologizing for making yet a third appearance, and an
equally lighthearted epilogue apologizing for a slip in the text—

"Good Ben slept there, or else forgot"—and he kept up the
same tone in the fortunes of the various members of the Privy
Council. He started with his old friend, the Earl of Pembroke,
and just brushed impudence.

> You never yet helped your master to a wench.
> 'Tis well for your honor he's pious and chaste,
> Or you had most certainly been displaced.

The Lord Treasurer, Baron Montagu, had just paid twenty
thousand pounds to attain his office, and as one who frequently
had to wait for his pension Jonson gave him a delicate hint,

> To put all that have pensions soon out of their pain
> By bringing th' Exchequer in credit again.

He brought in all the current Court events—the Marquis of
Hamilton's having been "lately employed" in Scotland and the
Earl of Buccleuch's new regiment—and managed to be as light
and knowledgeable at Windsor as he had been at Burley. Buckingham paid him a hundred pounds for the masque and Jonson
deserved it.

King James was equally pleased with his Court poet and presented him with the reversion of the mastership of the Office of
the Revels. If the current head of the Office, Sir George Buck,
died or became incapacitated, and if Sir John Astley, who held
the succession to the Office, died also, then Ben Jonson would
possess that very lucrative position. Jonson never became the
head of the Office of the Revels, since Astley outlived him, but
the grant had something of the same value as a second mortgage
on a piece of land. There was not much likelihood of getting
the property, but money could be raised on the reversion.

King James presented Jonson with the Revels patent on the
fifth of October, a month after the third showing of the gipsy
masque. He had apparently been planning a further gesture of
approval, for a Cambridge man reported in September: "A

friend told me, this fair-time, that Ben Jonson was not knighted but escaped narrowly . . . His Majesty would have done it, had there not been means made . . . to avoid it."

Knighthood was an expensive honor and one that Jonson almost certainly could not afford. It may have gratified him to feel that he could have been Sir Benjamin Jonson; but he was already an honorary burgess in Edinburgh and a Master of Arts at Oxford, and in London and Westminster he possessed a better title: Ben Jonson, poet.

# Chapter 24

A T ABOUT THIS TIME, Ben Jonson was approached by two
old friends from the world of the theatre, John Heminges and Henry Condell. They were planning a memorial volume of the works of William Shakespeare, which
they hoped to have in print by 1622, and they wanted Jonson
to write some commendatory verses for the front of it.

Jonson had been writing verses of this kind for the last
twenty years or so, starting with a contribution to a book of
emblems written by a fellow Catholic in 1598. He had been
turning out commendatory verses ever since, praising the books
of well-known writers like Chapman and Fletcher or lesser
men like Farnaby and Wright. It was a service that literary men
were usually glad to do for each other, and since Jonson had
been a friend of Shakespeare's it was a reasonable request for
Heminges and Condell to make of him.

John Heminges had worked with Shakespeare since the company was originally formed in 1594. Now that Richard Burbage
was dead, Heminges and his close friend and neighbor, Henry
Condell, were the last survivors of what had been known as the
Chamberlain's company and they were wearing the memorial
rings that Shakespeare had left them in his will.

The acting company of which Heminges and Condell were
now the senior members owned all the plays that Shakespeare had
ever written. Half of them were still in manuscript, and many
of the rest were being sold in the bookstalls in inaccurate ver-

sions. The only way to protect Shakespeare's work from mutilation or loss was to put it into permanent form in a folio edition that would include every script in the company's hands, and Heminges and Condell said they had no other motive in planning the volume. "We have . . . collected them, and done an office to the dead, to procure his orphans guardians; without ambition either of self-profit or fame; only to keep the memory of so worthy a friend and fellow alive as was our Shakespeare."

The folio they had planned would not be a handsome production like Jonson's. It would have no elaborately engraved title page, no expensive paper, no careful print work or proofreading. There was no extra money available for that sort of thing. The work was done by a second-rate printer, and even at that the publication of the folio had to be delayed for a year, apparently to reorganize the financing.

Yet many people would have said that the format was too good for the material, since the book contained nothing but plays. The idea of putting ordinary theatre scripts into permanent folio form was still very new in spite of the fact that Jonson had included some of his plays in his printed works. But in his case the plays had been carefully selected and appeared along with masques and poems, while in Shakespeare's case the purchaser would find himself with a folio volume that contained nothing but plays. Folio publication was usually reserved for books on medicine or theology or some other equally solemn subject, while the public was accustomed to getting its plays in cheap little quarto volumes.

Heminges and Condell were attempting to appeal to the well-to-do and cultivated reading public in their new venture—the kind of a public that could afford to buy folios—and they knew they were taking a real risk. It would have been a different matter if Shakespeare were one of the writers whom it was correct to admire and whom every gentleman of the period was expected to know. In that case, the members of the middle class could have bought a folio edition of his plays with the happy conviction that they were being cultured. But Shakespeare was a common playhouse poet and he did not belong among the elect. When Henry Peacham published *The Complete Gentleman* in 1622, as a kind of general guide to gentility, he of course included a section on poetry since every gentleman liked to be well read. But Peacham's list of contemporary poets did not include Shakespeare, for Shakespeare was not the kind of writer a gentleman needed to know.

Heminges and Condell were well aware of this difficulty but there was very little that could be done about it. The plays had to be printed in folio, since thirty-six plays in quarto would have made so short and thick a volume as to be unmanageable. The only thing to do was to issue the book under the best possible auspices, and with great wisdom the two actors dedicated it to the Earl of Pembroke and his brother, the Earl of Montgomery. Heminges and Condell admitted that the two earls could hardly be expected "to descend to the reading of these trifles" but in the case of the Earl of Pembroke at least they knew that they had a friendly and influential patron. As Lord Chamberlain and the supervisor of all entertainments at Court he had done many special services for the King's Men, and when Richard Burbage died the Earl of Pembroke had mourned him sincerely. He evidently knew and liked Shakespeare's plays, and Heminges and Condell could not have dedicated the book to a better man.

The position of the Earl of Pembroke at Court was the position of Ben Jonson in the world of letters. By 1622 Jonson was the leading poet in England and a kind of dean of literary affairs. He had for his readers just the people that Peacham would have called gentlemen, and a kind word or two from the poet laureate would give the Shakespeare folio the literary tone it needed. The other three poets who had agreed to contribute commendatory verses had no special reputation with the general public, and Heminges and Condell really needed Jonson.

Fortunately the two actors knew him very well and had worked with him over a period of many years. It was nearly a quarter of a century since they had both appeared in Jonson's first classical comedy, *Every Man in his Humour*, and since then they had appeared in *Every Man out of his Humour*, *Sejanus*, *Volpone*, *The Alchemist* and *Catiline*. The cast of his last play for the company, *The Devil is an Ass*, is not available, but it is probable that Heminges and Condell played in that one also. Heminges' son William had recently graduated from Jonson's Westminster School and gone to Christ Church on a scholarship. He was hoping to become a playwright, and after he started his literary career it was Ben Jonson he singled out for special praise.

Quite apart from his friendship for Heminges and Condell, Jonson had been a friend of Shakespeare's also. There was every reason to believe that he would be willing to help out two theatre colleagues and honor an old friend of his by writing a few suitable lines for the proposed volume.

On the other hand, the plays of Shakespeare stood for everything that Jonson disapproved of in the theatre and everything he had fought against in his long career as a playwright. Shakespeare had not followed the classical rules except in *The Comedy of Errors*, which came at the very beginning of his career. He had never written a realistic play that mirrored contemporary London and he had not kept to the dramatic types that were so clearly laid down by the rule-makers. He had mingled comedy and tragedy, clowns and kings, in a way that Sir Philip Sidney would have deplored. He had been careless about his sources, brought in farce and dances and melodrama to amuse the lowest elements in his audience, and in general had produced an untidy, sprawling body of work that a true classicist could only regard with something approaching despair. Over and over again Jonson had deplored the low state of the contemporary theatre and insisted that it could only be raised by following the classic ideal, and long before he mentioned it to Drummond he had made no secret of his conviction that Shakespeare lacked "art."

Heminges and Condell knew all this, and they would have been content with something from Jonson's pen that was brief, polite and generalized. Jonson could praise Shakespeare in a vaguely courteous way as a friend and fellow dramatist without committing himself to outright approval of a way of writing so unlike his own.

When Jonson sat down to write his verses on Shakespeare for the folio project of Heminges and Condell, he may have intended to write no more than a few noncommittal lines on the dead playwright who had been his friend. But Jonson was a great man and an honest one, and he found himself face to face with something older than the rules. He found in Shakespeare's plays what he had reverenced all his life and what had made him a classicist only because he had wanted to clothe it worthily—the spirit of poetry.

Jonson believed that the classical writers were the greatest in the world, but he had never reverenced them blindly. "They opened the gates, and made the way, that went before us; but as guides, not commanders." Shakespeare had opened his own gate and made his own way, and Jonson was able to forget a lifetime of traveling a different road and give Shakespeare the honor that was due him.

> Soul of the age!
> The applause! delight! the wonder of our stage!
> My Shakespeare, rise. I will not lodge thee by
> Chaucer or Spenser or bid Beaumont lie
> A little further, to make thee a room;
> Thou art a monument without a tomb,
> And art alive still, while thy book doth live,
> And we have wits to read, and praise to give.

Jonson refused to compare Shakespeare to the playwrights of his own generation, Marlowe and Lyly and Kyd. Instead the great classicist turned, not even to the Romans he had worshiped but to the Greeks who had themselves been worshiped by the Romans—"thundering Aeschylus, Euripides and Sophocles." Jonson refused to believe that Shakespeare was a local English playwright who wrote for his generation only. He be-

lieved that he was an immortal whose plays would last forever
and bring glory to England all over the world.

> Triumph, my Britain, thou hast one to show
> To whom all scenes of Europe homage owe.
> He was not of an age, but for all time.

This judgment of Jonson's is the only contemporary piece of
writing on Shakespeare that assigns him the position he now
holds. Several other contemporary playwrights—Drayton, Beaumont, Heywood and Webster—wrote favorably of Shakespeare
and his work, but there was usually a touch of patronage in
their remarks and never any indication that here was a giant
who towered over them all. In general, Shakespeare's contemporaries did not take him seriously as an artist or give him the
praise that is now considered his due. The only poet who was
capable of writing the magnificent and fitting tribute that stands
in the front of the First Folio was the classicist, Ben Jonson.
When Jonson was confronted directly with the plays as a whole
he had the greatness to see Shakespeare as he was; and there is
nothing in all Jonson's career that does him more honor than
the honor he was willing to do Shakespeare.

Long ago, in *Poetaster*, Jonson had written a description of
Vergil's work that might almost have served for Shakespeare's.

> 'Tis so rammed with life
> That it shall gather strength of life, with being,
> And live hereafter more admired than now.

It was this vitality in Shakespeare that Jonson recognized even
when later on, in one of his notebooks, he criticized him for it.
"He flowed with that facility, that sometime it was necessary
he should be stopped." In Jonson's eyes, Shakespeare was a kind
of torrent, while his own poetic ideal, like Horace's, was a
symmetrical lake; and it was an extraordinary feat of mental de-
tachment on Jonson's part to be able to praise so eloquently the

work of a man whose point of view as a writer was diametrically opposed to his own.

When Jonson's career is compared with Shakespeare's, the result is a curious paradox. It was Shakespeare, not Jonson, who led the narrowly dedicated life and who focused his colossal powers on one thing only. Jonson talked a great deal about reforming the stage but he spent a comparatively small part of his time writing for it, while Shakespeare worked for the theatre and for the theatre only. The great torrent flowed through narrow banks, gathering the strength, the intensity and the complete control that made his plays possible. Outside of his work for the stage, Shakespeare left nothing on paper except two narrative poems he wrote before he joined the company, a collection of sonnets whose date is unknown, and a brief contribution to "The Phoenix and Turtle." Of all the poets of the Elizabethan and Jacobean stage, it was only Shakespeare of whom it could be said that his collected plays and his collected works were almost the same thing. This whole-souled dedication has no parallel in any other writer of the period and certainly not in Ben Jonson.

The year in which the Shakespeare folio was issued there was a fire in Ben Jonson's house and all the manuscripts in his desk were burned. Jonson wrote a remarkably good-natured poem on the subject, a mock-heroic attack on the god of fire that he called "An Execration upon Vulcan," and in the course of the poem he gives a list of what his desk contained.

Among the manuscripts destroyed were "the parcels of a play" but nothing else in his desk had any connection with the theatre. He had been planning to write a full account of his journey to Scotland and hoped to include a survey of Scottish scenery and customs. He was working on an English Grammar. He had finished a survey of the art of poetry, with a discussion of the precepts of Aristotle and Horace. He had been working for the past twenty-four years on a religious work which he called "humble gleanings in divinity." He had been writing a life of Henry the Fifth and both Selden and Cotton had been lending him books on the subject. He had also been planning, as he told Drummond, a history of all the great men of England, told in couplets and designed as a kind of "epic poem." And he had also, as the Stationers' Register for that year testifies, nearly completed a translation of a Latin romance called *Argenis*.

A long list like this shows the vigor of Jonson at fifty but it also shows how thin he was spreading himself. He certainly did not have enough personal interest in *Argenis* to undertake the enormous job of turning nearly five hundred pages of Latin prose into English; but the author had been a friend of King James and the book itself was popular. *Argenis* was a political romance and since everyone felt that famous contemporaries could be recognized under the fictional names, the price of the Latin edition had tripled at the bookstores. Many English readers were no doubt delighted to hear that "the King hath given order to Ben Jonson to translate it"; but Jonson himself could have taken no pleasure in the book's ornate pseudoclassicism, and this was one manuscript whose destruction he probably did not mourn. He never attempted to replace it, and when the English version finally appeared it was by a translator so unsure of himself that he told his readers to compare his text "with the original Latin, and mend it."

Since Jonson was poet laureate, he could not very well refuse to execute a direct order from King James. On the whole, Jonson showed remarkable independence in his dealings with the Court and James never asked anything unreasonable of him. But there was nevertheless a kind of subtle, indirect pressure exerted on Jonson through the Court audience he worked for, the audience that preferred the cheap doggerel of his Cocklorell song to anything else he had written.

Long ago, at the beginning of his career, Jonson had dreamed of being able to attract an ideal audience that would help him, in turn, to become an ideal poet.

> Good men and virtuous spirits . . .
> Will cherish my free labours, love my lines,
> And with the fervor of their shining grace
> Make my brain fruitful to bring forth more objects
> Worthy their serious and attentive eyes.

Assisted by this select and sober audience he would be able to reform the drama, reform the masque, reform the epigram and even reform England, raising it up to the noble height of the Augustan days in Rome.

Unlike Shakespeare, Jonson could not accept things as they were and settle down to write for ordinary people. His theoretical temperament demanded an audience consisting of select and dedicated spirits, and of course he never found them. Instead he did most of his work for a stupid, self-indulgent and greedy Court, and searched earnestly for the great men he felt must be in it somewhere. As Jonson admitted in some verses to his friend John Selden, he had sometimes

> praised some names too much,
> But 'twas with purpose to have made them such.

The great moralist thought he could raise the little Jacobean lordlings to the height of his own dream by holding its image up before them, and the very loftiness of Jonson's attempt doomed it to failure. A masque like *Hymenaei*, with its massive, noble, scholarly appeal to virtue, was written for the wedding of the evil Frances Howard, and no one really cared that Jonson had taken the trouble to have it "grounded upon antiquity and solid learnings." His Court entertainments now had less and less learning in them and more and more topical jokes; and although *The Masque of Augurs*, which he wrote in 1622, bears witness to Jonson's laborious research in a huge mass of marginal Latin notes, the elaborate commentary keeps uneasy company with a comic introduction in prose and a ballad about dancing bears.

Jonson had not forsaken his dream. He never forsook it. But the enormous vigor that was required to put it into practice was beginning, little by little, to forsake him and there was nothing in the atmosphere of the Court to help him regain his strength. If Shakespeare's art was a river that found part of its strength through being forced to run through narrow banks, Jonson's was a river that was beginning to lose itself in dry sand.

# Chapter 25

**B**EN JONSON'S MASQUES were becoming so topical that they were almost journalistic. They had taken on a little of the tone of the "comical satires" he had written when he was a young man, and the masque that was produced on the 19th of January, 1623, included a direct personal attack on a fellow poet.

The poet was George Wither. He is chiefly remembered today for his lively love verses, and especially the famous

> Shall I, wasting in despair,
> Die because a woman's fair?

But Jonson looked upon him as a platitudinous and conceited fool who not only wrote bad verses but succeeded in selling them at the rate of thirty thousand copies in less than a year.

There was a certain amount of justification for Jonson's attitude. Most of Wither's verses were a commonplace glorification of middle-class virtues, chastising sin in interminable couplets that any sewing woman could repeat with satisfaction, and Wither himself showed a certain smugness in his championship of morality. He styled himself "Wither, the man that would not flatter" and inserted a self-portrait in the front of one of his volumes. It shows the poet crowned with laurel, spurning the world with his foot, leaning against a pillar to symbolize his fortitude and lit with divine rays that come from a cloud labeled "Jahveh."

Jonson was also a satirist with a reputation for attacking sin; and a man like George Wither, with his self-confidence, his sense of dedication and his very high opinion of himself, was a kind of second-rate imitation of Jonson. Jonson had been furious with John Taylor for imitating his foot-journey into Scotland, and he was equally furious with Wither for duplicating his own stand as virtue's champion and doing it in bad verse.

Jonson introduces Wither into his masque of *Time Vindicated* and has him announce his virtues in lines that are a skillful parody of Wither's own smug meters:

> When have I walked the streets but happy he
> That had the finger first to point at me . . .
> The sempster hath sat still as I passed by
> And dropped her needle. Fishwives stayed their cry . . .

It was not only the simple people of London who loved Wither and repeated his rhymes. The learned Dr. Alexander Gill, headmaster of St. Paul's School, had publicly compared him to Juvenal, and so Jonson introduced Dr. Gill into the masque also. Jonson had a profound admiration for Juvenal, and to have Wither exalted to so Roman an eminence was the final outrage in the eyes of that serious classicist.

Jonson's introduction of personal satire was not approved by some members of the Whitehall audience. "Ben Johnson, they say, is like to hear of it on both sides of the head for personating George Wither, a poet or poetaster as he terms him, as hunting after fame by being a . . . whipper of the time." The political atmosphere had become so hysterically touchy by 1623 that the whole subject of libel was getting more attention than it deserved. It had become "so tender . . . it must not be touched either in jest or earnest," and a few days earlier old Dr. White had made an inoffensive remark that was "interpreted as a kind of libel" merely because it mentioned the King and Prince Charles in connection with religion.

The basic reason why the question of libel had become so

"tender" was that Prince Charles was to be married to the Infanta of Spain and the English nation as a whole opposed the idea bitterly. James believed that such an alliance would remove permanently the threat of war and had been working over the match for years; when Jonson wrote a fortune for Prince Charles in the gipsy masque he gave him a Spanish bride with a "little James" to follow as an heir. But the Spanish were still making difficulties and Buckingham became convinced that everything could be ironed out if he and the Prince went to Spain in person.

When Buckingham had first arrived at the English Court, Charles was a suspicious adolescent who disliked him because of his ascendancy over King James, but since then he had fallen helplessly under the spell of the same sunny magic that had delighted his father. He came to depend on Buckingham's light heart, on his jokes and his tact and his affectionate teasing, and it was not long before he was signing his letters, "Your loving, faithful, constant friend." Anything that Buckingham suggested was agreeable to Charles, even so harebrained a project as a secret journey to Spain.

Both Charles and Buckingham had danced in Jonson's latest masque of *Time Vindicated* and normally they would have taken part in the Shrovetide festivities that followed. Instead the startled Court heard that they had left England secretly to get the Spanish Infanta and bring her back with them.

The two young men set out from London on horseback, "with disguised beards and with borrowed names of Thomas and John Smith." They were nearly detected at Gravesend because they tipped too lavishly, had to leap hedges at Rochester to avoid the coach of the French ambassador, and with difficulty became "untwined" at Canterbury after the local officials became suspicious of them. Buckingham sent a series of lively letters to their "dear dad," reporting to James that his son had been the first to be sick during the Channel crossing but Buckingham had kept it up longer, and that Charles had not fallen once from his horse on the way to Paris whereas Buckingham had tumbled four times. They were accompanied by Endymion Porter, who had played the third gipsy in Jonson's masque, and after various adventures they reached Madrid on the first of March.

King James lived for their letters and could repeat them almost word for word to anyone who would listen. The sentimental old Stuart had gone overseas for his own bride in his youth, and he felt that his two "sweet boys and dear venturesome knights" were acting out a real-life romance that no one could fail to admire. He became a kind of substitute father to Buckingham's small daughter, letting her play with his watch and sending off a bulletin that she now had four teeth. He also made her father a duke and sent his love by every boat that sailed. "God bless you, my sweet boys, and send you . . . a joyful, happy return to the arms of your dear dad."

The Spanish Infanta had no wish to marry a heretic, and the average Englishman did not want a Roman Catholic queen. Nevertheless the preparations for the marriage went forward, and by June matters were so near to completion that a committee was sent to Southampton to superintend the landing arrangements for the happy couple.

The committee included various high Court officials, to look impressive, but Inigo Jones and Edward Alleyn were expected to do most of the actual work. Both of them were men of experience in staging receptions and of high standing in the community. Alleyn had long since retired from acting but he still had a share in a London theatre and had been for many years in control of the royal bear-baiting. He was now a rather elderly man of property, highly praised for his founding of Dulwich College, and it was later in this same year that he startled London by marrying Dr. John Donne's young daughter Constance.

It annoyed Ben Jonson profoundly that Alleyn and Jones should have been appointed to the committee when he himself was not. He was so displeased, in fact, that he wrote a poem in which he stated loftily that he was quite above any petty personal annoyance in the matter. He said it was nothing to him that he had not been chosen to help with the "reception" and had been exposed to "neglect," although his reputation was hardly less than that of a puppet-master like Jones or a bear-warden like Alleyn. According to Jonson, the wise man lived secure within himself, where he could never be affected by the buffets of fortune.

The elaborate plans of the Southampton committee came to nothing, for the Infanta never arrived. Charles and Buckingham returned alone, and the people of England felt their prayers had been answered. They had been filling the churches for months, hoping that the Lord would deliver them from a marriage alliance with Spain, and when the Prince returned without his intended bride they went "mad with excess of joy" and lit bonfires all over England. Buckingham had made a complete failure of the intricate marriage negotiations, and so he became a hero in the popular mind for having saved the country from the dangers of popery.

Prince Charles returned to England in October, and a little later in the same month, Jonson was able to be of service to a woman whose husband had been destroyed because King James was hoping for an alliance with Spain. The wife of Sir Walter Raleigh was now a widow, and her son Wat was dead. Raleigh had gone on an expedition to look for gold on the Orinoco River, taking his son with him, and Wat had been killed in an abortive attack on a Spanish town. Raleigh had been brought up on the Elizabethan conviction that killing Spaniards was a worthy occupation, but when he returned to England he was beheaded on an old charge of treason that had been suspended but never withdrawn. The government was obliged to issue a special pamphlet justifying his death, and even the headsman knelt to ask the forgiveness of so gallant a foe of Spain. But James was trying to construct an alliance with Spain, and so Raleigh died.

His widow, the Lady Elizabeth, became involved in a suit with a London jeweler who was disposing of the family plate and jewels. He had sued her successfully and she was appealing the verdict in the Court of Chancery. Raleigh had made a listing of his debts, and Ben Jonson was called into court, as a document recently discovered by C. J. Sisson shows, to identify the handwriting. On the twentieth of October, 1623, he testified that he was "very well acquainted with the handwriting of Sir Walter Raleigh" and certified that the papers were his. It is pleasant to know that Jonson was able to be of service to the mother of his former pupil, for she had had what she would have called a "trubbellsum" life and needed friends.

Jonson testified at the time of the suit that his current residence was Gresham College. The splendid town house of Sir Thomas Gresham had been converted into a college for London merchants, with special quarters set aside for the professors, and it has been suggested that Ben Jonson was teaching there. The Professor of Rhetoric at Gresham College was Henry Croke, who had been given the position four years earlier as the youngest professor to be selected up to that time. If Jonson was doing any teaching it would have been as Croke's deputy, but there is no evidence that Croke ever had a deputy or that he ever failed to give satisfaction. He taught for "eight years with good reputation and esteem" and only left because he was going to get married. Nor was it necessary to be a teacher to live at Gresham College, since a friend of Jonson's, Sir Kenelm Digby, stayed there for some time after his wife's death. Jonson had a special reason for living in temporary quarters in the autumn of 1623, since there had just been the fire in his own house that he memorialized in the "Execration upon Vulcan."

Very little is known about Jonson's private life, and in general it is nearly impossible to say where he was living at any given time. Drummond shared this same difficulty with posterity, since in two of the letters he wrote Jonson from Scotland he explained that he had been delayed because he did not know what address to use. "The uncertainty of your abode was a cause of my silence this time past." Drummond finally sent off one packet while he still lacked a definite address, convinced that Ben Jonson was so famous that there could not be "any place either of the City or Court where he shall not be found out."

Jonson apparently did a great deal of visiting. He spent five years with Lord Aubigny, and there are records of his visits to country houses as the guest of men like Sir Robert Cotton, Sir Robert Sidney and Sir Henry Goodyere. But for many years he had a permanent address in the Blackfriars. The dedication of *Volpone* was written at "my house in the Blackfriars this 11 of February, 1607"; and in 1616, when Thomas Coryat wrote a letter from India to his friends in London, he sent a special message "to Master Benjamin Johnson, the poet, at his chamber at the Blackfriars."

By 1620 Jonson may conceivably have been living in Cripplegate, since one of Prince Charles' grooms went "by Cripplegate" to order his attendance at Court for a masque. And if this is true, he may very well have been the Benjamin Johnson who is listed in the parish register of St. Giles, Cripplegate, as having married one Hester Hopkins on the twenty-seventh of July, 1623. If the identification is correct, Jonson could not have been serving as a teacher in Gresham College that same autumn, since Sir Thomas Gresham had made it plain in his will that he shared the usual prejudice of the period against married teachers. "None shall be chosen to read any of the said lectures as long as he shall be married, nor be suffered to read any of the said lectures after he shall be married." This custom, which forced Henry Croke to leave his professorship as soon as he married, was the last remnant of the powerful medieval tradition that all teachers were "clerks" and therefore celibate.

If it is difficult to trace Jonson's places of residence, it is even more difficult to trace the members of his family. There was an "Elisib, daughter of Ben Johnson," christened in Whitechapel in 1610, who may have been an illegitimate daughter, and a second son named Benjamin who died while Jonson was living in the Blackfriars. Thomas Fuller, Jonson's first biographer and a careful man, said that he "was not very happy in

his children, and most happy in those which died first, though
none lived to survive him." Whatever else may be said about
Jonson's private life, it is clear that he was not a domestic man.
He would not have made a satisfactory husband for any woman
who longed for regular habits and a quiet, stable atmosphere.

When he was fifty Jonson was still writing love lyrics, and
his series of ten to "Charis" are as graceful a compliment as any
Court lady ever received. His love poems are those of a civilized
and experienced man, although towards the end he seems to relax into a willingness to make love in verse only.

> Let me be what I am, as Vergil cold,
>     As Horace fat, or as Anacreon old . . .
> Who shall forbid me then in rime to be
>     As light and active as the youngest he?

As he said, he had been working for twenty years among the
jewels and satins at Court and was not likely to be dazzled by
what looked so magical to an outsider.

> I who live, and have lived twenty year,
>     Where I may handle silk as free and near
> As any mercer . . .
> Have eaten with the beauties and the wits
>     And braveries of Court, and felt their fits
> Of love and hate . . .

Ben Jonson behaved with the ladies of the Court not as a
servant but as an equal. He could begin a sonnet to Lady Mary
Wroth with engaging familiarity—

> I that have been a lover, and could show it . . .

and his verses have the same tone he showed twenty years
earlier when he sent a special copy of *Cynthia's Revels* to the
"bright and amiable Lucy," Countess of Bedford.

Jonson's relations with women were similar to his relations

with men. He gave as much as he received and succeeded in behaving like an equal even in the Court atmosphere, thick with privilege and ceremony, in which so much of his time was spent.

One of the earliest of Jonson's friends, whom he had faithfully loved for more than forty years, died less than a month after Jonson had given his testimony for Lady Raleigh. William Camden had been failing in health for some time, and his many friends could not grieve too much when he died quietly at his home in Kent and was brought back to Westminster Abbey for burial. Camden had left most of his books and manuscripts to his former student, Sir Robert Cotton, to be added to Cotton's own collection, and the following year the University of Oxford issued a volume of tributes to him in Greek and Latin. Jonson was apparently not asked to contribute to the memorial to Camden, but the praise he had written already existed in Jonson's collected works and Camden had had the satisfaction of reading it.

What Jonson had learned from Camden he passed on to younger men; for whether or not he was ever formally a teacher Jonson had all the instincts of a schoolmaster and a good one. Part of Jonson's great success with young men came from the fact that he stimulated them mentally, giving them lively new visions of art and living, and yet at the same time made them feel that they had encountered something that was solidly rooted and thoroughly reliable. The young disciples he gathered around him were already beginning to be known as the Tribe of Ben; and Jonson, who was always at his best and most generous when he was being admired, expanded into a beneficent sun around which circled, like respectful planets, half the young writing men of London.

London was full of informal clubs, as it had been back in the days when Francis Beaumont was writing verses about the Mermaid Tavern. The group at the Mermaid had been meeting regularly enough to be called a club, since a letter from Coryat in 1616 mentions "the right worshipful fraternity of sirenical gentlemen that meet the first Friday of every month at the sign of the Mermaid in Bread Street." It was not, however, until eight years later that Jonson organized a real club of his own. It was started in 1624 and with a characteristic regard for the one great preoccupation of his life Jonson called it the Apollo.

The Apollo Club was housed in a large room at the back of the second floor of a popular tavern in Fleet Street which stood nearly opposite St. Dunstan's Church. The sign of the tavern commemorated that notable occasion on which St. Dunstan had tweaked the Devil's nose with pincers from his forge, and the full name of the tavern, the Devil and St. Dunstan's, had been conveniently shortened to the Devil. It was presided over by a skillful tavernkeeper named Simon Wadloe who had taken the place over in 1608 and built it up into one of the best taverns in the London area. By June of 1624 the Devil possessed a "fair room or chamber lately built" which housed the Apollo Club, and Jonson had composed a set of rules in Latin to indicate how the club was going to be run.

Except for the fact that Jonson was prepared to admit women to his gatherings, his principles would have been considered sound by any English clubman of a later generation. He expected good wine, good food and deft, silent waiters, and he did not wish to have any music with his meals. He expected his fellow members to be good talkers and good drinkers, with all fools, sulkers and arguers banished from the premises. He wished no one to break windows, tear down hangings or start drinking contests, and club members were not to repeat to the general public what had been talked about. Jonson put his twenty-four rules into elegant Latin prose, and they were passed about London with a good deal of interest.

Since Jonson was the acknowledged lord of the club, he had a raised seat at one end, with a handrail to help the increasingly stout poet to get up to it. The guiding spirit of the club— Apollo, god of poetry—was honored with a beautifully painted terra-cotta bust, crowned with a wreath; and beneath the bust was a warning, composed by Jonson, on the dire results of drinking nothing but water.

> He the half of life abuses
> That sits watering with the Muses.
> Those dull girls no good can mean us;
> Wine, it is the milk of Venus.

In the next century the Devil tavern was still flourishing, and Dr. Samuel Johnson gave a supper there to celebrate the publication of a friend's book. Dr. Johnson was also a literary dictator and a clubman and as convivial as his great predecessor, and the occasion went well. Dr. Johnson's large face "shone with meridian splendor" but the great days of the Devil tavern were nevertheless over. In fact, it is doubtful if Ben Jonson would have been willing to acknowledge his successor as a writer at all, for Dr. Johnson drank something almost worse than water. He went through the whole evening on lemonade.

# Chapter 26

B EN JONSON SUPPLIED HIS USUAL Twelfth Night masque
for 1624, since a Court poet was, as he said, "a kind of
Christmas engine, one that is used at least once a year."
It celebrated the return of Prince Charles, and Jonson called it
*Neptune's Triumph for the Return of Albion*. The masque
contained a running fire of topical references, and Jonson even
introduced a gift that the King of Spain had sent the previous
July—five elephants and a camel that were led through London
after midnight in the apparent hope that they would "pass
unseen."

Charles and Buckingham had practiced their parts in the
masque "diligently" but in the end it was not produced. The
Spanish match was still a possibility but a French match was
being increasingly discussed; and since there was no tactful way
to accommodate both the French and the Spanish ambassadors
in the audience at the Banqueting Hall, the only thing to do was
to call off the masque entirely.

By the following Christmas it was evident that Prince Charles
was going to marry the French princess and Jonson supplied a
masque called *The Fortunate Isles*. The comic material from
last year's masque did not fit this year's requirements, and Jonson thriftily used some of it in his next play. But much of the
lyric material could be kept intact except that the lines were
now celebrating a different marriage alliance, that of "the
bright Lily and the Rose."

The Rose was Prince Charles, and he and Buckingham were beginning to show signs of a political imbecility beside which King James was a tower of good sense. Encouraged by their current popularity with Parliament, they decided to declare war on Spain and avenge themselves on Buckingham's political enemies in England; and the old king argued in vain with his son and his protégé. He told Buckingham in his wrath what was the literal truth—"By God, Stenny, you are a fool"—and then he turned on Charles and told him with equal fury "that he would live to have his bellyful of parliaments."

Throughout the whole of his reign James had fought passionately to keep the peace. He had humbled himself repeatedly during the long negotiations with Spain because he believed that this was the best way to keep his country out of war; and he was currently enduring the ridicule of Europe and the displeasure of all right-minded Protestants for not rising in the "majestic indignation" that was expected of him to take the side of his Protestant son-in-law in Europe. If he had, he would have involved England in that hideous and meaningless conflict, the Thirty Years' War, but the average Englishman was nevertheless a little ashamed of his sovereign for being so unmartial.

Throughout this whole period the Continent was ravaged by wars, and 1610 was the only year in which all the European states were at peace. Yet no ruler except James seemed to be capable of realizing that these wars were not only preventable but solved nothing. As Sully said: "When I consider Europe as composed of such civilized people, I cannot but be astonished that she still continues to be governed by principles so narrow and customs so barbarous . . . War is the recourse of all places and upon all occasions; she knows no other way and conceives no other expedients . . . Why must we always impose on ourselves the necessity of passing through wars to arrive at peace?"

King James was almost the only sovereign in Christendom who could conceive of the possibility of "other expedients," but he knew that his subjects wanted war. As he lay dying, "he prophesied that, when he was dead, they should have more war than they knew how to manage." His prophecy came true, and the Englishmen of the next twenty years could look back to the lost tranquility of the Jacobean age as to something that had happened in a dream.

King James was in many ways a fool and in many ways weak, yet his long reign of twenty-two years cannot be called a failure. He kept his country out of war, which was something Queen Elizabeth had also struggled for but had failed to achieve. He avoided an open break with Parliament, although the basic problem of the rights of the people as opposed to the prerogative of the Crown had been gathering momentum in the previous reign and even Elizabeth, for all her tact, had trouble with her last Parliament. He advocated religious toleration, although he found few to agree with his conviction that no "religion or heresy was ever extirpated by violence or the sword"; and one of the greatest achievements of the seventeenth century, the King James Version of the Bible, was the direct result of his interest in religion.

James had many personal faults, but he was pathetically willing to admit most of them. He had, for instance, a violent temper, and when an old Groom of the Bedchamber named John Gib denied losing some valuable papers, the King kicked him. James was in a highly nervous state at the time, since the news from Protestant Europe was bad and the Spanish alliance was in danger. Then James found the papers and knew he had been unjust, and "he kneeled down to Gib and would not rise till he had pardoned him." After James went to bed at night he used to remember all the occasions during the day when he had been "overtaken with passion" and would call in some patient ecclesiastic to help him pray "for the forgiveness of his sins." James meant to be a good man and a good king, and on the whole he did not fail utterly.

He was unquestionably a good king as far as Ben Jonson was concerned. Jonson knew him well, and in *The Gipsies Metamorphosed* he gives a long rhymed survey of the royal tastes and point of view that is not far from being a full-length portrait. It is a half-teasing portrait, for James was not a monarch who insisted on formality, and Jonson's affectionate and admiring epigrams to "my James" are those of a contented subject.

King James can hardly be credited with the great flowering of English poetry and prose that occurred in his lifetime, but it is undeniable that he helped create the background against which it could flourish. If the King had disliked the theatre, for instance, and had failed to extend his full support to Shakespeare's company, the increasing Puritan pressure in London would almost certainly have forced the King's Men to disband. In that case *Macbeth* and *King Lear* would not have been written, and Jonson could not have produced *Volpone* and *The Alchemist*.

King James respected scholars and writers, although he did not always choose the best ones to support, and Robert Burton was not exaggerating beyond all reason when he called him a "patron, pillar and sustainer of learning." Towards the end of his life he took an active interest in a projected Royal Academy and discussed the final arrangements with Edmund Bolton on his summer progress in 1624. Bolton had made up a list of learned gentlemen, including Ben Jonson, John Selden, George Chapman, Sir Robert Cotton and so on, who were to meet once a year at Windsor Castle, each decorated with a green ribbon and a special device, as the members under a royal charter of what was to have been a kind of "English Olympus." But King James died the following year, and Edmund Bolton's dream of a Royal Academy died with him.

James fell ill early in March of what was called the tertian ague—a term about as vague as the modern use of "influenza." He bore his illness patiently for so impatient a man and died at his beloved Theobalds on the twenty-seventh of March, 1625. His body was brought back to London in a black velvet coach that went through the town by torchlight, accompanied by the "ceaseless rain" that had plagued England all that spring, and he was buried in the Abbey after a magnificent funeral. Inigo Jones, who designed the royal hearse, saved the government a great deal of money by forming the figures that supported the canopy of plaster of Paris and muslin instead of marble, but, even so, the funeral cost more than fifty thousand pounds. It was a fitting conclusion to the career of a monarch who had always spent money lavishly—a kind of final, expensive entertainment provided by the King who had given employment to so many masque-makers.

When Queen Elizabeth died in March of 1603 the plague had been creeping into London, and when King James died in March of 1625 a second disaster of the same sort was moving in on the city. It had been such a long time since anything of the kind had occurred that the official sealing-up of the first infected house in April attracted a crowd of curious sight-seers, but the ceremony was one with which the Londoners were soon to become bitterly familiar. When James was buried in May, thirteen parishes were already infected, and by August more than four thousand people had died of the plague. Shops were closed down, grass grew in the streets, and the chief activity in London was funeral sermons. The church of St. Clement Danes held a special communion service in August with three ministers officiating. One was stricken as he gave the sacrament and went home to die, the second was ill for thirteen weeks, and the third, who was "given to drink" and incapable of preaching a sustained sermon, survived unharmed, "officiated at every funeral, and buried all manner of people."

The coronation of the new king, Charles the First, had to be postponed until the following year. But many people lingered in town that summer, long after they should have left the stricken city, because they wanted to see the arrival of their new queen. Henrietta Maria, sixteen-year-old princess of France, had brown hair and bright black eyes, and was so small that she hardly reached to her young husband's shoulder. In her green suit she was pretty enough to make a highly favorable impression on the Londoners. One susceptible Puritan said there was little fault to find with her except that she was a Roman Catholic and he "could not abstain from divers deep-fetched sighs" because she lacked the knowledge of the "true religion." The English were a little inconsistent in being willing to accept a Catholic queen from France when they were terrified by the idea of getting one from Spain, but possibly the fact that the French had not sent an Armada against their shores had some-thing to do with the matter.

During the plague period all the theatres in London were of course closed, and the loss of revenue was so disastrous that most of the acting companies had to reorganize afterwards. The only acting company that survived the ordeal in triumph was the one that had once been Shakespeare's. It was still headed by those veterans of the theatre, John Heminges and Henry Con-dell, and they had no difficulty getting a royal patent from Charles so that they could continue as the King's Men.

Shortly after the coronation of the new King, which took place on the second of February, 1626, the King's Men pre-sented the first play that Jonson had written in ten years, *The Staple of News*.

Jonson claimed that he went backstage and harried the actors during the first performance, and his self-portrait is a classic picture of a playwright just before an opening. "Yonder he is within . . . i' the tiring-house . . . rolling himself up and down like a tun . . . His sweating put me in mind of a good Shroving dish." Like many of his fellow playwrights in a similar case he tried to drown his nervousness in drink, putting "himself to silence in dead sack." A quarter of a century earlier, the actors in Jonson's comedy, *Cynthia's Revels*, had assured the audience that the author was not backstage, "to prompt us aloud, stamp at the book-holder, swear for our properties, curse the poor tire-man, rail the music out of tune, and sweat for every venial tres-pass we commit." Jonson had changed his methods since then, or perhaps he was merely readier to admit it and to make mild fun of himself as an overanxious playwright.

Yet in one way Jonson had not changed in the least from the idealistic young man who had written *Cynthia's Revels*. He still wished to "steer the souls of men" in *The Staple of News*, as he said in the Prologue, and to mix "profit and delight" as he said in the Epilogue. And again he concentrated on what seemed to him to be the root of so much contemporary evil, the love of money.

The story that Jonson worked out for his play would have been better suited to a masque. The tale of the prodigal, the miser and Lady Pecunia is an allegory and there is no attempt to make it realistic. Pecunia's nurse is "old mother Mortgage"; "little Wax" is her chambermaid and Pawn her groom. Where Jonson achieves vividness is not in the characterization, for there is none to speak of, but in the sharp, accurate phrases with which he ridicules the current adoration of Lady Wealth —the courtiers who make "corpulent curt'sies to her till they crack for't" and the devotion that makes "aged knees to buckle."

Jonson named his lady Aurelia Clara Pecunia, the Infanta of the Mines, and since the Infanta of Spain was named Isabella Clara Eugenia it was natural to suspect that he was making a slanting reference to Charles' lost bride. But there is nothing in the play to support such an interpretation since the Lady Pecunia achieves a place of honor as soon as her real function is understood.

> Use her like a friend, not like a slave
> Or like an idol. Superstition
> Doth violate the deity it worships
> No less than scorn doth.

Jonson did not have a contempt for money but merely for its worshipers. He believed in the intelligent use of money, the "golden mean" that had been the ideal of the ancient world and which, as a classicist, he was trying to teach to an unheeding age.

The remainder of *The Staple of News*, which gives it its title, is a lively and topical satire on the current London interest in newspapers. The Infanta of the Mines is not intended to represent a real person, but there is no doubt of the identity of "Nathaniel," chief clerk of Jonson's office of news. Nathaniel Butter was one of the first Englishmen to edit a newssheet, launching the venture late in the reign of King James, and Jonson, who liked him no better than he liked George Wither, took a wicked delight in his last name. The first customer who appears at the news office is a butterwoman who wants

> A groatsworth of any news, I care not what,
> To carry down this Saturday to our vicar.

Because of her occupation she is naturally directed to Nathaniel, and Jonson keeps up references throughout the play to "the butter-box" and the news that is "beastly buttered." A stationer who has tried to freshen up old news is described as "buttering over again . . . his antiquated pamphlets with new dates" and when the news office finally collapses for lack of funds the unfortunate Nathaniel is "melted into buttter." It is no wonder that the real Nathaniel Butter had little love for Ben Jonson and showed his delight unmistakably when a later play of Jonson's was a failure.

Whatever Jonson's victim may have felt, the audience must have enjoyed the play, for Jonson had worked out the details of his imaginary news office with affectionate care. The staple was a monopoly,

> Where all the news of all sorts shall be brought,
> And there be examined, and then registered,
> And so be issued under the seal of the Office.

The office had its own staff of reporters, men

> that are sent abroad
> To fetch in the commodity from all regions
> Where the best news are made.

The duty of clerks like Nathaniel was to "sort and file" the news according to the time of year and the politics involved, whether Puritan, Protestant or Catholic—

> news o' the faction,
> As the Reformed news, Protestant news
> And Pontifical news.

The promoters of the office understood their customers, who were willing to "believe anything . . . they see in print," but for twopence a sheet they are willing to guarantee the complete accuracy of their product. Their sources are impeccable, and one of the Dutch eelboats moored at the London dock of Queenhithe has just reported a kind of submarine.

> It is an automa, runs under water,
> With a snug nose, and has a nimble tail
> Made like an auger, with which tail she wriggles
> Betwixt the coasts of a ship and sinks it straight.

There is also news of a Spanish plan to mount an army on cork and bring it across the Channel, a discovery by Galileo of a burning glass that can set any fleet on fire, and a more humane project, sponsored by a colony of cooks, to convert all American cannibals to the virtues of sauce on sausages so that they will "forbear the mutual eating one another." All this news is handled through a central office, well equipped with chairs and desks and other needful furniture, with Nathaniel busily supervising the sorting.

Jonson's imaginary Office of the Staple had such a bland air of reality about it that he had to add a note to his readers assuring them the whole thing was a joke and that his parody of European news had no "sinister" interpretation. He said he had invented his "ridiculous Office of the Staple" to show his fellow Englishmen the foolishness of their "hunger and thirst after published pamphlets of news, set out every Saturday . . . and no syllable of truth in them."

There had been a "hunger and thirst" after news in London long before Butter and his colleagues started putting out actual newssheets in the early 20's. But the earlier pamphlets and broadsides appeared spasmodically and usually recorded only what would appeal to a casual customer—local disasters, monstrous pigs and "wonderful strange news" from abroad. Whatever serious, consistent news was available in London was mostly supplied by well-informed men who lived in the various European capitals and wrote long, detailed letters to their English friends at regular intervals. The news was not always accurate, and one expert news gatherer who reported that Buckingham had contracted smallpox and then was forced to contradict himself put the problem philosophically. "These uncertainties of things so near us and as it were under our nose, make me not wonder at the poor intelligence we have from abroad."

Some of the European countries issued news reports, carefully censored to reflect the points of view of the various governments, but the only real newspapers were the ones printed in Holland. In 1620 the experienced Dutch journalists invaded the English market and a newssheet was printed in Amsterdam that was written in English and intended for English readers. London publishers could see no reason why the money of potential readers should take flight to Holland, and within two years *The Weekly News* made its appearance in England. The initials of its publisher were "N.B.," which could stand for Nicholas Bourne or Nathaniel Butter; but it was Butter who eventually headed the syndicate and he might be called the father of English journalism.

The development of newspapers in the seventeenth century was eyed by conservative people with great suspicion. "It was a great error in a state to have all affairs put into gazettes, for it overheats the people's brains and makes them neglect their private affairs by over-busying themselves with state business."

The average government of the period did not dare to permit any differences of opinoin. There was one church, Protestant or Catholic as the case might be, and there was one state. To welcome a second point of view would be to let in a tide of sedition that would destroy everything. The only government that permitted itself to relax was the loose federation of states called the United Provinces of the Netherlands, and visitors were startled by a Protestant regime which was willing to let Catholics have their churches and Jews their synagogues. "The violence and sharpness which accompanies the differences of religion in other countries seems to be appeased and softened here by the general freedom which all men enjoy."

Sharing in this "general freedom" was the Dutch press, and newspapers like the Leyden *News* and the Amsterdam *Gazette* were read all over Europe because they were not obliged to slant the news. When the King of France attempted to have a Dutch publisher suppressed he was told that it was impossible. The men of the Netherlands could not be forced into agreement either by a foreign king or by their own home governments, and therein lay their great strength.

No other government felt impelled to follow so revolutionary a policy, and certainly not the government of King Charles of England. The idea of a free press was no doctrine of his, and when he became displeased with the contents of Nathaniel Butter's publications the answer was simple. All news gazettes in England were suppressed by the Star Chamber just six years after Ben Jonson wrote *The Staple of News*.

It is only fair to remember that Queen Elizabeth disapproved also of freedom of the press and had her own system of censorship. The Tudors agreed with the Stuarts in considering the royal prerogative of vital importance and they had no wish to see ordinary citizens meddle in government affairs. But Elizabeth was a tactful woman, and she had a gift for compromise. England possessed a long tradition of personal liberty and the Tudors were usually careful not to push their own rights to extremes.

Charles, unfortunately, possessed no political tact, and to a man of his narrow, righteous temperament any compromise was a kind of disgrace. He believed that if Parliament were allowed its own way in anything it would cause a crack in the dike that would unloose a flood, and as soon as he found that Parliament was becoming unmanageable he merely ceased to call it into session. It was his curious conviction that if he blocked every expression of popular discontent, the discontent itself would somehow cease to exist, although any housewife could have told him that if the spout of a kettle is blocked the steam will accumulate enough force to blow off the lid.

On the fiercely contested subject of religion, Charles had been unlucky in his inheritance. King James disliked the Puritans intensely. He had been brought up in Scotland under Calvinists and had no wish to see those "fanatic spirits" in control of England also. But, with his usual bad luck, James took the one course of action that was sure to make Puritanism flourish. He tried to suppress the Puritans while at the same time protecting the Catholics, and as the Puritans fought back they became increasingly identified in the public mind as the one sure bulwark against popery.

James disliked the Puritans for the same reason that Elizabeth had disliked them; they were a threat to the royal prerogative. He could see a principle at work which was then considered sedition and is today considered democracy, when every "Jack and Tom and Will and Dick shall meet, and at their pleasure censure me and my Council." A foe of the Puritans once made a list of their shortcomings, their lack of charity, hatred of learning and so on, and he rose to a climax in his final charge that they believed in "equality, which is the nurse of error and confusion." There was no room for equality in the careful hierarchy of any Renaissance state, and the Stuart kings were on guard against anything that would undermine the base of the structure.

What saved King James from disaster was his fumbling good will and his dislike of going to extremes. He refused to advance William Laud in the church, for instance, because he distrusted Laud's temperament. "The plain truth is that I keep Laud back from all place of rule and authority, because I find he hath a restless spirit and cannot see when matters are well, but loves . . . to bring things to a pitch of reformation floating in his own brain." But Laud became Archbishop under Charles, who believed with the same uncompromising rigidity in an impossible

ideal, and between them the King and the Archbishop perse-
cuted the English moderates until they had harried them into
the camp of the enemy.

Most of Ben Jonson's friends disliked Puritanism, and yet it
was the Puritan party that was standing for the rights of the
people against the Church and the King. Anyone who valued
freedom was likely to find himself allied with that narrow, intense and bitterly partisan group which valued only its own
definition of freedom and was unwilling to concede any other.
It was becoming increasingly difficult for anyone in England to
take a moderate, middle-of-the-road position, and as the crack
between the King and the people widened no one could stand
astride it any longer.

The dilemma of many of Jonson's friends can be illustrated
by the case of John Selden. Selden had come a long way since
the big young lawyer attended the dinner Jonson had given
after *Eastward Ho*, and he was now honored for his learning
all over England. In 1618 he issued a scholarly history of the
tithes in which he said, among other things, that they were not
of divine origin. The fury of the bishops was unleashed against
him and Selden was brought up before the Court of High Commission.

King James took an interest in the affair, since he was always
fascinated by any theological discussion. He called Selden in
for an interview and Selden, who had never met the King, took
Ben Jonson along to make the proper introductions. James discussed minor points of doctrine with him at what turned out to
be a pleasant meeting, for James did not realize as clearly as his
bishops did the amount of damage that a liberal, skeptical mind
like Selden's could do to the intricate doctrine of church control. The churchmen themselves were not so easily silenced.
They not only suppressed the book but forced Selden to apolo-
gize publicly for having published it. "My good lords, I most
humbly acknowledge the error I have committed in publishing
the History of Tithes."

Selden did not feel that his apology was any reflection on the

accuracy of his book and remarked afterwards, "Is there a syllable in it of less truth because I am sorry for the publishing of
it?" His own private motto was "Liberty in all things," and
when the next Parliament began to attack governmental abuses
it found John Selden ranged on its side. Although he was not a
member, he helped to draw up the Protestation that was presented to James and was sent to prison for it. The next time
Parliament met Selden was a member, and from that time forward he put his vast learning and his steady courage at the disposal of the Parliamentarians.

Charles dissolved Parliament three years after his coronation
and put the blame on a small group of men whom he characterized as "vipers." This group included Selden. If Charles had
been willing to listen to the intelligent moderates instead of dis-
missing them as vipers, it is not impossible that the Civil War
could have been avoided. But Charles was serene in the knowledge of his personal integrity and his traditional privileges, and
with the most careful and painstaking precision he helped to
build the machine that destroyed him.

# Chapter 27

I T WAS OBVIOUS, from the moment of his coronation, that
King Charles was going to have a Court very unlike his
father's. King James had always been informal in his manners and grew increasingly so; he used "to call for his old shoes"
because they were "easiest for his feet." The new King, on the
other hand, made it clear from the beginning that he expected
to have elegance and correctness at Whitehall. Many of the nobility agreed, after his coronation, "that they had never seen
any solemnity . . . performed with so little noise and so great
order."

Charles made it equally clear that swearing and hard drinking would no longer be tolerated. After a profane old gentleman like King James, it must have been rather startling to have
an austere young monarch who would not permit in his presence "even the least sordid word." Whereas King James had
"the strongest antipathy to water," King Charles had an equally
strong antipathy to drunkenness. On one festive occasion, when
a nobleman drank more than was good for him and came "in
some gaiety" to show his royal master how well he could hold
his liquor, Charles told him coldly that he "deserved to be
hanged."

Ben Jonson was a talented and experienced drinker and he
must have felt a little out of place in this new and reformed
Whitehall. He had been brought up in Elizabethan and Jacobean ways and he was accustomed to a more spacious and re-

laxed way of doing things; he was alien to Charles' temperament and to his wish to live in a tight, formal world in which everything had its correct place. It was said of the new king that he "did not love strangers, nor very confident men," and while Jonson was no stranger, having been at Court since Charles was four years old, he was undoubtedly what might be called a confident man.

King Charles was kind to the poet laureate he had inherited and Jonson wrote many suitably admiring verses to his new sovereign, but the sprawling old dictator of the Apollo Club did not really fit into the strict and delicate lines of the new Whitehall. As Jonson cheerfully admitted to Lady Covell, he was "fat and old, laden with belly" and could

> hardly approach
> His friends, but to break chairs or crack a coach.

When he sat for his portrait, he told the painter that his shape was now "one great blot." Both the sense of humor and the voluminous shape were alien to the new king's sense of decorum, although they would never have been alien to his father's.

In one respect, however, Charles was exactly like his father, and that was in the love he bore the Duke of Buckingham. The new king was essentially a shy and reticent man who did not give his love easily, and that made it all the more intense when it was finally bestowed. Moreover, Charles looked to Buckingham to supply the lighthearted gaiety he lacked himself and he had admitted not long before he became king, "I . . . can enjoy nothing rightly while you are not here."

Unfortunately for England, Buckingham was as stupid politically as he was charming personally. Since he had never been crossed by anyone in his life, he was quite unprepared for the hostility of the new Parliament and struck back like a spoiled and infuriated child. Buckingham was not the vicious monster that the Puritans thought him, but he was certainly a foolish infant into whose hands had been thrust the weapon of too much power. He involved England in a war with France, "without any kind of provocation, and upon a particular passion very unwarrantable" and then committed the even worse mistake of not winning any battles. Charles sent his own coach to Portsmouth to pick Buckingham up when he came back from the Isle of Rhé, but most people remembered the dead soldiers that the Duke had left behind him and the "greatest and shamefullest" defeat that English arms had known for a long time.

King Charles was convinced that Parliament's hatred of Buckingham was the result of a kind of anarchy and that his dear friend was merely being used as an excuse for trying to destroy the government. The rising hysteria reflected in the popular broadsides, which by now were accusing the Duke of everything from cowardice to murder, merely convinced Charles of the need for special firmness in dealing with his fractious and childish subjects. He sent Parliament a message "absolutely forbidding them to meddle with the government or any of his majesty's ministers" and one member of the House of Commons was able to count more than fifty of his fellows who were in tears. They were tears of frustration. All of them were still convinced they could reach through to Charles and rouse his intelligence and good will if only Buckingham were out of the way.

In the end it was not Parliament that disposed of Buckingham. It was a lieutenant named John Felton who had left army life in a fury because Buckingham had not promoted him. A lonely, melancholy man, he read inflammatory pamphlets in his solitary London lodgings until he decided it was God's will he should kill the Duke.

Felton bought a tenpenny knife in a cutlery shop on Tower Hill and sewed the sheath into the lining of his pocket. Then he worked his way to Portsmouth, where the Duke was trying to raise recruits for his unpopular war, and walked into Buckingham's lodgings just as he had finished breakfast. The Duke, a tall man, was bending forward to speak to a friend when Felton drove the knife with a surgeon's precision through his lungs. Buckingham died in the hall, under the clock, with his blood all along the table; and his wife Kate, who was upstairs, tried to kill herself and her unborn child by throwing herself over the railing.

The news came to Charles at Whitehall while he was at prayer, and he heard of Buckingham's murder with a face that was rigidly motionless. He finished his prayers and then went and shut himself up in his room and did not come out for two days. The reaction of the people who lived around Portsmouth was somewhat different. "It was very remarkable that before the Duke's death we had rain every day, more or less, insomuch as those that were forward in cutting their harvest had it almost all spoiled. But after his death . . . such fair weather as all the country people wished he had been killed a month sooner."

When Felton was executed, it was popularly considered that he died a martyr for English liberty. A flood of admiring verses poured from the London presses and among them was a poem written by a young divinity student named Zouch Townley. Townley had been chosen to deliver Camden's funeral oration and he was a friend of Jonson's. He was also an admirer of Jonson's work and his verses in praise of Felton sounded enough like Jonson's to be mistaken in some quarters for his.

The government took the matter seriously, and two months after Buckingham's death Jonson was formally examined by the attorney general to find out if he had written the verses in Felton's praise. Jonson said he had not. He said that on one of his frequent visits to Sir Robert Cotton's house in Westminster he had seen the paper lying on the table after dinner and someone had asked him at the time if he had written it. Jonson said that rumor attributed the verses to Townley, a safe enough statement to make since his friend was safely across the Channel and staying at The Hague. Jonson was then asked how it had come about that Townley possessed a dagger of his and he told a story that throws a delightful light on the habits of the clergy. "On a Sunday after this examinant had heard the said Mr.

Townley preach at St. Margaret's Church in Westminster, Mr. Townley taking a liking to a dagger with a white haft which this examinant ordinarily wore at his girdle . . . this examinant gave it to him two nights after, being invited by Mr. Townley to sup."

Ben Jonson was living at the time in Westminster, in rented lodgings that stood between St. Margaret's Church and Westminster Abbey, not far from the house of his friend, Sir Robert Cotton. But there was to be no more visiting, for late in this same year of 1628 Jonson suffered a paralytic stroke. He became what he called a "bed-rid wit," suddenly cut off from the activities of what had been a very full and lively way of living.

Long ago, when Ben Jonson had been briefly imprisoned for helping to write *Eastward Ho*, he had spoken of learning to cultivate "the asinine virtue, patience." Now he was being forced to cultivate it whether he wished to or not, and it must have been a difficult art for so restless a man to learn. Moreover, Jonson was afraid that the disease would destroy his ability to write, which for him was the chief reason for living, and he described his muse lying

> blocked up and straitened, narrowed in,
> Fixed to the bed and boards, unlike to win
> Health or scarce breath . . .

Another enemy moved in upon Jonson at the same time: poverty. As Camden had once remarked, poverty was a "fate peculiar to poets," but Jonson had succeeded through his work in the theatre and his constant employment at Court in making a reasonable living. Now, in his old age, he had lost his chief source of revenue, for the King had not yet asked him to write a masque and neither had any of the Court noblemen. He still had his pension of a hundred marks a year, but that did not go far against the extra expenses of his illness and the loss of his earning power. Moreover, Charles had inherited his father's financial difficulties and the Court pension was liable to go unpaid. Jonson experienced the same difficulty that Geoffrey Chaucer had known in an earlier Court, and his rhymed protest shows an almost Chaucerian good temper.

> Father John Burges,
> Necessity urges
> My woeful cry
> To Sir Robert Pie . . .
> Tell him his Ben
> Knew the time when
> He lov'd the Muses
> Though now he refuses
> To take apprehension
> Of a year's pension
> And more is behind.

Jonson never lost his liveliness of mind, although for the last nine years of his life he lacked both health and money.

Since Jonson was a resident of Westminster and living in a house owned by the Abbey, the Dean and Chapter voted five pounds in January to send to "Mr. Benjamin Johnson in his sickness and want." Later on in this same year of 1629 King Charles sent him a hundred pounds as a gift, so that for the time being Jonson was not too badly off. Moreover the previous September the London aldermen had voted him the office of City Chronologer. The office had been left vacant through Thomas Middleton's death in July and it carried with it a salary of a hundred nobles a year.

The post of City Chronologer was completely unsuited to a man of Jonson's temperament. Its purpose was civic glorification and the Chronologer was expected to "collect and set down all memorable acts of this City and occurrences thereof." Anthony Munday, who continued John Stow's chronicle of London after that careful old historian died, possessed the civic pride that would have made a good chronologer; while Thomas Middleton, who had held the office for the past eight years, had been trained in the proper point of view by writing a series of

Lord Mayor's shows that glorified the mayor, the aldermen and the whole city of London.

Jonson was not interested in turning out hackneyed praise for what was rapidly becoming a Puritan city; and although, like Middleton, he was expected to earn his salary by writing a book "containing passages and occurrences proper to the honorable city of London," in actual practice he did nothing at all. To his indignant surprise the aldermen withdrew his pension after waiting in vain for three years for their new Chronologer to supply them with something, and Jonson had to enter into negotiations. He "promised at Christmas next" to present them with an account of the last four years of Sir Hugh Hamersley as mayor—a promise that must have made him feel he was back in the days of working for Henslowe, negotiating a twenty-shilling advance on a play for the Admiral's company "which he was to write for us before Christmas next."

But Jonson was no longer a hack playwright and he had many friends at Court. Six years after his appointment as Chronologer, the London aldermen finally capitulated to Jonson's private theory that he had been voted a pension rather than a salary and ceased to expect any work from him in return. It may have been just as well, for anything that Jonson wrote might have failed to supply the note of reverence that the city expected from its employees. A poet who could write of "two aldermen lobsters asleep in a dish" was not really suited by temperament to the post of City Chronologer.

Meanwhile, Jonson's friends did what they could to offset the loneliness of a paralytic's life. One of the most imaginative gifts that was sent to Jonson in the early days of his sickness came from Sir Thomas Badger, the Master of the King's Harriers. Sir Thomas was still breeding hounds with the skill and diligence that had made King James call him "sweet Tom Badger," and he sent Jonson the gift of a young fox. Jonson enjoyed the fox, "which creature, by handling, I endeavored to make tame, as well for the abating of my disease as the delight I took in speculation of his nature." The new pet was kept in a tub in the yard and made a strikingly suitable gift for the famous author of *Volpone, or the Fox.*

Jonson did not lack for visitors in his small house next to St. Margaret's Church. He was not only a famous man but a well-loved one, and the troop of young men who could no longer see him at the Apollo Club turned to his Westminster lodgings because Ben Jonson was there. He had a great gift both for making friends and keeping them, and it was a gift that served him well in the last years of his life.

Of all the young men who were attracted to Ben Jonson, one of the loveliest in spirit was Sir Lucius Cary. Cary was a rather shy young man and on their first meeting he apparently felt awkward in the presence of so prominent a writer.

> I thought you proud, for I did surely know
> Had I Ben Jonson been, I had been so . . .

But Jonson was not proud, at least with people he liked, and Cary soon relaxed into a delighted and grateful friendship with the man he called "noble father." It was said of Cary that he showed "the most incomparable gentleness . . . and even . . . submission to good and worthy and entire men" and Jonson was an "entire" man in the best sense of the word. Cary had the grace and intelligence to know how to use what Jonson could give him, and he signed his letters to the old man "your son and servant."

Cary's own father was a stubborn and bad-tempered spend-thrift, as courageous as his son but with none of his gentleness. Jonson had written of Sir Henry Cary's unfortunate capture by the Spaniards in his younger days, when he and Sir John Roe refused to run away and were taken by the enemy.

> No foe that day
> Could conquer thee, but chance who did betray.

The episode cost Sir Henry a great deal of money, and even when he became Lord Deputy of Ireland he was still struggling

with the financial worries he hoped to solve by marrying his son
to an heiress.

Lucius Cary's mother was a remarkable woman married to
the wrong man. As a child she was a voracious reader and her
family tried to stop her habit of reading in bed by depriving
her of light, so that she owed the maids for eight hundred candles they had smuggled in by the time she was twelve. Since no
tutor could handle her, she was self-taught in Latin and Spanish, and although she hated dressing up she tried to take a polite
interest in clothes after she married Sir Henry. She opened some
industrial schools in Dublin, in an effort to improve conditions
in Ireland, but she had no money sense (being "most subject"
to a tendency to pay the same bills twice) and the schools
failed. She then pursued the Catholic faith with equal intensity
and since her husband was a Protestant she left him. Her intense, dumpy little figure in shabby black became a familiar figure around London, where she had taken up a final project of
translating the works of Cardinal DuPerron.

Lucius Cary inherited his mother's idealism and his father's
valor, but his good sense he could have derived only from himself. Moreover, he had an awareness of other people's rights that
was lacking in both his parents. His "nature was so gentle and
obliging, so much delighted in courtesy, kindness and generosity, that all mankind could not but admire and love him."

In Ireland Cary had formed an intense friendship with the
son of one of his father's friends. Young Henry Morison was
a devoted reader of Latin poets and an ardent idealist, and the
two young men became inseparable. They were like a pair of
young Sidneys, solemnly determined to build something great
and good out of their lives, and they could not have found a
better friend in London than Ben Jonson.

Sir Henry Morison died in the summer of 1629 and Jonson,
now a paralytic, wrote a long poem "To the immortal memory
and friendship of that noble pair, Sir Lucius Cary and Sir H.
Morison." He chose the difficult form of the Pindaric ode, the
first time it had been used in English, to express his profound

conviction that Morison's life had not ended broken and unful-
filled.

> It is not growing like a tree
> In bulk, doth make man better be,
> Or standing long an oak, three hundred year,
> To fall a log at last, dry, bald and sere.
> A lily of a day
> Is fairer far in May
> Although it fall and die that night;
> It was the plant and flower of light.
> In small proportions we just beauty see,
> And in short measures life may perfect be.
>
> Call, noble Lucius, then for wine
> And let thy looks with gladness shine.
> Accept this garland, plant it on thy head,
> And think, nay, know, thy Morison's not dead.

In Jonson's view, nothing worthy or noble could ever die, and
the poem is a fitting tribute to two very good and honorable
young men. Lucius Cary later said of Jonson that he

> did our youth to noble actions raise,
> Hoping the meed of his immortal praise,

so that in a sense Jonson had helped to produce what he so
nobly praised.

After Morison's death, Cary married his friend's sister, and
since she was not an heiress his father never forgave him. When
the relentless old man died four years later Cary became Viscount Falkland, and he made his house at Great Tew, near Oxford, a center of graceful hospitality and political liberalism.
He probably saw less of Jonson after his marriage but he evidently kept up his gifts to him, "having naturally such a generosity and bounty in him, that he seemed to have his estate in
trust for all worthy persons who stood in want of supplies or
encouragement, as Ben Jonson and many others."

It might be said in passing that anyone who met Sir Lucius Cary for the first time would have seen a dwarfish little man with a rather stupid-looking face, a jerky way of walking and a badly pitched voice. But no one noticed his outward appearance twice, and when he was killed in the Civil War England lost an heroic and lovely spirit.

Very unlike Lucius Cary was another young man who was also a close friend of Jonson's, the tall, handsome and self-confident Sir Kenelm Digby.

When Kenelm was three his father was executed for his part in the Gunpowder Plot; and although he kept all his father's letters in two silk bags and reread them when he was alone, he never let the tragedy darken his buoyant and theatrical temperament. In 1623 he married the notorious Venetia Stanley, adding to his career one more of the "disadvantages . . . which would have suppressed or sunk any other man but never clouded or eclipsed him." Far from feeling apologetic about the reputation of his beautiful wife, Sir Kenelm wrote a book about her past career, blaming the whole scandal on rumor but adding that chastity was no more important in a woman than in a man. "There are innumerable vices, incident to them as well as to men, that are far more to be condemned than the breach of this frozen virtue." Sir Kenelm was convinced that the whole question of chastity had assumed undue importance because of "men's interests," not women's, and it is worth recording that his marriage was a happy one.

Sir Kenelm was the hero of his own book, and it is clear that he gave himself great satisfaction. He speaks of the "noble temper of his mind," the "great strength and well-framing of his body" and his skill in "the study of philosophy and other deepest sciences." All this was quite true, and he might have added what one of his friends attributed to him, "a wonderful graceful behavior, a flowing courtesy and civility, and such a volubility of language as surprised and delighted." Sir Kenelm was a philosopher and a scientific experimenter and he was also, by 1629, a successful pirate, for he was just back from an expedi-

tion in which he had attacked foreign shipping in the neutral
port of Scaderoon.

Jonson thoroughly enjoyed his young friend's expansive
nature.

> His breast is a brave palace, a broad street
> Where all heroic, ample thoughts do meet,
> Where Nature such a large survey hath ta'en,
> As other souls, to his, dwell in a lane.

Sir Kenelm, in his turn, took an almost reverent attitude towards Jonson and testified to "the great value and esteem I have
of this brave man, the honor of his age."

One reason why Sir Kenelm loved Jonson was that Jonson
loved Venetia. Jonson was always attracted to women of wit
and spirit, and Sir Kenelm said truly of his lovely wife: "The
excellency of her wit I cannot describe better than in saying it
is a masculine and vigorous one, and every way correspondent
to her fair outside." Jonson's own relationship to her was very
close, and he felt the deepest gratitude for the part she played
in his life.

> All that was good or great in me she weaved
> And set it forth.

Venetia Stanley was found dead in her room one May morning when she was thirty-three, and her husband commissioned
a painter to do a life-size portrait of her as she lay in bed. He
then buried her in a black marble tomb and retired for a time to
Gresham College and scientific experiments. For two years he
went about unshaved, in a mourning cloak and high-crowned
hat, and since Sir Kenelm could not even grieve without doing
it theatrically he had his portrait painted in his new garb.

Jonson reared his own monument to the Lady Venetia, an
elaborate ten-part poem that he called "Eupheme." Jonson's
grief, like that of her husband's, is transmuted into something
intricate, ornate and rather theatrical, in complete contrast to
the noble, sober poem he wrote for Sir Lucius Cary on a some-

what similar bereavement. The grief was as real, but the people involved were very unlike; and the measure of the difference is accurately reflected in Jonson's lines.

Another young man who belonged to Jonson's circle in London was a lawyer from the Middle Temple named Edward Hyde. Later on, when Mr. Hyde became the Earl of Clarendon, he wrote his autobiography for his children and advised them to select worthy friends in youth. His own closest friend, he said, was Sir Lucius Cary, but "whilst he was only a student of the law and stood at gaze, irresolute what course of life to take, his chief acquaintances were Ben Jonson, John Selden . . . Sir Kenelm Digby . . . and some others of eminent faculties." He admired Jonson for his learning but considered him something of an autocrat. "His conversation was very good, and with the men of most note; and he had for many years an extraordinary kindness for Mr. Hyde, till he found he betook himself to business, which he believed ought never to be preferred before his company."

The future Earl of Clarendon was a lawyer, not a poet; and the poets, at least, found little in the way of "business" that was more important to them than Ben Jonson's company.

> To him how daily flocked, what reverence gave,
> All that had wit or would be thought to have.

All of them longed to be sealed of the Tribe of Ben, and when young Thomas Randolph attained that coveted distinction and was accepted by Jonson as a "son," he wrote sixty-four jubilant lines congratulating himself: "Boast I must." Randolph was a friend of young William Heminges, the actor's son, and in 1629 was still at Cambridge. His clever, youthful verses were more admired in their own day than they deserved to be, but Randolph was eager to give Jonson the credit for everything that was good in his work.

> That which is best in me
> May call you father; 'twas begot by thee.

James Shirley, in 1629, called Jonson "our acknowledged master," and he spoke for a whole troop of younger poets. Thomas Carew and William Cartwright could have said the same, for Jonson had a great deal of influence over them both and felt a special pride in Cartwright. "My son Cartwright writes all like a man." But popular young versifiers like these were never able to understand the great vision of antiquity that had fired Jonson in his youth. They accepted as part of their literary creed the fact that he had reformed the English stage, but none of them understood what he had really been trying to do in his plays. Jonson never succeeded in bringing the young Caroline poets up to the high level of his solid, sober, humanistic standards and he never succeeded in transmitting his own sense of dedication. They were graceful young versifiers rather than poets, and although he might call them his sons they would never grow up to be his equals.

Of all the Tribe of Ben, the one who came nearest to reflecting Jonson's brilliance was a young divinity student from Cambridge. Two years earlier this young man had served as Buckingham's chaplain on the ill-fated military expedition to the Isle of Rhé, and in 1629 he left London to become a country vicar. His name was Robert Herrick, and he was the greatest of Jonson's "sons."

Herrick's father was a goldsmith and he himself had been brought up in the trade. He would have made an excellent jeweler, for his work has a polished delicacy and a technical perfection almost unrivaled in English literature. Added to it was a gay charm all his own, the product of his light-hearted determination "to live merrily and to trust to good verses."

Herrick wrote six poems on Ben Jonson, and they are very unlike the solemn literary tributes that most of Jonson's disciples proffered him. Herrick remembered best the "lyric feasts" they had shared in various taverns throughout London, where

each verse of thine
Outdid the meat, outdid the frolic wine.

In this he resembled Francis Beaumont, remembering an earlier revelry from the country, but even Beaumont could not match the lighthearted grace of the final prayer that Herrick wrote for the man who helped him become a poet.

> When I a verse shall make,
>     Know I have prayed thee
> For old religion's sake,
>     Saint Ben to aid me.
>
> Make the way smooth for me
>     When I, thy Herrick,
> Honoring thee, on my knee,
>     Offer my lyric.
>
> Candles I'll give to thee
>     And a new altar;
> And thou Saint Ben, shalt be
>     Writ in my psalter.

# Chapter 28

BEN JONSON WAS NOW FIFTY-SEVEN, five years older than
Shakespeare had been when he died. He was gray-haired
and bed-ridden and might very well have been expected
to settle down to a quiet and resigned old age. But there had
never been anything quiet about Ben Jonson, and his old age
was as argumentative as his youth had been.

Jonson opened the year of 1629 by having a new play produced at the Blackfriars by the King's Men. He called it *The
New Inn* and had worked out a comic-opera plot, depending on
disguises and long-lost children, that might have taxed the ingenuity of W. S. Gilbert. Jonson himself did not take it very
seriously, and as the chief guest at the inn remarked when the
plot was finally unwound,

> Is this a dream now, after my first sleep?
> Or are these phant'sies . . .
>                         sold i' the New Inn?

Jonson had evidently been reading Chaucer and there are
several slanting references in the play to that "reverend" poet
as well as the introduction of a vaguely Chaucerian Court of
Love. There is also a long discussion of valor, and Ben Jonson,
onetime soldier and duelist, had a different conception of valor
now. In his old age it seemed to him that the highest valor was
fortitude.

The things true valor is exercis'd about
Are poverty, restraint, captivity,
Banishment, loss of children, long disease . . .
 Here valor is beheld
Properly seen; about these it is present.

These were the things that Jonson himself was enduring, and no doubt he was able to believe, however momentarily, that death was the "least" of them.

Jonson also gave it as his opinion that a truly valiant man would not stoop to notice any injuries that were done him,

knowing himself advanced to a height
Where injury cannot reach him, nor aspersion
Touch him with soil.

Jonson was honestly convinced that he habitually treated insults with quiet scorn and never answered back, and at the moment this imaginary portrait of himself was especially real to him. He even sent an Epilogue along with the play that was humbly suited to his changed circumstances. "The maker is sick . . . but . . . he meant to please you."

Jonson could not attend the opening performance and do his worrying backstage, and it was left to his friends to bring him the reluctant report that the play had been hissed. Obviously hoping to soften the blow, they explained that the audience thought it detected a personal allusion in the name of the chambermaid. Moreover, they reported that the play had been carelessly produced by the King's Men and that only two of the actors had done their parts well.

What made the situation especially infuriating from Jonson's point of view was the fact that the same company produced a play called *The Lovesick Maid* a few weeks later and scored a great success. *The Lovesick Maid* was written by a former servant of Jonson's called Richard Brome, and Jonson spoke bitterly of "Brome's sweepings." Later on, his natural sense of justice reasserted itself and he wrote some affectionate verses for a subsequent play of his "old faithful servant and . . . loving friend," but in 1629 Jonson was too angry to be reasonable.

Having quite forgotten all the wise remarks he had just made about true valor rising superior to insults, Jonson wrote a long, vigorous and furious poem to inform the playgoing public exactly what he thought of it. He described the poem as having been born of "the just indignation the author took at the vulgar censure of his play by some malicious spectators," and the strength of his language showed that he had lost none of his vigor since the old fighting days of *Poetaster*.

This was too much for Jonson's numerous enemies to accept in silence. Owen Feltham wrote a malicious parody in the same meter, and an even more vicious attack, wisely anonymous, lashed out at "decaying Ben." In prompt answer, the Tribe of Ben turned out a string of verses of their own. Thomas Randolph assured Jonson's critics that they were "bacon-brains" and a young man who signed himself "I. C." informed the world that only men of weak minds would attack so great a poet. Thomas Carew, a little less blindly adoring, pointed out that Jonson's play had not really been a masterpiece and that the poet might well, in the sunset of his life, leave the reform of the stage to his disciples.

What Jonson apparently could not endure was the imputation that he was too old to be able to write well any longer. Towards the end of the year he petitioned King Charles for an increase in his pension and mentioned the envy of the "less poetic boys" who tried to maintain that he was becoming "decayed" through his illness. "But we last out," said Jonson triumphantly. He felt that if Charles would increase his pension his rivals would burst with envy, a prospect he evidently looked forward to with deep interest.

Jonson hoped to have his Court pension changed from marks to pounds, which would increase its value by about a third. In March of the following year his petition was granted, with Charles signing the document in April. Because of "the good and acceptable service done unto us and our said father by the

said Benjamin Johnson and especially to encourage him to pro-
ceed in those services of his wit and pen which . . . we expect
from him," he was to receive henceforth a hundred pounds a
year in quarterly payments. He would also be given an annual
cask of canary wine from the Whitehall cellars, a gift which
Jonson welcomed both for its own sake and because it was
suited to a Court poet. Jonson's copy of Chaucer's poetry carried the information that his great predecessor had been given
a similar grant of wine, and what had been suitable for Chaucer
was clearly right for Jonson also. When there was a delay in the
delivery of the cask Jonson wrote a brisk epigram on the subject.

> What can the cause be, when the King hath given
> His poet sack, the household will not pay?

Jonson was an alert man when it came to his rights, especially
since he had worked long enough in Whitehall to know how
inefficient some of the departments could be.

In this same year of 1630, Jonson received a better gift than
wine. He was commissioned to write the masques for both the
King and the Queen in the coming Christmas season, his first
opportunity of that kind since the coronation.

Jonson's masque for the King was produced on the ninth of
January, 1631, and called *Love's Triumph through Callipolis*.
Callipolis was Plato's ideal city, where beauty and goodness
dwelt, and King Charles and his fourteen fellow masquers personified true love. A comic antimasque in fantastic Italian costumes showed the foolish lovers who lived in the suburbs of Callipolis, the boasting, the jealous, the sensual and so on. Jonson
was still firmly convinced that masques "ought always to carry
a mixture of profit with them, no less than delight," and his
masque for King Charles was a skillful combination of Court
compliment and Jonson's own sober idealism.

The masque for the Queen was called *Chloridia*. According
to Ovid, Chloris was the goddess of flowers, and Jonson sur-

rounded Henrietta Maria with a spring masque full of trees and garlands. The antimasque was supplied by dancers dressed as thunder, lightning and rain, with the Queen's dwarf as a prince of hell, all of them threatening the radiance of spring-time as personified by the Queen.

Once again Jonson found himself working with Inigo Jones; and, being Jonson, he was incapable of realizing how completely their positions had become reversed. Under King Charles, Inigo Jones had completed the upward climb he had begun under King James and he was now the undisputed master of the Court masque as he was of English architecture. The hawklike, handsome old man was accustomed to profound respect from his subordinates, and when he agreed to repair St. Paul's Cathedral with the stipulation that he was to be "sole monarch," the phrase reflects the position he had achieved in his field.

Even in his dealings with royalty Inigo Jones did not permit himself any abasement. His costume drawings for *Chloridia* had to be sent to the Queen for her approval, and Jones wrote at the bottom of one of his sketches: "The colors are in her Majesty's choice; but I should humbly—" At this point he reconsidered, crossed out the last four words with an extra stroke through *humbly* and wrote instead: "but my opinion is that several fresh greens mixed with gold and silver will be most proper."

Ben Jonson was quite willing to admit that Inigo Jones had worked hard on both masques and when the King's masque was published he had the designer's name put beside his own on the title page:

The Inventors
Ben Jonson        Inigo Jones

Jones, however, was displeased because he thought his own name should have come first. He waited for Jonson to make amends when the Queen's masque was published and Jonson solved the question in his own fashion; he left Jones' name off the title page of *Chloridia* entirely.

If Jonson had been willing to humble himself, no doubt Jones would have been quite willing to forgive him. On an earlier occasion when they had quarreled, Jones had eased himself with some verses entitled "To his false friend, Mr. Ben Johnson," in which he remarked rather plaintively that he had done everything possible to make Jonson like him. He had even been willing to listen to the "tedious story" of Jonson's trip to Scotland,

> though
> I was as tired as thou couldst be to go.

At the time, Jones had denounced Jonson as "the best of poets but the worst of men," and there was nothing in their latest difference of opinion to make him change his mind.

Jonson greeted the new warfare with some verses of his own. Inigo Jones had recently become a justice of the peace for Westminster, and Jonson put down exactly what he thought of "tireman, mountebank and Justice Jones." What maddened Jonson was what had always maddened him, the glorification of scenery and costumes at the expense of the script.

> O shows! Shows! Mighty shows!
> The eloquence of masques! What need of prose,
> Or verse, or sense, t' express immortal you?

As long as "wisest Inigo" was available it was clear that no mere poet was needed.

> Painting and carpentry are the soul of masque.
> Pack with your peddling poetry to the stage,
> This is the money-get, mechanic age.

Jonson poured out his scorn on everything connected with Jones' side of the work, the slit deal boards, the painted cloth, the engineering and lighting effects. He, at least, was not going to "fall down" in worship before it, whatever the audiences at Whitehall might do, and he said so with vigor and with fury.

There could be only one ending to the controversy, for the foes were no longer evenly matched. Inigo Jones was now a great power at Court, and if the two men could not work together harmoniously it would not be the architect that was set aside. The next Christmas, the commission to write the royal masque was given to Aurelian Townshend, a suitably respectful young poet who announced that a masque was "nothing else but pictures with light and motion" and who knew how to take a satisfactorily subservient position to Inigo Jones.

Everyone at Court knew why Townshend had been given the commission. Jonson was "for this time discarded, by reason of the predominant power of his antagonist, Inigo Jones, who, this time twelvemonth, was angry with him for putting his own name before his on the title page." The letter writer who sent out this report had his information correct enough as far as it went, but he could not look into the future. It was not "for this time" only that Jonson was discarded. He never again was permitted to write a royal masque.

Jonson needed money badly, and if he had been willing to humble himself a little, something might have been arranged. But the old warrior had never humbled himself, and he would not do so now. He refused to agree that the role of the writer was subordinate to that of the stage designer, and neither old age nor weariness had the slightest effect upon his point of view. Inigo Jones might be able to take away most of his livelihood, but he could not make him change his mind.

In what may have been an effort to raise money, Jonson spent part of 1631 struggling to bring out an edition of three of his plays—*Bartholomew Fair, The Devil is an Ass* and *The Staple of News*. His printer was John Beale, who was admittedly "a very contentious person" and was not a very careful or competent workman. Jonson could no longer visit the print shop, as he had done with his folio, and he struggled helplessly to maintain the same high standards of presswork under almost impossible conditions. "My printer and I shall afford subject enough for a tragicomedy, for with his delays and vexations I am almost become blind." Beale was especially unco-operative on what Jonson felt to be the vital matter of punctuation, and Jonson said that if a play were written on the subject of their warfare he was prepared to cast his printer as the Absolute Knave. In the end the edition came to nothing and the plays were not offered to the public until after Jonson's death.

It was at the end of this year that the London aldermen discontinued Jonson's fee as City Chronologer. The old poet was reduced to writing begging letters, which he did with his own kind of dignity, too honest to shelter under the soothing fiction that he was only asking for a loan. "I have no faculty to pay; but my needs are such, and so urging, as I do beg what your bounty can give me, in the name of good letters." In another letter Jonson made the same point. "I send no borrowing epistle to provoke your Lordship, for I have neither fortune to repay or security to engage." If he had to beg at least he would do it honorably and not pretend to be asking for a loan.

In the same year of 1631, Jonson sent a begging letter in rhyme to the Treasurer, Lord Weston. He compared himself to a besieged city, with "Disease, the enemy, and . . . Want" threatening to crumble all his defenses. It was inevitable that he should have his moments of profound depression and a visitor named Nicholas Oldisworth caught him in one of them. Oldisworth went to see the famous poet when he was in London, hoping apparently for a few brilliant remarks and instead found Ben Jonson sunk in gloom.

> His whole discourse
> Was how mankind grew daily worse and worse,
> How God was disregarded, how men went
> Down even to Hell and never did repent.

George Morley, who visited Jonson frequently during this period, reported an even lower state of theological melancholy. He said that during his sickness Jonson became "much afflicted that he had profaned the Scripture in his plays, and lamented it with horror." Almost exactly the same story was told of Geoffrey Chaucer when he also lay dying in Westminster more than two hundred years earlier, and in both cases the story comes from a churchman. Moreover, in Jonson's case the story becomes almost wholly unreliable since it appears in a highly inaccurate little sketch of Jonson's life that was jotted down by Izaak Walton from memory when he was eighty-seven.

There is no doubt that Jonson and Chaucer were sometimes frightened by the idea of hell-fire, for they both lived in an age of faith and both of them were good Christians. But it is equally improbable that either poet thought about the matter continually or that Jonson really repented having written so much nonreligious poetry.

On the basis of most of Jonson's writing it would be easier to conclude that he was a Senecan Stoic than that he was a Christian. He wrote a certain amount of religious verse, but none of it can match the furious and subtle intensity of Donne or the luminous conviction of George Herbert. This is not to deny the strength and reality of Ben Jonson's religious convictions. It is merely to say that they did not penetrate that layer of his mind where his best poetry was made. Like Chaucer, he was a man of this world and he could not focus his whole attention on the world to come. What Nicholas Oldisworth saw in him was true enough, just as Drummond's report was true enough also as far as it went; but it did not go very far, since neither man really understood Jonson.

If Jonson's "whole discourse" was on hell-fire, his mind certainly was not. For he was working on a new play and he had it ready for production by the middle of October, 1632. He called it *The Magnetic Lady* and presented it to the King's Men, having apparently forgiven them for their share in the failure of *The New Inn* three years before.

It was a rather heroic achievement to have written a new play after so long a period of helplessness and pain, and one Londoner reported in some surprise that Ben Jonson, "who I thought had been dead," had come out with a new script. Jonson knew he would not be writing many more Humour comedies and he gave his new play the subtitle of *Humours Recon-ciled* because he found himself "now near the close, or shutting up of his circle." It was like Jonson to try to round out into a logical whole his series of comedies and to speak of his own death as the closing of a circle, just as it was like him to make a pun on *The Magnetic Lady* and maintain that his play had at least an "attractive" title. It was also characteristic to announce that only intelligent theatregoers would like his play. "Careless of all vulgar censure . . . not depending on common approba-tion, he is confident it shall super-please judicious spectators, and to them he leaves it."

Jonson's play is not a good one, chiefly because the idea of various "humours" being attracted to a magnetic lady is too artificial to be successful. But the writing is careful and con-sistent, with no sign of slackening, and the play is weak because it lacks vigor, not because it lacks intelligence. There is an excellent piece of characterization in a chatty old dame named Polish, and when Polish promises a gift to a midwife, there is still room in Jonson's script for his rich delight in detail.

> You shall have a new, brave, four-pound beaver hat
> Set with enamelled studs, as mine is here,
> And a right pair of crystal spectacles—
> Crystal o' the rock, thou mighty mother of dames—
> Hung in an ivory case at a gold belt,
> And silver bells to jingle as you pass
> Before your fifty daughters in procession.

The play is thin, but it is not a complete failure. Moreover, it is the work of a man who had a clear reason for everything he did and who explained these reasons with almost passionate carefulness.

Because Jonson had frequently been in trouble with the au-thorities over his plays, he was careful to point out that he was not satirizing any particular alderman in Sir Moth Interest or any well-known lawyer in "the ridiculous Mr. Practice." Nevertheless, the play did not escape trouble with the authorities, and for a reason that would have startled an Elizabethan. The actors had interpolated a few oaths when they acted the play, and this was so grave a matter in the delicate world of Charles the First that the King's Men were summoned before the ecclesiastical Court of High Commisson. The actors first said that the oaths had been in the original script and then changed their minds, and the Archbishop of Canterbury was able to hand down a solemn decision that Ben Jonson was guiltless in the matter. So was the Master of the Revels, who was involved in the discussion because he had licensed the script and thereby given it official approval.

The Master of the Revels was Henry Herbert, brother of George Herbert the poet. He had no real right to the office since Sir John Astley, who held the patent, was still alive; but Astley had rented the position to Herbert for a hundred and fifty pounds a year, and Herbert made enough money in the first four years to buy himself an estate in Worcestershire. In theory, the Master of the Revels could collect fees only for licensing new scripts, but Herbert managed to collect from showmen who were dealing in nothing more theatrical than elephants and opossums. He demanded an extra pound a year from the King's Men for permitting them to have music in their theatre, and he discovered an additional source of revenue in the fact that all the old Elizabethan and Jacobean plays needed re-censoring. Herbert announced firmly that "all old plays ought to be brought to the Master of the Revels . . . for which he should have his fee, since they may be full of offensive things . . . In former time the poets took greater liberty than is allowed them by me."

Jonson was a poet from a former time, and Herbert found that he had to be on the alert with him. Jonson wrote a new play, called *A Tale of a Tub*, and Herbert was informed by Whitehall that the play was not to be licensed until Jonson removed a character called Vitruvius Hoop. Inigo Jones had objected vigorously to Vitruvius Hoop "as a personal injury unto him," and Herbert sent word to the actors that the play would have to be rewritten before it was licensed. Jonson rewrote his script, since there was nothing else to do, and Herbert licensed the emasculated version on the seventh of May, 1633, charging two pounds for his services.

Since Jonson had been obliged to remove Vitruvius Hoop, he gave some of the original lines to a character named Medlay. They do not fit Medlay, but there is no doubt that they fitted Inigo Jones. The architect was evidently fond of issuing pronouncements when he made his estimates, and of using the words *feasible* and *conduce*. Nothing is feasible with Medlay in *A Tale of a Tub* unless something else conduces to it, and another character remarks truly that those are "his ruling words." Medlay also expects to have everything his own way when he designs a masque for Squire Tub.

> He will join with no man . . .
> He must be sole inventor.

As he surveys the ground for the masque he discusses his "knowledge in design," and Squire Tub is awed into respectful submission. "I will leave all to him." The fragments of the original characterization that survive in Medlay show what a merciless caricature Jonson must have achieved in Vitruvius Hoop, and it is not surprising that Inigo Jones used his influence to have part of the play suppressed.

The remainder of the play is a lightweight little story about a series of rustic suitors trying to marry one Audrey Turf on St. Valentine's Day. *A Tale of a Tub* is sometimes said to have been an earlier play composed in Elizabethan days and then rewritten, but it mirrors an interest in country customs that Jonson first showed in his gipsy masque and that concerned him increasingly as he grew older. He set the play back in the days of Queen Mary's reign and the plot is too trivial to be taken seriously. Yet Jonson put some good writing into it and a careful use of dialect, and he showed an accurate memory for local country customs in spite of his years as a "bed-rid wit."

For the first time in nearly twenty years, a new play of Jonson's was not presented by the King's Men. Perhaps he did not offer the script to them, since they had acted *The New Inn* carelessly and tampered with *The Magnetic Lady*. Heminges and Condell were both dead, and although John Lowin had been acting in Jonson's scripts since the days of *Sejanus*, he was perhaps not as sympathetic to the poet as the former heads of the company had been.

At any rate, Jonson's new play was presented by the Queen's Men, a group of actors who had been growing in prestige under the skillful handling of Christopher Beeston. Beeston had started his career as a boy apprentice in Shakespeare's company and had acted in the original production of *Every Man in his Humour* with Shakespeare and Burbage; but he eventually lost interest in acting and developed into a theatre manager not unlike Philip Henslowe. Beeston built his own theatre in a fashionable location near Whitehall and made it an indoor playhouse illuminated with candles in gilded candlesticks. It was used by a series of acting companies, with Beeston always listed as a member, and he would oust the current acting company as soon as he found a more profitable one to serve as his tenant.

Beeston would never have accepted Jonson's play for sentimental reasons, and *A Tale of a Tub* must have seemed a good investment to him or the popular Queen's Men would never have presented it. Moreover, it must have found favor with the audience, since Beeston included it among the plays that his company presented that Christmas at Court.

That year the Christmas season at Court was an unusually gala one. The Queen had just recovered from the delivery of a son and was taking a lively interest in all the festivities, even going so far as to lend the King's Men some costumes for their revival of John Fletcher's pastoral, *The Faithful Shepherdess*. The King's Men also presented several of Shakespeare's plays and were highly applauded for *Richard the Third*, *The Taming of the Shrew*, *Cymbeline* and *The Winter's Tale*.

But the star of the occasion was Inigo Jones, whose hand was everywhere. He did the sets for *The Faithful Shepherdess*. He did the designs for a magnificent masque given by the Inns of Court, which was in answer to a Puritan attack on expensive Court shows and cost a thousand pounds for the music alone. Jones had also done the designs for the King's own masque, which had been written by Thomas Carew and which outglittered everything else in the magnificence of its spectacle. Henry Herbert noted reverently in his office book that "it was the noblest masque of my time."

As for *A Tale of a Tub*, which was also presented during the Christmas season, Herbert dismissed it in a single laconic phrase: "not liked."

Ben Jonson had one consolation at least. His work might not be welcome at Court, but his days as a masque-maker were not quite over. The previous summer the King had passed through Nottinghamshire and the Earl of Newcastle had asked him to Welbeck for dinner. The Earl had commissioned Jonson to write the entertainment and Jonson had supplied a song to be delivered during dinner and a lively sketch for a country wedding afterwards. His "Entertainment at Welbeck" was an unqualified success, and when the King came north the following year, this time with the Queen accompanying him, he indicated that he was prepared to be entertained again by the Earl of Newcastle.

The Earl of Newcastle had been a friend and patron of Ben Jonson's for more than seventeen years. He was a man of a literary bent, who scribbled verses and even wrote an occasional play, and his adoring second wife maintained that he was "the best lyric and dramatic poet" of his time. He was hardly that, but he knew enough about the difficulties of writing to be generous to poets and he had always been especially kind to Jonson. Not long after Jonson returned from Scotland, he wrote a delightful if somewhat rowdy christening entertainment for his patron's eldest son. He also wrote an epitaph for his lordship's father, another for his aunt, three poems in praise of his mother and two epigrams honoring the Earl himself. Jonson praises him for his horsemanship and his fencing, but he might equally well have mentioned Newcastle's gentleness, his dislike of formality and the courtesy that made him take off his hat "to the meanest person."

The Earl may have given the Welbeck commission to Jonson partly through kindness but it was also in part shrewd common sense. The Earl was in financial difficulties (as he remarked mournfully, "Children come on apace") and he was currently angling for the lucrative post of tutor to Charles' eldest son. He had about given up hope since, as he admitted frankly, he did not know of "any reason why the King should give me anything," but the King's arrival at Welbeck stirred him to optimism. When Charles returned the following year, bringing Queen Henrietta Maria with him, the Earl of Newcastle gathered together all his resources and spent about fifteen thousand pounds in a final effort to get the post of tutor. He moved out of Welbeck, which he turned over to the royal pair, and planned a new entertainment at his castle at Bolsover. He furnished Bolsover with everything that might contribute to the success of the great event, down to a set of napkins and tablecloth that cost a hundred and sixty pounds, and he then chose Ben Jonson, as an experienced Court poet, to write the script for the entertainment.

In the letter of thanks Jonson wrote his "best patron," he expressed his sense of obligation not only for the commission itself but for the courteous way in which it had been handled. The Earl left the negotiations to Robert Payne, a man of learning who knew Jonson well. "Your Lordship could not have employed a more diligent and judicious man," or, added Jonson, one who treated him with "more humanity." Jonson was grateful for the money, which, as he said, "fell like the dew of heaven" upon his needy household, but he was equally grateful for not being treated like a hired lackey who could be made to do anything for pay.

The script that Jonson sent up to Bolsover was a charming one. Since the Queen was present, the song at the banquet was in honor of love, and Jonson gave it a noble and beautiful definition:

> a lifting of the sense
> To knowledge of that pure intelligence
> Wherein the soul hath rest and residence.

A second banquet was brought in by two cupids, one garlanded with lilies and the other with roses and both neatly outfitted with gloves and perukes like any proper little cupid of the period. At the end there was an eloquent speech on the importance of a loving king and of dutiful subjects, and it is a pleasure to be able to report that the Earl of Newcastle eventually became the Prince's tutor.

At the end of the first banquet Jonson introduced a comic dance given by some mechanics. It is organized and supervised by one Colonel Vitruvius, an extremely bossy man who is a surveyor. The King's own Surveyor, Inigo Jones, was evidently not at Bolsover, but even if he had been he could not have objected very strongly to Jonson's light and good-natured foolery. "Colonel Vitruvius" shows none of the malice that went into "Vitruvius Hoop" and the war ended lightly enough on Jonson's side at least.

While Charles was being entertained at Bolsover, the miners in the district were assembling to present a petition to the King that the authorities felt was mutinous. The Earl of Newcastle had been warned to disperse them, "that their Majesties may peaceably enjoy the honor you intend them without distraction or trouble." At the beginning of his career at Court, Jonson had celebrated a "hallowed union" that ended in murder; and now he wrote of "this excellent king and his unparalleled queen" while the clouds thickened for civil war.

Jonson had no real interest in politics and no special reason to find fault with his king. Charles had always been kind to him, for he meant well although he sometimes "paused too long in giving." In this same year of 1634, Jonson was given his pension by the London aldermen, including a full payment of arrears, and the Court of Aldermen made the move because it was "his Majesty's pleasure signified unto them by the right honorable the Earl of Dorset."

In return, Ben Jonson behaved as a loyal Court poet should. He wrote occasional pieces for the King's birthdays and celebrated the births of some of his numerous children. He opened 1635 with "a New Year's gift sung to King Charles," and if he thriftily re-used some of the lines that had already served him well for King James that only showed that one monarch is very like another. Moreover, the song is charmingly done. For the past thirty-five years Jonson had been writing New Year's verses, to present as gifts to various people at Court, and his last is by no means his worst. He was old and tired and had only two more years to live, but he was a poet still.

# Chapter 29

T HE EARL OF CLARENDON said that Ben Jonson lived to be "very old" and until paralysis had "made a deep impression upon his body and his mind." Jonson died when he was about sixty-four, which does not make him a "very old" man even by seventeenth-century standards, and although disease was slowly destroying his body there is no evidence that it was destroying his mind.

There is a letter extant which Jonson wrote in his last years to Sir Thomas Cotton, the son of his now-dead friend and the inheritor of his library; and it is not the letter of a man whose mind is weakening. "I salute you. And by these few lines request you that you would by this bearer lend me some book that would determinately satisfy me of the true site, and distance, betwixt *Bauli* or *portus Baiaru* and *Villa Augusta*, into which (if I err not) runs *Lacus lucrinus*. They are near by my historical aim to *Cumae Chalcidensium Misenu, Avernus*, in *Campania* . . . The book shall be returned this night."

As Jonson lay dying not far from Westminster School, he was still the Westminster schoolboy, Camden's scholar, who had found delight and stimulus and rest in the printed word. At the end of his life, as at the beginning, he kept his face turned towards the great world of books.

Long ago, when Jonson was a small boy, Camden had trained him to keep a commonplace book and to jot down any quotations from his reading that happened to impress him. Every schoolboy in England was trained to keep one of these books and most of them were dutiful patchworks of familiar quotations. But they flowered into complete literary justification when Bacon used his as the basis for his famous *Essays,* and Jonson had planned something along the same line as a testament to a lifetime of ardent reading. The loose sheets were found in his desk after he died and published under the title, *Timber, or Discoveries made upon men and matter, as they have flowed out of his daily readings.*

The title is Jonson's, a continuation of the image he had already used in "The Forest" and "Underwoods," but the book itself is incomplete. It is mostly scraps and jottings, set in no particular order and sometimes without even much rewording of the original quotation. A passage in praise of Bacon, for instance, comes almost word for word from a letter written by a Venetian at the time of the Chancellor's fall, and Jonson apparently copied it out on a slip of paper for ultimate incorporation in his book. A section on education must have been copied from a letter of Jonson's own since it begins with its original introduction: "It pleased your Lordship, of late, to ask my opinion touching the education of your sons . . ." Even the most nearly complete section of the book, the discussion on style that brings it to a close, was left unfinished. Almost the last sentence in the book is Jonson's hopeful remark that he will have more to say on the subject, "of which hereafter."

If the book does not read like an unfinished patchwork, it is chiefly because it is unified by Jonson's own lucid, vigorous and solid prose. He wrote clearly because he thought clearly, and although the book is actually a composite of other men's opinions they seem to be Jonson's because he made them his own.

The section on the art of writing is not only an excellent example of the simple, un-Elizabethan straightforwardness of Jonson's style but it also shows, almost in a series of layers, the

men to whom he was especially indebted. The base of the structure is of course supplied by Quintilian, the great Roman
schoolmaster whose advice, as Jonson told Drummond, was "not
only to be read but altogether digested." Then comes Vives,
the Spanish educationalist who had done so much to improve
the Tudor school system and whose independence and good
sense had always appealed to Jonson. And lastly there was Jonson's own contemporary, Daniel Heinsius, the great Dutch
scholar whose rational, solid classicism attracted Jonson in his
old age very much as Sir Philip Sidney had attracted him in his
youth. This same section also includes a long quotation from
Jonson's lively friend John Hoskins, a lawyer who had written
a textbook for a young gentleman who needed instruction in
speaking and writing. But Hoskins derived most of his material,
in turn, from another great Dutch classicist, Justus Lipsius, so
that Jonson, Hoskins and the Dutch scholars were all drawing
from the same source. They were all classicists and all taught
by Rome.

All Roman theories on style were heavily influenced by the
fact that the Roman schools were trying to produce not writers but orators. Quintilian did not write his great treatise for
poets but for speechmakers, and all the excellent advice Jonson
got from him on the need for revision and patience and self-
control was intended for orators who were trying to persuade
a judge and who needed the firm and orderly advice that Quintilian was able to give. While Quintilian did not wholly object
to poetry, he felt it should be read cautiously and written only
in one's idle hours as a relaxation from the more difficult forms
of composition. This was certainly not Jonson's own strenuous
approach to poetry; but he wanted to give his verses all the
solidity and persuasiveness possible, and to the end of his life
Quintilian remained his chief teacher.

The more Jonson read the advice of the Roman and Dutch
classicists, the more clearly he could see what was wrong with
Shakespeare. Shakespeare had taken too undisciplined an ap-

proach to the art of writing. He was somewhat like a very emotional and fluent Roman orator named Haterius, who had been gently reproved by Seneca the Elder for his flow of words, and when Jonson wanted to describe Shakespeare he transferred the whole passage in which Seneca had described Haterius.

Heminges and Condell had described Shakespeare as writing with such "easiness that we have scarce received from him a blot in his papers." Jonson was trained in a more arduous school of revision and he had apparently argued with the King's Men on the subject.

I remember the players have often mentioned it as an honor to Shakespeare that in his writing (whatsoever he penned) he never blotted out line. My answer hath been, 'Would he had blotted a thousand,' which they thought a malevolent speech. I had not told posterity this, but for their ignorance who choose that circumstance to commend their friend by, wherein he most faulted, and to justify mine own candor (for I loved the man and do honor his memory, on this side idolatry, as much as any). He was indeed honest and of an open and free nature; had an excellent fantasy, brave notions and gentle expressions . . .

This much Jonson was writing in his own person. The rest of the paragraph on Shakespeare is a direct quotation from Seneca, except for the illustration that Jonson supplies from Shakespeare's *Julius Caesar*.

He flowed with that facility that sometime it was necessary he should be stopped. *Sufflaminandus erat* [He needed a brake] as Augustus said of Haterius. His wit was in his own power; would the rule of it had been so too. Many times he fell into those things, could not escape laughter: As when he said in the person of Caesar, one speaking to him, 'Caesar, thou dost me wrong,' he replied 'Caesar did never wrong but with just cause,' and such like; which were ridiculous. But he redeemed his vices with his virtues. There was ever more in him to be praised than to be pardoned.

Jonson's own advice to young writers was to follow the reverse of Shakespeare's method and take infinite care in the revision. "All that we invent doth please us in the conception, or birth; else we would never set it down," but if there had been too much "easiness" in the act of composing the author should eye himself with mistrust. "So did the best writers in their beginnings. They imposed upon themselves care and industry. They did nothing rashly. They obtained first to write well, and then custom made it easy . . . Good writing brings on ready writing. Yet when we think we have got the faculty, it is even then good to resist it; as to give a horse a check sometimes with a bit . . . doth not so much stop his course as stir his mettle." Shakespeare drove with a free rein as far as Jonson could see, and although he admitted that Shakespeare achieved astonishing results he was still convinced that the method was wrong.

No one can agree with everything that Jonson put down in his book, and Jonson himself, who valued independence, would not have expected full agreement. But it remains a vigorous and intelligent piece of work and even in its unfinished state it is excellent reading.

Also left unfinished was another project of Jonson's, the *English Grammar* that was published after his death. Jonson had always been interested in grammar, and while he was in Scotland he discussed with Drummond the intricacies of *them*, *they* and *those*. Jonson was convinced that it should be possible to reduce the untidy luxuriance of his native tongue to its basic principles, although he confessed to a friend of his that "the further he proceeded, the more he was puzzled."

Jonson's *Grammar* drew heavily on earlier authorities, English, French and Latin, but his book was nevertheless a pioneering attempt to find some kind of order in the jungle of English syntax. He had a sharp struggle with verbs, which, as he said, "need much the stamp of some good logic to beat them into proportion" and it cost him some "painful churning" to find any logical order in them. His solution in this case was remarkably successful but he held no special brief for it. "If it seem to any to be too rough-hewed, let him plane it out more smoothly, and I shall . . . most heartily thank him for so great a benefit." Since Jonson had no wish to confuse his readers, he preferred to omit a point rather than baffle anyone by it. "The tripthong is of a complexion rather to be feared than loved, and would fright the young grammarian to see him. I will therefore let him pass and make haste to the notion of the syllables."

It was not only the grammar of his own country that interested Jonson; he built up a collection of books on the subject in various languages. Only three years before his death an obliging neighbor named James Howell tracked down a Welsh Grammar that Jonson had been coveting for a long time and presented it to him. Jonson wrote the name of the giver and the date of the gift on the title page and added the motto he put in most of his books: *Tanquam explorator*. It was a suitable motto for Jonson, who remained a persistent and youthfully minded explorer throughout the whole of his life.

Even in his final years Jonson kept up the warm interest he had always shown in the work of younger men. Two years before Jonson's death, a young admirer of his named Joseph Rutter published a pastoral tragicomedy which had been successfully shown at Whitehall and which was called *The Shepherds' Holiday*. Jonson wrote a commendatory poem for the printed version, addressing it "to my dear son and right-learned friend" and giving Rutter a criticism that must have gratified him.

> I have read
> And weighed your play; untwisted every thread,
> And know the woof and warp thereof; can tell
> Where it runs round and even, where so well,
> So soft and smooth it handles, the whole piece
> As it were spun by nature off the fleece.

This was not the first time Jonson had praised a stage pastoral. A quarter of a century earlier he had written commendatory verses for John Fletcher's *The Faithful Shepherdess*, which had also been presented recently at Whitehall.

After Jonson's death, an unfinished pastoral drama of his own was found among his papers. *The Sad Shepherd* is written with such liveliness and brilliance that some people feel it cannot have been the work of his old age, but to judge by Jonson's Prologue he designed it as the final play of his life.

> He that hath feasted you these forty years . . .
> He prays you would vouchsafe, for your own sake,
> To hear him this once more.

Jonson had opened his career as a playwright with *The Isle of Dogs* in 1597; and if the "forty years" is to be taken literally he must have been working on *The Sad Shepherd* in 1637, the year that he died.

Jonson had been thinking for many years of writing a true English pastoral to take the place of the ones that had Greek or Sicilian backgrounds. When he was in Scotland he told Drummond that he had written a pastoral called *The May Lord* and hoped to do another with Loch Lomond as a background. Neither of these survived and perhaps they were burned, along with the first draft of his *English Grammar*, in the fire that destroyed all his papers in 1623. But Jonson refused to give up the idea, and the success at Whitehall of the two pastorals by Fletcher and Rutter may have brought the idea back to him again.

The full title of Jonson's pastoral is *The Sad Shepherd, or A Tale of Robin Hood* and the scene is Sherwood Forest. The Lord Warden of Sherwood Forest was Jonson's patron, the Earl of Newcastle, and when Jonson wrote the "Entertainment at Welbeck" he mentioned the

> odd tales
> Of our outlaw, Robin Hood,
> That reveled here in Sherewood.

Jonson's play might almost be called one of the "odd tales," for it tells the story of old Maudlin, "the witch of Paple-wick,"

who goes about Sherwood Forest making trouble for Robin
Hood, Maid Marian and their assorted guests. The witch is
assisted in her wicked spells by Puck and gallantly resisted by
Robin Hood himself.

In spite of its echoes from Theocritus the play is an English
fairy tale, written by a man who might be bedridden but whose
remembering heart could still re-create the English countryside.
The play is full of the things that Robert Herrick, Jonson's dis-
ciple, also loved—"span-long elves" and "giddy flittermice with
leathern wings"—and it has in it the spirit of play that Jonson
had excluded so ruthlessly from most of his work.

*The Sad Shepherd* takes place in "youthful June" and the
writing matches the month. Jonson laid aside his preoccupation
with satire, naturalism and morality and set out instead to enjoy
himself, and all the lyric gifts that he normally suppressed came
to the surface and flowered in the sunlight. Jonson is not usually classified as a romantic writer, yet he opens the play with a
shepherd searching for his lost love in language that the early
Keats might have used.

> Here she was wont to go, and here, and here,
> Just where those daisies, pinks and violets grow.
> The world may find the Spring by following her,
> For other print her aery steps ne'er left.
> Her treading would not bend a blade of grass
> Or shake the downy blow-ball from his stalk.

The shepherd believes his lady has been drowned; and when
Robin Hood tries to offer him the "solace of the Spring" the
bereaved lover replies in the tone of a nineteenth-century romantic.

> A Spring now she is dead? Of what? Of thorns?
> Briars and brambles, thistles, burrs and docks?
> Cold hemlock, yew, the mandrake or the box?
> These may grow still, but what can spring beside?
> Did not the whole earth sicken when she died?

Fortunately, the lady is not really drowned. She has been shut up in a tree by the wicked witch, who wants her to marry her son. The witch's son is a swineherd, a sort of junior Caliban with a little of the pathos of Shakespeare's monster, and he conducts his unsuccessful wooing with a gift of a badger cub and two hedgehogs. What happens in the end is not known, for the manuscript was never finished. It was found among Jonson's papers after his death and printed by his editor as "a piece of too much worth to be laid aside." And so *The Sad Shepherd* remains, a romantic fragment that shows what Jonson could do when he laid his own rules aside and wandered off into Sherwood Forest.

Jonson had been hoping that he might somehow get there in person as well as in his imagination, going first to visit his friend Falkland at Great Tew and then traveling north into the Robin Hood country. As Falkland himself said,

> Not long before his death, our woods he meant
> To visit, and descend from Thames to Trent.

Jonson did not reach "old Trent" except in his imagination, but the river runs glittering through his play, with its mills and its weirs and the spring flowers on its banks.

Another unfinished play was found among Jonson's papers after his death. *Mortimer, his Fall* exists only in a fragment—the opening soliloquy and a brief exchange of dialogue—but there is enough to show that Jonson had been planning to write the most rigidly classical play of his life. He had never considered *Sejanus* altogether satisfactory, since it lacked "a proper Chorus," and both *Sejanus* and *Catiline* had casts too large to fit within the strict limits of Roman tragedy. But when he planned *Mortimer*, Jonson supplied a Chorus, kept the cast down to nine people and was apparently intending a rigid observance of all three of the unities. If he had deliberately designed the play to be in complete contrast to *The Sad Shepherd* he could hardly have succeeded better; and the two scripts—the easy-going English one and the austerely Senecan—stand at the two poles that mark Jonson's career as a writer. It may be that the vigor with which he championed classicism came in part from his determination not to succumb to a romanticism that was as much a part of him as of the most lyrical Elizabethan.

In any case, *Mortimer* was never completed. Jonson's attempt to graft the technique of Roman tragedy on to English history remains an experimental fragment, with the editor's note at the end: "He died and left it unfinished."

Ben Jonson died on the sixth of August, 1637, and apart from the manuscripts that were found in his desk he left very little behind him. A wicker chair, "such as old women used," was later exhibited as his, but the total valuation of his goods came to the pathetic sum of eight pounds, eight shillings and ten-pence.

Thirty-three years before, a poet named Thomas Churchyard had died in Westminster and his name had become a byword for poverty.

> Poverty and Poetry this tomb doth enclose,
> Therefore, gentlemen, be merry in prose.

Yet Churchyard had been rich enough to draw up a will, and he had left enough money to be buried "like a gentleman." He was not like Jonson, who left no money at all.

Jonson had his funeral nevertheless. He was buried in Westminster Abbey with as great a train of mourners as though he had been a nobleman. Because it was summer many people were in the country, but his funeral was attended by "all or the greatest part of the nobility and gentry then in the town."

He was not buried in the Poets' Corner near Chaucer and Beaumont and Spenser, but in the north aisle of the nave. There is a story that Jonson was joking one day with the Dean of Westminster about being buried with the other poets and said that he could not afford the honor. "I am too poor for that, and no one will lay out funeral charges upon me. No, sir, six feet long by two feet wide is too much for me; two feet by two feet will do." The Dean of Westminster was a friend of Jonson's, the learned and lavish Bishop Williams who had clung to his deanship throughout the whole of his meteoric rise to high office in case he had "need of a covering." Jonson told his fortune in the gipsy masque, and Williams was always generous to men of learning. According to the story, he told Jonson that he could have his "two feet by two feet" in the Abbey and Jonson was buried accordingly.

It was later decided that the story was a legend, invented to account for the small, square stone under which Jonson had been buried. But his grave was disturbed early in the nineteenth century, while a Lady Wilson was being buried next to it, and the workmen discovered that Jonson's cheap coffin had in fact been set in upright instead of lengthwise. Whether or not it was because of a joke with the Dean, Ben Jonson refused to lie down even in Westminster Abbey.

After the funeral was over, Sir Kenelm Digby took over the task of going through Jonson's papers and preparing them for publication. He wanted the world to share in "those excellent pieces (alas, that many of them are but pieces!) which he hath left behind him and that I keep religiously by me." Sir Kenelm also wrote approvingly to the Dean of Christ Church, Dr. Brian Duppa, who was planning to issue a collection of memorial verse written by Jonson's friends: "I believe . . . that these compositions, delivered to the world by your hand, will be more grateful obsequies to his great ghost than any other that could be performed at his tomb." Jonson's neighbor, James Howell, also wrote Dr. Duppa in praise of his "very worthy" project and the book was issued the following March.

It was called *Jonsonus Virbius, or The Memory of Ben Johnson Revived by the Friends of the Muses,* and it is doubtful if Jonson's "great ghost" would have thought much of it. It was printed on poor paper with rather smudged type, and Jonson's name was not even spelled the way he would have liked. The thirty-three contributions came mostly from Oxford graduates or from people about the Court, and the same platitudes were repeated in apparently endless couplets. Most of them mentioned that Jonson had reformed the stage and too many were unable to resist the temptation to rhyme *hearse* and *verse*. Even Lord Falkland, who had loved Jonson dearly, was not able to rise above the level of the commonplace, and the only contributor who caught a real echo of Jonson's spirit was an anonymous poet who may have been that remarkable young man, Sidney Godolphin.

The thin little book issued with such good intentions shows clearly how little of himself Jonson had been able to transmit to his "sons." There was only one poet of the period who was capable of understanding Jonson's great Roman vision, the exalted conviction without which all the rules were worthless, and that was young John Milton. His masque of *Comus* was published the year Jonson died, and it possessed the heroic moral content that Jonson had dreamed of as well as the golden, lucid, gravely controlled poetry that he had longed to see written in England. There is no evidence that the two men ever met, yet of all England's poets it was the young Puritan only who was capable of being Jonson's "son" and inheritor.

Since every poet was supposed to have his monument, Jonson's friends started a collection to have a suitable one erected in Westminster Abbey. Perhaps they had in mind something like the monument Inigo Jones designed for his friend George Chapman, "built after the way of the old Romans." A considerable sum of money was collected for the purpose and then had to be refunded; for the Civil War had broken loose upon England and there was no longer any talk of building but only of destruction.

Yet Ben Jonson got his monument. A brief inscription was carved on the small square of marble that marked his grave, and the story goes that a passer-by ordered it done on impulse and gave the stonecutter eighteenpence for the work. If so, the impulse served Jonson better than long meditation would have done, for the natural thing would have been to give so distinguished a classicist an ornate description in Latin. Instead he got four words in English which are brief, admiring and truthful, and they constitute the perfect epitaph for that lively and incomparable Englishman:

O RARE BEN JONSON

# Selected Bibliography

I would like to make special mention of the eleven-volume edition of *Ben Jonson* by Herford and Simpson, published by the Oxford Press. The edition is indispensable to any biographer of Ben Jonson, and he himself would have been very proud of it.

JOSEPH QUINCY ADAMS, "The Bones of Ben Jonson," *Studies in Philology*, 1919.

WILLIAM ALEXANDER, *The Poetical Works of Sir William Alexander, Earl of Stirling*, edited by L. E. Kastner and H. B. Charlton, Volume I, London: William Blackwood and Sons, 1921.

ROBERT ALLOTT, *Englands Parnassus*, London, 1600.

ROGER ASCHAM, *The Scholemaster*, London, 1570.

J. W. H. ATKINS, *English Literary Criticism: the Renascence*, London: Methuen and Company, Ltd., 1947.

J. W. H. ATKINS, *Literary Criticism in Antiquity*, 2 volumes, Cambridge: Cambridge University Press, 1934.

CHARLES SEARS BALDWIN, *Renaissance Literary Theory and Practice*, New York: Columbia University Press, 1939.

T. W. BALDWIN, *William Shakspere's Small Latine & Lesse Greeke*, 2 volumes, Urbana: University of Illinois Press, 1944.

WALTER GEORGE BELL, *Fleet Street in Seven Centuries*, London, 1912.

WALTER GEORGE BELL, *A Short History of the Worshipful Company of Tylers and Bricklayers of the City of London*, London: H. C. Montgomery, 1938.

GERALD EADES BENTLEY, *The Jacobean and Caroline Stage*, 2 volumes, Oxford: Clarendon Press, 1941.

GERALD EADES BENTLEY, *Shakespeare & Jonson*, 2 volumes, Chicago: University of Chicago Press, 1945.

THOMAS BIRCH, *The Court and Times of James the First*, 2 volumes, London, 1848.

E. W. BLIGH, *Sir Kenelm Digby and his Venetia*, London: S. Low, Marston and Company, 1932.

REGINALD BLOMFIELD, *A History of Renaissance Architecture in England, 1500–1800*, 2 volumes, London: George Bell and Sons, 1897.

JOHN BODENHAM, *Belvedere; or, The Garden of the Muses*, Manchester: Spenser Society, 1875.

JESSE FRANKLIN BRADLEY and JOSEPH QUINCY ADAMS, *The Jonson Allusion-Book*, New Haven: Yale University Press, 1922.

LEICESTER BRADNER, *Musae Anglicanae; A History of Anglo-Latin Poetry, 1500–1925*, London: Oxford University Press, 1940.

EDWARD WEDLAKE BRAYLEY, *The History and Antiquities of the Abbey Church of St. Peter, Westminster*, 2 volumes, London, 1818–1823.

WILLIAM DINSMORE BRIGGS, "On Certain Incidents in Ben Jonson's Life," *Modern Philology*, 1913.

WILLIAM DINSMORE BRIGGS, "Studies in Ben Jonson," *Anglia*, 1913, 1914, 1915.

JOHN BRINSLEY, *Ludus Literarius; or, The Grammar Schoole*, edited by E. T. Campagnac, London: Constable and Company, Ltd., 1917.

EDMUND KEMPER BROADUS, *The Laureateship*, Oxford: Clarendon Press, 1921.

DOUGLAS BUSH, *English Literature in the Earlier Seventeenth Century, 1600–1660*, Oxford: Clarendon Press, 1946.

DOUGLAS BUSH, *The Renaissance and English Humanism*, Toronto: University of Toronto Press, 1939.

WILLIAM CAMDEN, *Annales, the True and Royall History of the Famous Empresse Elizabeth*, London, 1635.

WILLIAM CAMDEN, *Britain, or a Chorographicall Description of the Most Flourishing Kingdomes, England, Scotland and Ireland*, London, 1610.

WILLIAM CAMDEN, *Remaines Concerning Britain*, London, 1657.

GEORGE CAREW, *Letters from Sir George Carew to Sir Thomas Roe, 1615–1617*, edited by John MacLean, Royal Historical Society Publications 76, London, 1860.

GEORGE CAREW, "A Relation of the State of France" in *An Historical View of the Negotiations Between the Courts of England, France and Brussels* by Thomas Birch, London, 1749.

W. A. CATER, "Some Letters from William Camden," *British Archaeological Association Journal*, 1913.

CATHOLIC RECORD SOCIETY, *London Sessions Records, 1605–1685*, Catholic Record Society Publications 34, London, 1934.

ALGERNON CECIL, *A Life of Robert Cecil*, London: John Murray, 1915.

JOHN CHAMBERLAIN, *Letters*, edited by Norman Egbert McClure, 2 volumes, Philadelphia: American Philosophical Society, 1939.

EDMUND K. CHAMBERS, *The Elizabethan Stage*, 4 volumes, Oxford: Clarendon Press, 1923.

ROBERT CHAMBERS, *The Life of King James the First*, 2 volumes, Edinburgh, 1830.

GEORGE CHAPMAN, *The Plays and Poems of G. Chapman*, edited by Thomas Marc Parrott, 2 volumes, London: George Routledge and Sons, Ltd., 1910–1914.

GEORGE CHAPMAN, *The Poems of George Chapman*, edited by Phyllis Brooks Bartlett, London: Oxford University Press, 1941.

JOHN CLAPHAM, *Elizabeth of England*, Philadelphia: University of Pennsylvania Press, 1951.

EDWARD, EARL OF CLARENDON, *The History of the Rebellion and Civil Wars in England*, 2 volumes, Oxford: Oxford University Press, 1840.

EDWARD, EARL OF CLARENDON, *The Life of Edward, Earl of Clarendon*, 3 volumes, Oxford: Clarendon Press, 1827.

ANDREW CLARK, editor, *Register of the University of Oxford*, Volume II, Part 1, Oxford: Clarendon Press, 1887.

BARRETT H. CLARK, *European Theories of the Drama*, New York: D. Appleton and Company, 1929.

DONALD LEMEN CLARK, *Rhetoric and Poetry in the Renaissance*, New York: Columbia University Press, 1922.

G. N. CLARK, *The Seventeenth Century*, Oxford: Clarendon Press, 1947.

CHARLES M. CLODE, *The Early History of the Guild of Merchant Taylors*, Volume I, London, 1888.

WILLIAM COBBETT, *Parliamentary History of England*, Volume I, London, 1806.

WILLIAM G. CRANE, *Wit and Rhetoric in the Renaissance*, New York: Columbia University Press, 1937.

ALBERT CREW, *The Old Bailey*, London: Ivor Nicholson and Watson, Ltd., 1933.

C. G. CRUICKSHANK, *Elizabeth's Army*, London: Oxford University Press, 1946.

PETER CUNNINGHAM, *Extracts from the Accounts of the Revels at Court in the Reigns of Queen Elizabeth and King James I*, London: Shakespeare Society, 1842.

FOLKE DAHL, "Amsterdam—Cradle of English Newspapers," *The Library*, 1949.

ROBERT DALLINGTON, *The View of France*, with an introduction by W. P. Barrett, London: Oxford University Press, 1936.

SAMUEL DANIEL, *The Complete Works in Verse and Prose of Samuel Daniel*, edited by Alexander B. Grosart, 5 volumes, London, 1885–1896.

THOMAS DEKKER, *Dramatic Works*, edited by R. H. Shepherd, 4 volumes, London, 1873.

THOMAS DEKKER, *The Non-dramatic Works of Thomas Dekker*, edited by Alexander B. Grosart, 5 volumes, London, 1884–1886.

SIMONDS D'EWES, *The Autobiography and Correspondence of Sir Simonds D'Ewes, Bart.*, edited by James Halliwell, 2 volumes, London, 1845.

THOMAS FROGNALL DIBDIN, *Bibliotheca Spenceriana*, Volume V, London, 1822.

KENELM DIGBY, *Private Memoirs*, London, 1827.

BERTRAM DOBELL, "Newly Discovered Documents of the Elizabethan and Jacobean Periods," *The Athenaeum*, 1901.

WILLIAM DRUMMOND, *The Poetical Works of William Drummond of Hawthornden*, edited by L. E. Kastner, 2 volumes, Manchester: University of Manchester Press, 1913.

O. JOCELYN DUNLOP, *English Apprenticeship and Child Labour*, London: T. Fisher Unwin, 1912.

MARK ECCLES, "Jonson and the Spies," *Review of English Studies*, 1937.

MARK ECCLES, "Jonson's Marriage," *Review of English Studies*, 1936.

EDWARD EDWARDS, *The Life of Sir Walter Ralegh*, 2 volumes, London: Macmillan and Company, 1868.

HENRY ELLIS, editor, *Original Letters Illustrative of English History*, 3 volumes, London, 1824.

KATHARINE A. ESDAILE, "Ben Jonson and the Devil Tavern," *Essays and Studies by Members of the English Association* 29, Oxford: Clarendon Press, 1944.

FLORENCE M. GREIR EVANS, *The Principal Secretary of State*, Manchester: University of Manchester Press, 1923.

WILLA McCLUNG EVANS, *Ben Jonson and Elizabethan Music*, Lancaster: Lancaster Press, Inc., 1929.

NATHAN FIELD, *Plays,* edited by William Peery, Austin: University of Texas Press, 1950.

F. J. FISHER, "The Development of London as a Centre of Conspicuous Consumption in the Sixteenth and Seventeenth Centuries," *Royal Historical Society Transactions,* fourth series, Volume 30, 1948.

ASTRID FRIIS, *Alderman Cockayne's Project and the Cloth Trade,* Copenhagen: Levin and Munksgaard, 1927.

THOMAS FULLER, *The History of the Worthies of England,* London, 1662.

SAMUEL RAWSON GARDINER, *History of England, 1603–1642,* 10 volumes, London, 1863–1884.

EDMUND GIBSON, "The Life of Mr. Camden," preface to Camden's *Britannia,* Volume I, London, 1772.

ALLAN H. GILBERT, *The Symbolic Persons in the Masques of Ben Jonson,* Durham: Duke University Press, 1948.

GODFREY GOODMAN, *The Court of King James the First,* 2 volumes, London, 1839.

D. J. GORDON, "The Imagery of Ben Jonson's *The Masque of Blacknesse* and *The Masque of Beautie*," *Journal of the Warburg and Courtauld Institutes* 6, 1943.

WALTER WILSON GREG, *Dramatic Documents from the Elizabethan Playhouses,* 2 volumes, Oxford: Clarendon Press, 1931.

WALTER WILSON GREG, *Pastoral Poetry & Pastoral Drama,* London, A. H. Bullen, 1906.

WALTER WILSON GREG, "The Riddle of Jonson's Chronology," *The Library,* 1926.

FULKE GREVILLE, *Life of Sir Philip Sidney,* edited by Nowell Smith, Oxford: Clarendon Press, 1907.

JOHN HACKET, *Scrinia Reserata, a Memorial Offer'd to the Great Deservings of John Williams,* London, 1693.

JAMES ORCHARD HALLIWELL, editor, *Letters of the Kings of England,* 2 volumes, London, 1846.

JOHN HARINGTON, *Nugae Antiquae,* 3 volumes, London, 1792.

PHILIP HENSLOWE, *Henslowe Papers,* edited by Walter Wilson Greg, London: A. H. Bullen, 1907.

PHILIP HENSLOWE, *Henslowe's Diary,* edited by Walter Wilson Greg, 2 volumes, London, A. H. Bullen, 1904–1908.

HENRY HERBERT, *The Dramatic Records of Sir Henry Herbert, Master of the Revels, 1623–1673,* edited by Joseph Quincy Adams, New Haven: Yale University Press, 1917.

HAROLD NEWCOMB HILLEBRAND, *The Child Actors*, 2 volumes, Urbana: University of Illinois Press, 1926.

HORACE, *Complete Works*, edited by Casper J. Kraemer, Jr., New York: Modern Library, 1936.

J. LESLIE HOTSON, *I, William Shakespeare . . .* , New York: Oxford University Press, 1938.

JAMES HOWELL, *Epistolae Ho-Elianae*, London, 1754.

JOSEPH HUNTER, "An Account of a Scheme for Erecting a Royal Academy in England in the Reign of King James the First," *Archaeologia*, 1847.

JAMES I, *The Workes of the Most High and Mightie Prince, James*, London, 1616.

JOHN CORDY JEAFFRESON, editor, *Middlesex County Records*, Volume I, London: Middlesex County Records Society, 1886.

AUGUSTUS JESSOPP, *William Cecil, Lord Burghley*, London, 1904.

GEORGE W. JOHNSON, *Memoirs of John Selden*, London, 1835.

BEN JONSON, *Ben Jonson*, edited by C. H. Herford and Percy Simpson, 11 volumes, Oxford: Clarendon Press, 1925–1952.

BEN JONSON, *The Workes of Beniamin Jonson*, London, 1616.

*Jonsonus Virbius: or, the Memorie of Ben Johnson Revived by the Friends of the Muses*, London, 1638.

W. K. JORDAN, *The Development of Religious Toleration in England*, Volumes I and II, London: George Allen and Unwin, 1932–1940.

A. V. JUDGES, editor, *The Elizabethan Underworld*, London: George Routledge and Sons, Ltd., 1930.

GEORGE LYMAN KITTREDGE, "King James I and *The Devil Is an Ass*," *Modern Philology*, 1911.

L. C. KNIGHTS, *Drama & Society in the Age of Jonson*, London: Chatto and Windus, 1937.

ARTHUR F. LEACH, *Educational Charters and Documents, 598–1909*, Cambridge: Cambridge University Press, 1911.

M. ANTONIN LEFÈVRE-PONTALIS, *John de Witt*, 2 volumes, Boston: Houghton Mifflin and Company, 1885.

LONDON COUNTY COUNCIL, *Survey of London*, Volumes 13, 14, 18 and 20, London: P. S. King and Son, 1900–1950.

W. H. MANCHÉE, *The Westminster City Fathers (the Burgess Court of Westminster) 1585–1901*, London: John Lane, 1924.

J. A. R. MARRIOTT, *The Life of John Colet*, London: Methuen and Company, Ltd., 1933.

JOHN MARSTON, *Works*, edited by A. H. Bullen, 3 volumes, London: John C. Nimmo, 1887.

DAVID MASSON, "Ben Jonson in Edinburgh," *Blackwood's Magazine*, 1893.

DAVID MASSON, *Drummond of Hawthornden*, London: Macmillan and Company, 1873.

DAVID MATHEW, *The Jacobean Age*, London: Longmans, Green and Company, 1938.

FRANCIS MERES, *Palladis Tamia, Wits Treasury*, New York: Scholars' Facsimiles and Reprints, 1938.

ARNOLD OSKAR MEYER, *England and the Catholic Church under Queen Elizabeth*, London: K. Paul, Trench, Trübner and Company, Ltd., 1916.

FYNES MORYSON, *An Itinerary*, 4 volumes, Glasgow, 1907–1908.

KENNETH B. MURDOCK, *The Sun at Noon*, New York: The Macmillan Company, 1939.

THOMAS NASHE, *Works*, edited by R. B. McKerrow, 5 volumes, London: A. H. Bullen, 1904–1910.

MARGARET, DUCHESS OF NEWCASTLE, *The Life of the First Duke of Newcastle and Other Writings*, New York: E. P. Dutton and Company, Inc., 1916.

BERNARD H. NEWDIGATE, *Michael Drayton and His Circle*, Oxford: Shakespeare Head Press, 1941.

JOHN NICHOLS, *The Progresses of King James the First*, 4 volumes, London, 1828.

ALLARDYCE NICOLL, *Stuart Masques and the Renaissance Stage*, London: George G. Harrap and Company, Ltd., 1937.

JOHN OGLANDER, *A Royalist's Notebook*, London: Constable and Company, Ltd., 1936.

HENRY PEACHAM, *The Compleat Gentleman*, London, 1634.

FRANCIS PECK, *Desiderata Curiosa*, London, 1779.

HENRY TEN EYCK PERRY, *The First Duchess of Newcastle and her Husband as Figures in Literary History*, Boston: Ginn and Company, 1918.

*The Pilgrimage to Parnassus with the Two Parts of the Return from Parnassus*, edited by W. D. Macray, Oxford: Clarendon Press, 1886.

MARIO PRAZ, *Studies in Seventeenth-century Imagery*, Volume I, London: The Warburg Institute, 1939.

*Proceedings and Debates in the House of Commons, 1620 and 1621*, Oxford: Clarendon Press, 1766.

G. W. PROTHERO, *Select Statutes and Other Constitutional Documents Illustrative of the Reigns of Elizabeth and James I*, Oxford: Clarendon Press, 1913.

QUINTILIAN, *Institutio Oratoria,* translated by H. E. Butler, 4 volumes, London: William Heinemann, 1921–1922.

WALTER RALEIGH, *The History of the World,* London, 1617.

PAUL REYHER, *Les Masques Anglais,* Paris, 1909.

CESARE RIPA, *Nova Iconologia,* Padua, 1618.

JOHN SALTMARSH, "Plague and Economic Decline in England in the Later Middle Ages," *Cambridge Historical Journal* 7, 1941.

JOHN EDWIN SANDYS, *A History of Classical Scholarship,* Volume II, Cambridge: Cambridge University Press, 1908.

JOHN SARGEAUNT, *Annals of Westminster School,* London: Methuen and Company, 1898.

JULIUS CAESAR SCALIGER, *Select Translations from Scaliger's Poetics* by Frederick Morgan Padelford, New York: Henry Holt and Company, 1905.

F. L. SCHOELL, *Études sur l'Humanisme Continental en Angleterre à la Fin de la Renaissance,* Paris: H. Champion, 1926.

WILLIAM ROBERT SCOTT, *The Constitution and Finance of English, Scottish and Irish Joint-Stock Companies to 1720,* Volume I, Cambridge: Cambridge University Press, 1912.

MATTHIAS A. SHAABER, *Some Forerunners of the Newspaper in England, 1476–1622,* Philadelphia: University of Pennsylvania Press, 1929.

EDGAR SHEPPARD, *The Old Royal Palace of Whitehall,* London: Longmans, Green and Company, 1902.

PHILIP SIDNEY, *An Apologie for Poetrie,* London: Henry Olney, 1595.

PHILIP SIDNEY, *The Correspondence of Sir Philip Sidney and Hubert Languet,* edited by William Aspenwall Bradley, Boston: Merrymount Press, 1912.

PERCY SIMPSON and C. F. BELL, editors, *Designs by Inigo Jones for Masques and Plays at Court,* Oxford: Oxford University Press, 1924.

C. J. SISSON, "Ben Jonson at Gresham College," *London Times Literary Supplement,* September 21, 1951.

G. GREGORY SMITH, editor, *Elizabethan Critical Essays,* 2 volumes, Oxford: Clarendon Press, 1904.

JOHN EDWARD SMITH, *A Catalogue of Westminster Records,* London, 1900.

THOMAS SMITH, *The Common-wealth of England,* London, 1621.

JAMES SPEDDING, *The Letters and the Life of Francis Bacon,* 7 volumes, London, 1861–1874.

J. E. Spingarn, *Critical Essays of the Seventeenth Century*, Volume I, Oxford: Clarendon Press, 1908.

J. E. Spingarn, *A History of Literary Criticism in the Renaissance*, New York: Columbia University Press, 1920.

Mary Susan Steele, *Plays and Masques at Court during the Reigns of Elizabeth, James and Charles*, New Haven: Yale University Press, 1926.

Lawrence Stone, "The Anatomy of the Elizabethan Aristocracy," *Economic History Review* 18, 1948.

John Stow, *Annales, or a Generall Chronicle of England*, with additions by Edmund Howes, London, 1631.

John Stow, *The Survay of London*, with additions by Anthony Munday, London, 1618.

John Strype, *Annals of the Reformation*, 4 volumes, Oxford: Clarendon Press, 1824.

Mary Sullivan, *Court Masques of James I*, New York: G. P. Putnam's Sons, 1913.

Duke of Sully, *Memoirs*, 4 volumes, London, 1856.

Elizabeth J. Sweeting, *Early Tudor Criticism*, Oxford: Basil Blackwell, 1940.

J. R. Tanner, *Constitutional Documents of the Reign of James I*, Cambridge: Cambridge University Press, 1930.

Lawrence E. Tanner, *Westminster School; a History*, London: Country Life Ltd., 1934.

Henry L. Thompson, *Christ Church*, London, 1900.

J. A. K. Thomson, *The Classical Background of English Literature*, London: George Allen and Unwin, Ltd., 1948.

William Trumbull, "Papers of William Trumbull the Elder," edited by E. K. Purnell and A. B. Hinds, *Great Britain, Historical Manuscripts Commission, Report on the Manuscripts of the Marquess of Downshire*, Volumes 2, 3 and 4, London, 1936, 1938, 1940.

Celeste Turner, *Anthony Munday: an Elizabethan Man of Letters*, California University Publications in English, Berkeley, 1928.

George Unwin, *The Gilds and Companies of London*, London: George Allen and Unwin, Ltd., 1938.

George Unwin, *Industrial Organization in the Sixteenth and Seventeenth Centuries*, Oxford: Clarendon Press, 1904.

John Ward, *The Lives of the Professors of Gresham College*, London, 1740.

Foster Watson, *The English Grammar Schools to 1660*, Cambridge: Cambridge University Press, 1908.

KURT WEBER, *Lucius Cary, Second Viscount Falkland*, New York: Columbia University Press, 1940.

ANTHONY WELDON, *The Court and Character of King James*, London, 1650.

H. F. WESTLAKE, *St. Margaret's, Westminster*, London, 1914.

BULSTRODE WHITELOCKE, *The History of England*, London, 1713.

BULSTRODE WHITELOCKE, *Memorials of the English Affairs*, London, 1732.

JAMES WHITELOCKE, *Liber Famelicus*, edited by John Bruce, Westminster: Camden Society, 1858.

ROGER WILBRAHAM, *The Journal of Sir Roger Wilbraham, 1593–1616*, edited by Harold Spencer Scott, London: Royal Historical Society Publications, series 3, no. 4, 1902.

HUGH ROSS WILLIAMSON, *King James I*, London: Duckworth, 1935.

DAVID HARRIS WILLSON, *The Privy Councillors in the House of Commons, 1604–1629*, Minneapolis: University of Minnesota Press, 1940.

ARTHUR WILSON, *The History of Great Britain, Being the Life and Reign of King James the First*, London, 1653.

F. P. WILSON, *The Plague in Shakespeare's London*, Oxford: Clarendon Press, 1927.

RALPH WINWOOD, *Memorials of Affairs of State in the Reigns of Queen Elizabeth and King James*, 3 volumes, London, 1725.

ANTHONY WOOD, *Athenae Oxonienses, London*, 1721.

HENRY WOTTON, *Reliquiae Wottonianae*, London, 1651.

FRANCES A. YATES, *John Florio*, Cambridge: Cambridge University Press, 1934.

# Index

# Index

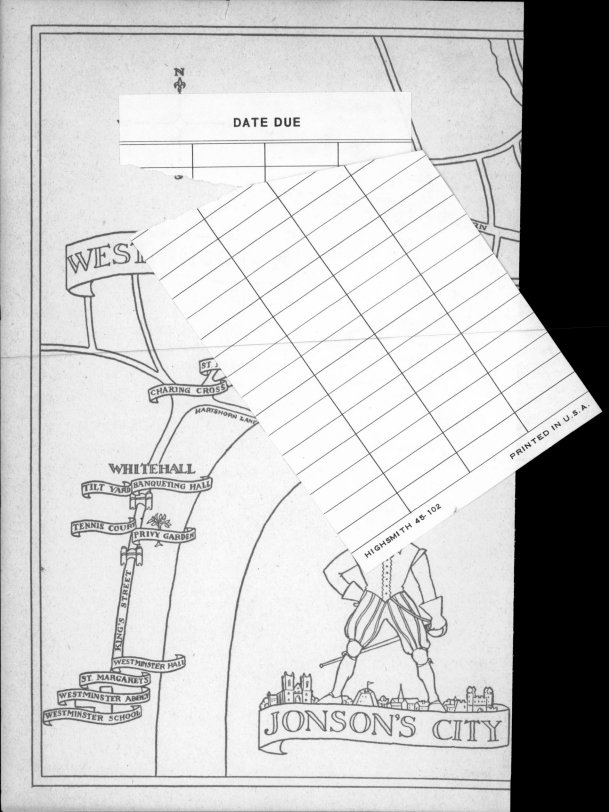

N

WES

ST.
CHARING CROSS

HARTSHORN LANE

WHITEHALL
TILT YARD BANQUETING HALL
TENNIS COURT
PRIVY GARDEN
KING'S STREET
WESTMINSTER HALL
ST. MARGARETS
WESTMINSTER ABBEY
WESTMINSTER SCHOOL

JONSON'S CITY